Jeff Maynard is an author and documentary maker. His books include *Niagara's Gold*, *Divers in Time* and *The Letterbox War of Kamarooka Street*. Jeff is a former editor of *Australian Motorcycle News* and retains a keen interest in classic motorcycles. He is a former field editor of *Australasian Scuba Diver*, a member of the Explorers Club and President of the Historical Diving Society: South East Asia, Pacific. He lives in Melbourne, Australia, with his wife, Zoe, and their family.

www.jeffmaynard.com.au

For Jennifer, Rebecca, Sean, Warren and Zoe.
Five who make a difference.

WINGS
OF ICE

JEFF MAYNARD

VINTAGE BOOKS
Australia

A Vintage book
Published by Random House Australia Pty Ltd
Level 3, 100 Pacific Highway, North Sydney NSW 2060
www.randomhouse.com.au

First published by Vintage in 2010

Addresses for companies within the Random House Group can be found at www.randomhouse.com.au/offices.

National Library of Australia
Cataloguing-in-Publication Entry

Maynard, Jeff.
Wings of ice: the air race to the poles.

ISBN 978 1 74166 934 3 (pbk).

Wilkins, G. H. (George Hubert), Sir, 1888–1958.
Byrd, Richard Evelyn, 1888–1957.
Arctic regions – Aerial exploration.
Arctic regions – Discovery and exploration.

910.9113

Cover photograph courtesy Byrd Polar Research Center, Ohio State University.
Richard Byrd (centre) stands in front of the *Josephine Ford* with George Noville
(left) and Floyd Bennett, before a failed attempt to depart from Kings Bay, May 1926.
Cover design by Darian Causby/www.highway51.com.au
Typeset in 12/16 pt Bembo by Midland Typesetters, Australia
Printed and bound by Griffin Press, South Australia

Random House Australia uses papers that are natural, renewable and recyclable products and made from wood grown in sustainable forests. The logging and manufacturing processes are expected to conform to the environmental regulations of the country of origin.

10 9 8 7 6 5 4 3 2 1

Contents

Author's Note

Generally, I refer to places, people, measures or objects as the explorers of the period referred to them. Where I refer to *Eskimo*, for example, I am of course referring to the people today known as *Inuit*. Now the name *Spitsbergen* refers only to the main island, while the archipelago is called *Svalbard*. This preference for historical authenticity does not guarantee consistency in the quoted passages. As an Australian of his era, George Wilkins generally used English spellings: *aeroplane* instead of *airplane*, *recognise* rather than *recognize*, and so on. Obviously, Richard Byrd used American spellings. However, many of Wilkins' books (including *Flying the Arctic* and *Under the North Pole*) were published by American publishing houses and his text was edited. Only when I feel the reader may be confused have I taken the liberty of altering spellings or adding information in brackets.

The word *mile* comes from the Latin *milia passuum*, meaning 'a thousand paces'. The length of a mile, therefore, varied, depending on who was stepping it out, until it was standardised at 1760 yards or 1.609 kilometres. A 'land mile' is known as a *statute mile*. At sea it is not possible for mariners to measure distance by stepping it out, using lengths of chain or fixing a distance between two points. Distance is measured in latitude and longitude, and these, in turn, are measured in degrees, minutes and seconds against a fixed point in space as the Earth revolves. A 'sea mile' or *nautical mile* is one minute of latitude. Sixty nautical miles equal one degree of latitude. This method of measuring distance at sea was used long before the technology was available to ascertain how long a nautical mile actually was, in relation to a statute mile. When it became possible to accurately measure the circumference of the Earth the nautical mile was standardised at 1.151 statute miles or 1.852 kilometres. Mariners measure speed at sea in *knots*. One knot is one nautical mile per hour.

There are passages in this book where the explorers refer to specific distances. Byrd, for example, writes '20 miles to go'. It would be confusing to quote this in the text as '32.187 kilometres to go'. Accordingly, the expression of distance has not been standardised, and the most appropriate form has been chosen in each instance.

Foreword

The Ballyhoo Years

When Christopher Columbus stepped ashore on a remote island in the Bahamas in 1492 he was met by a people who, having lived there for more than 15,000 years, would not have considered the place a 'new world'. When Captain James Cook sailed up the east coast of Australia in 1770 he was greeted by a people who had been there for 50,000 years. And so it was for the 'discoverers' and 'explorers' of Africa, Asia and the Americas. They followed human migration, albeit many years later, and were often assisted in some way by local knowledge. Certainly the fact that these places were inhabited meant the existence of food and the availability of shelter.

But human migration never ventured far into the polar regions, stopping just past the tree line in the lands of the north. Similarly, it never crossed the Southern Ocean. Here the explorer could truly claim to be the first human to set eyes on the secrets to be revealed. At the beginning of the twentieth century, hardy men made small inroads into these frozen regions. They offered to the mapmaker a few degrees of longitude and latitude by travelling as explorers had always travelled: sailing on water and walking on land. Nevertheless, at the end of World War One large areas at the top and bottom of the globe were still vast, cold mysteries. These areas may have contained mountainous continents, deep oceans or numerous islands. No one knew.

Into these last unknown areas explorers would, for the first time, fly. The aeroplane became their ally – but also their enemy. Now they could sail over mountains and cross vast tracts of land in hours instead of weeks or months, but the smallest faulty part – a blocked carburettor, a cracked bolt – could send them plummeting to their death. And the polar regions held unique challenges for powered machinery. Manufacturers of internal combustion engines did not imagine an environment where hot oil drained from a sump could be a frozen lump as it hit the ground, or where touching a metal component with bare hands might mean having to have fingers amputated.

The first aerial explorers would also fly into a new social phenomenon. Eager to follow their exploits was a world embracing moving pictures, radio broadcasts and photographs in newspapers. Thus, the last of the planet's explorers became its first media superstars. They were urged on by their publicity-seeking sponsors to achieve headline-grabbing firsts, and by their governments to discover and claim new lands.

For a brief time in these 'Ballyhoo Years' of ticker-tape parades, when pioneer aviators could easily draw crowds of 100,000 people to watch them drive by, when the world wanted to celebrate anything and everything, these men were celebrities, the like of whom had never been seen before. When they began their work, an area larger than the United States and Canada combined was still unmapped. When, a few years later, they were finished, there remained only details to fill in.

Many brave men flew into these enormous white wildernesses, but three stand out. There was Roald Amundsen, who had survived the 'heroic age' of polar exploration but would not survive this one. There was Richard Byrd, who understood the machinery of celebrity better than he understood the machinery of aeroplanes. And there was George Hubert Wilkins, who believed scientific exploration could raise mankind to a higher state of civilisation.

On 8 May 1926 these three were locked in a race to fly to the North Pole. Wilkins was at Barrow, Alaska, anxiously waiting for the weather to clear so that he could get airborne in his Fokker Trimotor. Amundsen was at Kings Bay, Spitsbergen, preparing an airship. Byrd was also at Kings Bay, building a runway for his plane. Shortly after midnight Byrd flew north. He returned sixteen hours later and declared he had reached the North Pole.

A year later, while Amundsen was involved in the bitter dispute that would cost him his life, Byrd announced his intention to fly to the South Pole. Wilkins, who had just completed a record-breaking flight in the Arctic, was hired to beat him. Late in 1928 Byrd and Wilkins unloaded their planes on opposite sides of Antarctica and prepared for the last great race in polar history.

But the story of the air race to the Poles has remained untold for over eighty years. The reason is simple. A race needs a minimum of two competitors; should one of them disappear from the history books, so does the suggestion of a contest. This happened with Wilkins. It is difficult to find a twentieth-century figure, in any field of endeavour, who achieved so much yet is so little remembered. Any number of his expeditions should allow him to stand equal with the likes of Scott, Amundsen, Shackleton, Peary and Mawson. Yet today few people have heard of him.

With Wilkins reinstated to his rightful place in history, and with his story told against those of Byrd and Amundsen, an entirely new picture of this thrilling era emerges. And we gain a new perspective of the men who raced to fly to the ends of the Earth.

1

An Unspeakable Secret

The eradication of Sir George Hubert Wilkins from the pages of history began on the afternoon of 1 December 1958. Earlier that day his body had been found lying fully clothed on the floor of Room 4A at the Park Central Hotel, Framingham, Massachusetts, USA. After a doctor pronounced him dead, his body was taken to a nearby funeral home. On learning of her husband's death, Suzanne, Lady Wilkins, travelled from New York to inspect the modest room in which he had lived alone for five years. She completed her inspection, locked the door and instructed the proprietor to let no one in. As Suzanne turned the key she began a process that locked away the secrets of Wilkins' life. Many of them forever.

Shortly after Wilkins' death, author John Grierson approached Suzanne with a request to write her husband's biography. Suzanne agreed, on condition that she received thirty per cent of Grierson's royalties. Grierson was initially allowed access to Wilkins' collection of films and writings, but Suzanne soon had second thoughts when she realised she was losing control of her husband's story. When Grierson wrote to Wilkins' family in Australia, Suzanne also wrote to them, insisting they not reply. Information about Wilkins, she said, was to come only from her.

In a very short time she and Grierson were no longer on speaking terms. She demanded the return of all of Wilkins' material and threatened to sue Grierson if he published. Grierson countered by threatening to sue her if she tried to stop him. The next news disturbed Suzanne even more: Grierson was planning to sell the film rights to his book. Suzanne would have no control over this. More to the point, she would make no money from the deal. She consulted her lawyer and was advised there was not a lot she could do, except demand the return of her property.

Suzanne decided the best way to stop Grierson would be to have someone else write a book about Wilkins. She wanted a popular author who would outsell Grierson and thereby diminish the value of his book, hopefully to a point where no one would want to base a film on it. She turned to one of Wilkins' friends, the author and filmmaker Lowell Thomas, believing:

> A book with Lowell's name on it should sell . . . as to Grierson I think any book he writes will have a far more academic quality, probably more scientific and scholarly in his way, whereas Lowell's should be more racy while still truthful and very readable. I don't care about all this beyond the fact that [were] Grierson able to sue successfully I might very well wind up the loser.

To assist both authors Suzanne handed over a copy of *Thrills*, an autobiographical radio serial that Wilkins had written in the 1950s. However, in the hope of keeping a radio audience enthralled, Wilkins had added many fictitious events to his life. For example, he wrote that when he stopped at Algiers on his first trip to England he was captured by slave-traders and carried off into the desert, only to be rescued by a beautiful maiden. That when he was filming the Balkans War he kept ending up in harems. That gypsy girls would stow away on his aeroplanes. That he fought duels, ran spy missions and had narrow escapes from death. In short, *Thrills* could best be described as semi-fictitious. It followed the major events of Wilkins' life but dramatised them with a great deal of fiction. Unfortunately, not knowing better, both authors relied heavily on *Thrills* for their biographies. In fact, unlike Grierson, Lowell Thomas didn't check any independent sources or do any other research at all. He simply omitted some of the more incredulous *Thrills* stories and published the rest as they were written by Wilkins. The only alterations he made were to change some Australian words to American: *paddock* became *field*, *station* became *ranch*, and so on.

Sir Hubert Wilkins – His World of Adventure. An Autobiography recounted by Lowell Thomas was published in 1961. Thomas's book sold well, was reprinted several times and has remained a standard reference for the life of George Hubert Wilkins ever since. Until now, no one has known it is largely fiction. Grierson's book, *Sir Hubert Wilkins – Enigma of Exploration*, was, as Suzanne predicted, not nearly as 'racy'. It enjoyed only one print run and copies are hard to find today.

After her experience with Grierson, Suzanne became extremely difficult towards anyone wanting to promote Wilkins or publicise his remarkable life. Harold Sherman, who had collaborated with Wilkins on a book exploring mental telepathy, recorded an example:

> I am sorry to say, I have a most unhappy memory of
> Suzanne. Wilkins had told me that if anything happened to
> him the complete ownership of our book *Thoughts Through*

Space was to belong to me. I trusted him completely. When Wilkins died it wasn't too long before Suzanne made demands on me. The book had gone through several editions but it has never been a big seller and is now out of print. It should be kept in print as it is considered a pioneering classic of its kind. I own the copyright.

In 1964, when I was on the West Coast, Ivan Tors ... drew up a contract with his producing company to make a feature picture out of *Thoughts Through Space* ... and his lawyers said he would need a clearance from Suzanne. The moment she heard about it she said she would not grant a clearance unless she was hired for $1,000 per week and all expenses to work on the picture as a personal consultant – that no one knew Sir Hubert as she did, and she must protect his name. This killed the deal. The word in the industry was that she was an impossible person and I can believe it from such experiences as I have had with her.

People soon stopped asking Suzanne for permission to write about, or make films about, her remarkable husband. No further biographies were written. No films were made. Wilkins became a footnote in the history books. The man who tried to reach the North Pole by submarine in 1931. The man who was first to fly in the Antarctic. The man who was first to fly an aeroplane across the Arctic Ocean. And there were lesser-known achievements that rarely, or never, rate a mention. The two years he spent in the Australian outback studying flora, fauna and the Aboriginal Australians. His participation in the England–Australia Air Race in 1919. How he organised the first crossing of the Antarctic continent. His role in the ill-fated Canadian Arctic Expedition in 1913. Or his photographic work at the Western

Front in World War One. Forty-five years of exploring, filming, photographing and recording – and Wilkins had kept everything. The scope and magnitude of his collection at his death must have been breathtaking.

Wilkins had devoted his life to exploring. He believed that with a better understanding of the environment, particularly the polar regions and their influence on the weather, the human race could raise itself above famine and war. It could secure a more just future for all its citizens, so that individuals, relieved of the daily struggle for survival, could unlock the power of their minds and elevate themselves spiritually. Wilkins' collection was, therefore, more than a record of his life. It was his gift to humanity. But after his death, Wilkins' legacy began to unravel.

Coincidentally, although it was entirely different, so too did Admiral Richard Byrd's.

* * *

When Richard Byrd died on 11 March 1957 he was firmly established as an American icon. His ascendency to this status began in 1926, when he was credited as the first man to fly over the North Pole. It had continued with his flights in Antarctica until he was forever frozen in the public imagination as the 'Admiral of the Antarctic' and 'America's Greatest Polar Explorer'.

In the 1920s the new American industrial age was creating mass production, mass consumerism, mass culture and the frenzy of mass media. Americans wanted heroes who would personify the growing dominance of America in world events, who were youthful, strong and pioneering. There were many heroes in the 1920s who were swept up in the public fascination with those who stood out, but no one understood the emerging power of the media – or manipulated it – like Byrd. Some, like the shy Charles Lindbergh, sought privacy and shunned adulation. Others, like Babe Ruth, revelled in it until it drowned them in a life of waste and dissipation. Not Byrd. He strode centre stage and commandeered the spotlight. He used the media while never allowing it to use him, and three decades later his public image remained carefully groomed and intact. When he died it was almost too perfect.

At the time of Byrd's death, Bernt Balchen was writing his autobiography. Balchen had known Byrd well and been his pilot on the first flight over the South Pole. A few months after Byrd's death, Balchen delivered his manuscript to his publisher, E. P. Dutton. Almost immediately, Dutton began getting warnings from members of Byrd's family, as well as his supporters and expedition members, not to publish anything that might be detrimental to Byrd's memory. Dutton ignored the warnings and circulated unbound galleys to reviewers in February 1958. The warnings soon escalated into legal threats. After taking advice, Dutton destroyed the galleys and removed the offending paragraphs. The expurgated version of Balchen's autobiography was finally published, and for the time being Byrd's public image stood unchallenged.

Five years later Eugene Rodgers became Public Information Officer for the US Antarctic Research Program. Rodgers started looking for books about Byrd, but the only ones he could find were written by Byrd himself, or his men, and were dated. Also, they only gave technical details of the expeditions and did not explain the personalities or the human side of the stories. Rodgers decided to write his own book, to 'give the late Admiral his due'. He began contacting Byrd's associates in an effort to interview them and was astounded at the animosity he encountered. Many refused to talk to him. Others tried to intimidate him or warn him off the story. He was told to interview only men of 'good character' and not 'Byrd's detractors'. He learnt that Byrd's eccentric son, Richard E. Byrd Jr, was refusing to let researchers access his father's papers, and that it was Byrd Jr who had orchestrated the attack on Bernt Balchen's book. Rodgers wrote that:

> [nothing could] explain the degree of evasion and animosity I encountered. I felt as if Byrd's intimates were sitting on some unspeakable secret. Byrd's idolators seem so opposed to complete, frank treatments of Byrd and his expeditions that they would rather he be forgotten than that the legend that he and they created be compromised.

Undaunted, Rodgers continued his research.

In 1971 an American journalist, Richard Montague, published a book titled *Oceans, Poles and Airmen*. 'The late twenties and early thirties,' wrote Montague, 'were aviation's most romantic years. Neither before nor since has flying produced such a host of eager adventurers.' His book, he explained, 'was an effort to keep their memories bright a little longer'. Montague then went on to explain a secondary aim of the book – to 'expose a fraud':

> That Byrd's claim to have reached the [North] Pole was a fraud seems clear beyond any reasonable doubt. In fact it seems to have been the biggest and most successful fraud in the history of polar exploration.

Montague had interviewed Bernt Balchen, who, more than ten years after his autobiography had been forcibly edited, was willing to talk frankly about what had been left out. What's more, Montague sought Byrd's original charts, which, back in 1926, had been handed over to a committee of the National Geographic Society in order to verify that Byrd had reached the North Pole:

> When the committee of experts finished with them, it gave them back to the Navy. The Navy says it gave them to the National Archives. And the Archives say that if the Navy did, they can't be located.

Following the release of *Oceans, Poles and Airmen*, theories began to fly thick and fast. Not content merely to suggest that Byrd might not have reached the North Pole, writers began to publish theories about conspiracies that had protected him for thirty years. Byrd, some authors claimed, had simply taken off, flown a little way up the coast and then circled his plane for some fifteen hours, before returning to say he had reached the North Pole.

A further indictment of Byrd came with the eventual publication of Eugene Rodgers' book, *Beyond the Barrier*, in 1990. After many years of research, Rodgers dealt primarily with Byrd's first Antarctic expedition; his well–documented research destroyed any lingering myth of the righteous upstanding hero. Byrd was paranoid, vindictive, lied about many of his discoveries and stole kudos unfairly from his men. What's more, he probably didn't know where he was when he flew to the South Pole and had got drunk before his plane had returned to base. According to Rodgers, all Byrd's discontent seemed to have its origin in the North Pole flight.

The debate about Byrd and his achievements continues today. Ironically, his legacy is not what he would have wished.

The image of the towering hero striding valiantly across the globe on some noble quest did not last. His critics call him a cheat and a liar and claim he never flew to the North Pole. His supporters say that he did, or at least genuinely believed that he had reached it. But no one has yet provided a definitive answer to the question of what really happened on the North Pole flight. Knowing this will go to the core of the Byrd legend and finally expose the true man.

When Byrd's actions are examined closely, along with those of Wilkins and Roald Amundsen, not only does the riddle of the polar air race present itself, but so too does a solution. Wilkins and Amundsen provide some of the clues, as do contemporary newspaper reports and independent observers. Ultimately, however, it is Byrd himself who tells us what really happened, clearly and in his own handwriting. In effect, he solves the mystery that he created for the world eighty years ago.

2

The Seeds of Disaster

There is nothing at the North Pole. No gold to be mined. No ancient civilisation to convert to Christianity. There is neither strategic advantage to be used in a time of war nor revelation regarding our history. There is no reason for an individual to go there, other than to say he has been to an imaginary point on which the globe rotates. The ability to be able to say this has driven men to extraordinary feats of heroism and deception. With a compulsion that far outweighs mere scientific or geographic curiosity, they have fought, struggled, lied and sometimes died as they obsessively inched their way forward to reach a point that, in practical terms, means nothing.

The North Pole is a goal, like the summit of Mount Everest, against which people feel a need to measure themselves. And so rarely do they say they have simply 'reached' it. Instead they feel they have 'conquered' it, while in truth they have really conquered fears, shortcomings and limits of physical endurance within themselves to demonstrate to the rest of society that they are somehow different – that they are special.

Central to this compulsive behaviour is the ability to travel in this inhospitable environment. A naked man would not last a minute. So, in their quest to stand apart from society, each adventurer has also had to take and adapt the best technology for polar travel that his society could provide. In 1888, the year that both Wilkins and Byrd were born, the technology of polar travel underwent a transformation. The architect of this transformation was a Norwegian, Fridtjof Nansen, and to understand it we need to look briefly at the attempts to explore the Arctic up until this time.

Seafarers travelling north had been bumping into what they described as a 'wall of ice' almost from the beginning of recorded history. About 330 BC the Greek Pytheas reached the Arctic ice pack. The Vikings who roamed the Arctic waters in the Middle Ages may have reached Spitsbergen. They certainly reached America and colonised Greenland.

When Ferdinand Magellan's expedition sailed around the world in 1519–22 it confirmed that the earth was in fact a globe and not a flat surface. As a spinning globe, it must have a north and south 'pole'. With the Spanish and Portuguese dominating the trade routes to China, Asia and the Pacific Ocean, the British and the Dutch began wondering if it were possible to reach these areas by sailing over the top of the globe.

Various European expeditions set out, heading north in sailing ships and navigating between either Spitsbergen and Greenland or Greenland and Canada. But they kept coming up against the wall of ice. Some tried to push their way through it, expecting that an open polar sea on the other side would give them clear sailing to the North Pole, and then on to the Barents Sea, which they knew was the gateway to the Pacific Ocean. The further they pushed their ships into the ice the more difficult, and sometimes disastrous, things became. By the 1820s the British Admiralty, who were mounting the most expeditions, began to accept that the Arctic might be covered by ice, or at least that the wall of ice might conceal land closer to the North Pole. Either way, attempts to find a clear, open sailing route to the Pacific seemed futile.

It was about this time that the idea of reaching the North Pole purely for the sake of reaching it began to take shape in explorers' minds. In 1827 the British Admiralty despatched an expedition with 'sledge boats'. The expedition, under John Franklin and William Parry, would sail north from Spitsbergen until it reached the ice, then it would attempt to man-haul the sledge boats to the Pole. Of course, if open sea was found again, the sledge boats would be put back in the water and the expedition would keep sailing. It was the first realistic and organised effort to reach the North Pole, but it didn't get very far due to the impossibly heavy sledge boats, each of which weighed some 3753 pounds (1702 kilograms).

The British sent Franklin back in 1845 but the expedition disappeared. In the 1840s and 1850s some thirty expeditions searched for Franklin, and between them they succeeded in mapping a great deal of the Canadian Archipelago. But in the end both the Admiralty and the public became thoroughly sick of the expenditure and effort being wasted on exploring the Arctic, for little or no return.

Arctic exploration was revitalised in 1875 when a Franklin search veteran, Captain George Nares, was appointed to command an expedition, one of whose objectives was to reach the North Pole. The expedition's two ships successfully sailed to the north-eastern extremity of Ellesmere Island, where the crew wintered over. A polar sledge party, led by Commander Albert Markham, set out in April 1876 to make a dash to the Pole. The party consisted of two large sledges and fifteen men, but little seemed to have changed since the Franklin–Parry sledge boat expedition forty-nine years earlier. Their 'dash' became a slow slog, made more difficult by their ill-suited equipment.

They refused to learn from the Scandinavians and chose poor clothing and tents. After less than a week, Markham reported that their clothing was frozen and the temperature inside their tents was minus twenty-two degrees Fahrenheit. Their method of getting the two heavy sledges over the rougher ice was to make a road with picks and shovels, then to drag their sledges along it. Four weeks out, the men were breaking down physically and they were still over 400 miles from the North Pole. On 9 May Markham wrote:

> We have at great length arrived at the conclusion, although with a great deal of reluctance, that our sick men are really suffering from scurvy, and that in no mild form. Should our surmise be correct, we can scarcely expect to see any of the afflicted ones improve until they can be supplied with fresh meat and vegetables.

The next day Markham turned around and headed back.

The expedition had reached 83° 20' 26" north latitude: a new record 'farthest north'. But it had again sated any appetite the British Admiralty and public had for expeditions attempting to reach a global pole. The press called the expedition a failure; in hindsight, the shortcomings of hauling sledges, not being properly equipped and not allowing for the onset of scurvy seem glaringly obvious. But Markham went on to become Vice Admiral Sir Albert Markham and Commodore of the Royal Navy Training Squadron. In 1887 he was in the West Indies when he invited his cousin Sir Clements Markham to dinner. Sir Clements was the secretary of the Royal Geographical Society and was planning to sponsor an expedition to Antarctica. The cousins discussed polar travel and Albert introduced Sir Clements to a young midshipman under his command. The midshipman's name was Robert Falcon Scott, and the seeds of another British disaster in polar exploration were sown.

Into this arena of wilful self-sacrifice in the name of polar travel stepped the Norwegian Fridtjof Nansen. In the summer of 1888 he and five companions crossed Greenland from Umivik to Godthaab. The Greenland ice cap had never been crossed before, but more importantly, no one had ever travelled like Nansen. He introduced a catalogue of innovations: a light, one-person wooden sledge running on skis, as well as special clothing and tents, and a lightweight saucepan that became known as the 'Nansen cooker'. He developed sledging rations based on a man's needs rather than on his comfort. At the heart of Nansen's innovation was the idea that the best way for a man to travel over snow and ice was on skis. Nansen returned to Christiana (now Oslo) a triumphant hero. Among the crowd that cheered him, as his ship sailed up the fjord, was a seventeen-year-old schoolboy named Roald Amundsen.

Nansen's next idea was as bold as it was brilliant: take a ship, provision it for Arctic travel and a long stay away from civilisation, then purposely sail it into the ice pack somewhere north of Siberia. Then simply wait and let the moving ice pack do the work. The ship might drift close to the North Pole. In the spring it would sail out of the ice pack, perhaps near Spitsbergen or Greenland. Nansen had a special ship built, the *Fram* (Forward). Its strong wooden hull had rounded sides, so that when squeezed by ice it would ride up instead of being crushed.

In a famous Arctic voyage, the *Fram* entered the ice north of the New Siberian Islands in September 1893 and began to drift slowly westward. But it became apparent to Nansen that the ship would drift no closer than 400 miles from the Pole – and it was going to be a very slow voyage.

A year later, still on board the *Fram*, which was still locked in the ice, Nansen began planning a dash for the North Pole using dogs, skis, his lightweight sledges and kayaks for when they reached open water. With a companion he set out on 14 March 1895. Initially they made very good progress, travelling up to twenty miles a day, but they discovered the ice closer to the Pole was impassable and turned back on 8 April. More dogs, Nansen believed, would have allowed them to continue. He had got as far as 86° 13' 06" north: a new record by nearly three degrees.

Fourteen months later, after walking 500 miles and wintering in a makeshift hut on the ice, Nansen and his companion reached one of the islands in Franz Josef Land north of Siberia. He returned to Norway a hero again. The *Fram*, with its crew of eleven men still on board, was freed near Spitsbergen after a three-year ice drift.

* * *

Roald Engebreth Gravning Amundsen was born on 16 July 1872 at Hvidsten, Norway. His ambitions turned towards polar exploration on the day he stood with the crowd welcoming Nansen back from his Greenland crossing. That same year, Amundsen went on the first of many long ski tours to condition himself for life as a polar explorer. He made his own sleeping bag, based on Nansen's design, and his own jacket with a sewn-in hood, again copied from Nansen, who in turn had imitated an Eskimo design. Amundsen also made improvements to skis, boots and bindings.

In 1896 Amundsen was appointed second mate aboard the *Belgica*, which the Belgian Adrien de Gerlache was preparing for an expedition to Antarctica. Amundsen travelled south, wintered over on the *Belgica* when it became stuck in the ice in the Bellinghausen Sea, then returned to Norway in 1899.

Having served his apprenticeship as a polar explorer it was now time for Amundsen to lead his own expedition. This, he decided, would be to sail the Northwest Passage. The ability to sail north on the Atlantic Ocean, 'over the top' of America and Canada and down into the Pacific Ocean, had been a goal of sailors for 300 years. Various expeditions had attempted the Northwest Passage from both directions, but none had succeeded. Amundsen's idea, however, was not to take a large, fully provisioned ship and a large crew. Like Nansen, he realised that success in polar travel lay in small numbers, light weight and, where possible, living off the land. Whereas the British had attempted the Northwest Passage with 200-ton, three-masted ships holding a crew of upwards of 40 men, Amundsen purchased a small coastal fishing boat, the *Gjøa*. With a crew of five men, he slipped away from Christiana at midnight on 16 June 1903. He sailed up the west coast of Greenland, around the Boothia Peninsula, through the James Ross and Rae Straits, and into the Simpson Strait. He put the *Gjøa* into a small bay and by 3 October 1903 the ship was frozen in. It would remain so for almost two years.

Amundsen now began training for polar exploration in earnest. He was a competent skier but had little experience at driving dogs. He began practising daily with the pack he had brought with him. A month after reaching Gjoa Haven, as Amundsen named the bay, the men were visited by Eskimos, and Amundsen was careful to gain their trust and friendship. One Eskimo family camped by the *Gjøa* and each morning Amundsen would practise building igloos under their guidance. He also built up his stock of Eskimo clothing and learnt techniques for making sledges slide on any kind of snow, especially at very cold temperatures. On 13 August 1905 the *Gjøa* sailed out of Gjoa Haven and continued its journey west. Two weeks later a whaling ship out of San Francisco was sighted. Amundsen had sailed through the Northwest Passage. He was a famous man.

Amundsen's ambition and restless energy now turned to the greatest goal in Arctic exploration: the North Pole. He wanted to repeat Nansen's drift in the ice pack, but to enter it further to the east, hoping to drift to a higher latitude, possibly even to the Pole itself. In any event, Amundsen intended to be close enough to reach it with ski, sledge and dogs. He needed a ship and the ideal one was Nansen's *Fram*. Amundsen met with Nansen and eventually convinced him to loan him the *Fram*. Amundsen then toured and lectured, trying to pay off his debts and raise money for the new expedition. It was a slow process. He announced his intentions on 10 November 1908 and, while still trying to raise money, began the task of equipping the *Fram*. Amundsen hoped to leave in January 1910. But everything changed when his departure was just four months away.

On 1 September 1909 Amundsen opened his newspaper to read that Dr Frederick Cook, a friend who had been on the *Belgica* in Antarctica with him, had announced that he had reached the North Pole on 21 April 1908 and had wintered in Greenland before returning. A week later, Robert Peary claimed to have reached the North Pole a year after Cook – on 6 April 1909. (Today the debate over whether either, both or neither man reached the North Pole continues to such a degree that it can safely be called an industry in itself.) Neither Cook nor Peary produced navigational readings, or independent witnesses, to prove they had reached the Pole. No one will ever know if either of them actually did.

But to Amundsen, these questions were irrelevant. The North Pole had been claimed and he understood the significance of that. He knew the importance of exploring 'firsts' and how they equated to newspaper column inches, audience sizes and, ultimately, sponsorship dollars. He had the *Fram*, a small and trusted crew, the experience of travelling over ice and snow, and most of the required money and equipment. He quickly made a decision: he would be the first to the South Pole.

Then, less than a week after Peary announced his attainment of the North Pole, a newspaper article appeared announcing that Captain Robert Scott was planning another British expedition to Antarctica for scientific purposes, along with the intention of reaching the South Pole. Amundsen was now in a race with Scott; it was a race that Amundsen won on 14 December 1911. Amundsen's South Pole journey was his crowning achievement and the most brilliantly executed success of the heroic age of polar exploration. It was a masterpiece of planning and organisation, confidently carried through, and aided by no small amount of luck.

But Amundsen was less adept in the civilised world, where the significance of his achievement was not always understood. A year later he was in America, touring the lecture circuit yet again to pay debts, when the news came that Scott's party had died on their return journey from the South Pole. Amundsen returned to Norway and resurrected his plan of taking a ship on an Arctic drift, but the idea now seemed hollow. The North and South Poles had been reached and the Northeast and Northwest Passages navigated by ship. All that remained was to fill in the blanks on the world map. And Amundsen rightly foresaw that this would not be done by using the techniques of dogs, sledges and skiing that he had mastered, but by applying a new invention: the aeroplane.

Amundsen saw his first plane flight in Germany in 1913 and immediately learned to fly. He obtained Norway's first civilian pilot's licence in 1914, but World War One broke out before he could mount an expedition to explore the Arctic from the air. After the war he was unable to find planes capable of flying the long distances he required, so, impatient to return north, he built his own ship modelled on Nansen's *Fram*. Amundsen named his *Maud*, after the Queen of Norway, and sailed it through the Northeast Passage, commencing in 1918. The expedition achieved little and attracted scant attention. Aviators were now grabbing the headlines with their daring, record-breaking flights. Amundsen realised that planes were the key not only to the future of exploration, but to gaining the sponsorship and audiences he needed to survive financially. He decided he would become the first person to fly to the North Pole.

He purchased two small planes and took them to Wainwright, Alaska, but crashed them both before he was able to get airborne. He returned home in debt again and declared himself bankrupt. But, with the single-minded focus that was both his strength and his downfall, Amundsen ordered two of the latest German-designed Dornier-Wal flying boats. These planes, he decided, would be more suitable for flying in the Arctic because they could take off and land on water, or even on smooth ice. To pay for them, Amundsen went to America on a lecture tour, but a decade and a war had dimmed the memories of the public, and he found himself talking to empty seats. Then, on 7 October 1924, while locked in a hotel room in New York, refusing to meet callers lest they be creditors, Amundsen received a phone call that would once more lead him to the centre stage of world exploration.

* * *

'I am frankly a hero-worshipper and always have been,' wrote Lincoln Ellsworth. 'Three great men have stood out before my eyes – three who have inspired me most and whom I have tried most to emulate – Theodore Roosevelt, Roald Amundsen, and the Western frontiersman Wyatt Earp. Rated by their influence on me, the greatest of these was Wyatt Earp, but the one I knew was Amundsen.'

Lincoln Ellsworth was a shy, sensitive child of delicate health whose mother died when he was eight. Ellsworth grew up in fear and awe of his father, a rich and powerful American industrialist who had developed coal mines in Washington County, Pennsylvania. After studying engineering in college, Ellsworth's love of the outdoors led him to go looking for Incan relics in Colombia. To satisfy his father's ambition, he put his engineering qualifications to work building railways in Canada, but soon found himself following 'Indian trails' that led to Alaska where, for the first time, he stood on the coast and looked north to the frozen Arctic. Here, he said, his ambition to be a polar explorer crystallised.

Crystallised it may have, but it would be two decades before Ellsworth transformed his dream into action. In 1924, at the age of forty-four, Ellsworth had just returned from an expedition gathering fossils in Peru and was living in New York, preparing for another trip to South America. He noticed a small item in the newspaper announcing that Roald Amundsen had arrived in New York the previous day. Ellsworth rang the famous explorer and asked for a meeting. Amundsen consented. Their meeting extended to dinner, over which the two men discovered they had much to offer each other. Ellsworth wanted adventure, fame and to prove himself to a domineering father. Amundsen was tired of battling creditors and now wanted to return to the Arctic; he just needed someone to foot the bill.

Ellsworth wrote:

> Thus I came to Amundsen as a godsend, bringing not only
> new blood and enthusiasm to bolster up his spirits, but a
> chance as well to secure financing for some magnificent
> adventure.

Over the dinner the pair discussed plans for a flight over the Arctic Sea, with Ellsworth hoping to secure the finance from his father. Otherwise, Ellsworth would invest what money he had of his own to make exploratory flights to areas that had not been completely mapped. 'Failing to do that, we might both go to his cabin at Wainwright, Alaska, and make a study of Arctic birds,' Ellsworth later wrote.

But their first ambition was to fly to the North Pole and across the Arctic Sea. Amundsen instructed the factory to resume building the Dornier-Wal flying boats he had ordered. Ellsworth pledged $20,000 of his own money and set out to convince his wealthy father to put up another $50,000. Ellsworth Senior alternately supported the project and attempted to stop it. Father and son bickered continually but eventually the money was forthcoming. To get it, Lincoln Ellsworth had to promise his father that he would only fly from Spitsbergen to the North Pole and back. That is, he would not make the longer flight over the Arctic Sea to Alaska.

On 8 April 1925 the expedition ship, carrying equipment, crew and the two unassembled flying boats, left Tromso for Spitsbergen, where they arrived at the small coalmining settlement of Kings Bay. The flying boats were unpacked and assembled. Ellsworth, who claimed the entire focus of his life to this point had been directed towards polar exploration, attempted skiing for the first time.

There was still confusion about whether the expedition would fly to the North Pole and back to Kings Bay, or continue to Alaska. Amundsen was aware of Ellsworth's promise to his father but was keen to make what he called 'the big trip'. The real unexplored area was between the North Pole and Alaska, and if there was any new land to be discovered – perhaps even a new continent – then this was where it would be found. On 28 April Amundsen had a meeting with Ellsworth and the two pilots, Hjalmar Riiser-Larsen and Lief Dietrichson, to outline the plan.

The two planes, he proposed, with three men in each plane, would fly to the North Pole, where they would land and take observations. Then Amundsen, Riiser-Larsen and a mechanic would take off and continue onto Alaska in one plane. Ellsworth, Dietrichson and the other mechanic would return to Kings Bay. The two pilots were opposed to the idea and refused. The planes were untried and their fuel consumption unknown, they argued. Even being able to get to the Pole and back was uncertain. Splitting the expedition was unwise. If they stayed together, should one plane crash, then there was a chance the six men could return in the other. Amundsen grumbled and agreed not to make the big trip, but the pilots expressed doubts he would keep his word.

With the planes assembled, the expedition waited for suitable weather for flying. Three weeks later Amundsen climbed into the nose seat of the plane designated *N-25*. Behind him were pilot Riiser-Larsen and, in the rear of the plane, mechanic Karl Feucht. Ellsworth climbed into the nose seat of the *N-24*, Dietrichson took the controls, and mechanic Oscar Omdal sat in the rear. Neither plane carried a radio.

The first aeroplane flight to explore the Arctic ice pack, and attempt to reach the North Pole, lifted off from Kings Bay, Spitsbergen, at 5.15 pm on 21 May 1925. The coalmines were shut for the day so the miners could watch the historic undertaking. Riiser-Larsen throttled up the Dornier-Wal *N-25*, which bumped its way along the ice. Amundsen sat quietly, staring intently ahead: the man again going where no man had gone before. A cheer went up from the miners as the *N-25* lifted into the air. Ellsworth's plane got stuck and had to be rocked back and forth before it could begin to taxi. As it slid along the ice Dietrichson heard a ripping sound and thought the duralumin hull had been torn. Nevertheless, he got the plane into the air and followed Amundsen's course. The two planes circled Kings Bay before heading north.

As they flew north they opened a new era in exploration. Ellsworth would later write:

> At 3,000 feet of altitude a simple calculation told us that with glasses we could see between sixty and seventy miles in every direction. Thus, into one of those white patches of the map which had so struck my wonder as a child I was now helping to draw an explored band, 125 miles wide. Heavy transport planes were not so fast then as now. Our cruising speed of 75 miles an hour seemed tremendous in 1925. Every hour we were putting behind us a journey that would take a sledge-party a week to accomplish. Every hour we added to known geography more than nine thousand square miles of the earth's surface.

The two planes flew steadily north, side by side, until the sun directly ahead told them that it was midnight. They had been flying seven hours. An hour later they flew over a lead (an area of open water in the ice) and the *N-25*, flown by Riiser-Larsen and with Amundsen on board, dipped and banked, seemingly waving the *N-24* to follow. To Ellsworth the landing looked precarious, almost impossible, but without radio he couldn't confirm Amundsen's intentions. He had no choice but to signal the pilot to follow them down onto the ice. Dietrichson searched for clear water on which to land, eventually choosing a small lagoon. Their flying boat bounced across the water to end nose-up, against the ice on the far side.

Ellsworth, Dietrichson and Omdal scrambled clear and Ellsworth took observations. They had landed at 87° 44' north – 136 nautical miles short of the pole. And they had drifted well to the west. They also found the hull of the *N-24* was leaking as a result of the damage sustained during take-off. Their flying boat was sinking. Omdal set to work pumping it out while Ellsworth and Dietrichson went to look for the *N-25*. From the tops of the ice hummocks they could see nothing of the other plane or the three crew members.

The crew of the *N-24* assessed their position. One of their engines was wrecked. Their flying boat was leaking badly and had to be dragged up onto the ice to stop it from sinking. The chances of getting airborne again were virtually nil. They were stranded on the ice and had no idea where the *N-25* was. Dietrichson commented that, knowing Amundsen, he would have flown on to the Pole alone. Dejected, the men set up their tent to prepare a meal and rest. A few hours later Ellsworth and Dietrichson climbed to the top of a tall ice ridge and spotted the *N-25* about three miles away.

Five days later, after a risky trip across the thin ice, the three men from the *N-24* reached Amundsen, Riiser-Larsen and Feucht, who were camped by the *N-25*, trying to repair it. When the plane had descended to the ice it was not a planned landing; a break in the air intake had caused a temporary engine failure. Amundsen had not been signalling the *N-24* to follow them down onto the ice. Just the opposite. The positive news was that the *N-25* was undamaged and ready to fly. However, there was no open lead in which the flying boat could take off. Using small tools and their hands, the men hacked out a 500-yard runway and packed it flat. It was exhausting work that took three weeks to complete. To some extent, it was Amundsen's survival skills that kept the six men alive on the ice during this period.

On 15 June all six climbed into the *N-25* and, with Riiser-Larsen at the controls, they took off. Despite the hopelessly overloaded plane, they still managed to reach a remote area off the coast of Spitsbergen. A passing sealing boat picked them up and three days later they arrived back at Kings Bay. The world had not heard from them in four weeks. Most people had assumed they were dead.

Ellsworth learned that on 2 June, while they had struggled to cut a runway on the ice, his father had died. He felt a tremendous sadness at the loss of his father but also, as we can sense from his writing, a feeling of relief. Ellsworth would inherit a fortune and could finally make decisions for himself.

Amundsen, on the other hand, could only reflect that his latest expedition was another failure. More bad press, more debt and more standing in front of half-filled theatres showing his glass slides in an attempt to sell his books. The wily Amundsen had a better idea: he flattered Ellsworth. Didn't the now-rich American have the same initials as the legendary Norse explorer, Leif Ericson? Surely this was a sign Ellsworth was destined to be a heroic figure in polar exploration.

Ellsworth didn't need much convincing. Before leaving Kings Bay, Amundsen had successfully pitched a new idea to him. A more expensive idea. An idea that would allow them to return to Spitsbergen in the northern summer of 1926 and become the first men to fly to the North Pole and cross the Arctic Sea.

3

Aviation Will Conquer the Arctic

Richard Evelyn Byrd was born on 26 October 1888. He was born into a family that could trace its roots in Virginia, USA, back to 1671. It was a family accustomed to wealth and influence. It was also a family that kept its skeletons securely in the closet. Byrd's father fought a losing battle with alcoholism, but despite his addiction still became a successful lawyer and pursued a political career, serving as the Speaker of the House in the Virginia State Assembly. His ability to do this was largely due to Byrd's mother. Eleanor Bolling Byrd was herself from a proud and traditional family and knew the importance of maintaining a public image. She instilled her beliefs in her son. Young Richard was encouraged from childhood to do many things, but above all he was instructed never to bring shame to the family name. Byrd learnt his lessons well.

The young Byrd seemed suited to a life of physical, rather than intellectual, activity. He was adequate at academics but excelled in sport. He played football for the University of Virginia and decided, along with his mother, that his best career possibilities lay in the United States Navy. Between 1904 and 1907 he attended the Shenandoah Valley Academy and then the Virginia Military Institute. He entered the United States Naval Academy in Annapolis in 1908. During his first year at the Academy Byrd broke his foot in three places while playing football, which ended his prospects in the sport. The athletic Byrd switched to gymnastics, where he also excelled, but he re-injured the same foot in a fall from the flying rings. This time the injury had long-reaching consequences for his naval career.

Byrd graduated from the Naval Academy in 1912 and served as a junior officer on various battleships. In 1914 he joined the USS *Washington* and travelled to the Gulf of Mexico with the US invasion forces. While there, he rescued drowning seamen on two occasions and received the Congressional Life-Saving Medal. He also experienced his first flight aboard a Curtiss flying boat.

By 1915 Byrd had married his lifelong companion, Marie Ames. Around this period, his good looks and athletic prowess, along with his family influence, began to tell on his career. He was assigned to the yacht of the Secretary of the Navy, and soon after to the yacht of President Woodrow Wilson, who was also a Virginian and a friend of the Byrd family. However, Byrd was unable to stand the long watches required of a junior officer and his classmates were promoted while he was not. In 1916, because of his disability, Byrd was granted retirement from active service.

It would be a short retirement. America was preparing to enter the war in Europe and naval officers were needed. Byrd worked as an administrator, first with the naval militia for the state of Rhode Island, and then with the Bureau of Naval Personnel in Washington DC. He found, almost by accident, that he was an excellent organiser and administrator. He made influential contacts and, still wanting a more active career, he won an appointment as a naval aviation cadet. Flying, Byrd reasoned, would be exciting, and he wouldn't have to stand on his injured foot in an aeroplane.

In 1917 he earned his pilot's wings. There was no US Air Force in 1917. All flying in the armed forces was undertaken by either the Army or the Navy. As a flyer, Byrd's Navy career had restarted. He became expert at night flying and developed an interest in the problems of navigation from planes. Using the traditional instruments of navigation, the compass and the sextant, in the cramped cockpit of a plane flying at speed, often through cloud and buffeted by winds, was far more difficult than using them on the deck of a ship. At the same time, the war in Europe was advancing aeroplane technology quickly. What had begun the war as underpowered, unreliable box kites were, by 1918, machines capable of crossing continents and oceans.

Byrd was assigned the administrative task of getting US planes to Europe. He suggested they be flown, rather than shipped, across the Atlantic. At the time, the Navy was building the largest flying boats yet seen, and Byrd proposed that they could be flown in stages across the Atlantic, landing on the water to be refuelled by waiting Navy warships. In this way they could fly from America to Newfoundland, then in sea hops to the Azores, then on to Europe. Byrd raised this idea in 1917, then again in May 1918:

> And in the following week I learned confidentially that Walter Camp and Admiral Peary, discoverer of the North Pole, had gone to the Navy Department and urged that the flight be undertaken. This touched me in a tender spot also because I had long thought a flight across the North Pole was possible.

Although the US Navy was seriously considering the idea of the transatlantic flight, Byrd wasn't selected for the leading role he would have liked. Instead, in August 1918 he was sent to Halifax, Nova Scotia, to construct a Navy Air Station that could be used by seaplanes looking for German submarines. This gave Byrd his first opportunity to organise men, materials and aeroplanes in a remote area, and he took to the job with relish, seeing it as a stepping stone to the transatlantic flight.

> Meanwhile . . . with fading hopes I continued to work on the Trans-Atlantic Flight problem. We could not understand the silence of Washington on the subject. At every mail, at every dispatch blank that was handed to me, I braced myself for the great news that the NC-1 [flying boat] was at last ready to start. But always I was disappointed. Storms were getting more and more frequent. Days were growing shorter. Temperature was slowly falling towards the inevitable zero. But . . . [I] clung to the belief that if the big flying boat would only show up we would be capable of taking her safely to the Azores, and thence to France.

Byrd also worked on the problems of navigating a plane out of sight of land. Flyers of the time were still navigating by following rail lines, roads and other landmarks. Through his work on these problems Byrd helped develop the bubble sextant and the drift indicator, both of which would later be vital for his polar flights.

After the armistice was declared on 11 November 1918, Byrd was ordered to hand the airbase he had established over to the Canadians and return to Washington. There he learnt, to his surprise, that the Navy was now planning to make the transatlantic flight. But personnel who had served on foreign soil, including Canada, would not be permitted to take part in the actual flying. Byrd was disappointed but wrote: '. . . after all, the important thing is for an American navy plane to prove that it can first fly the Atlantic Ocean.'

The Secretary of the Navy approved the flight in February 1919. The Navy didn't have confidence in the aerial navigation of the time, so the plan was to have warships positioned fifty miles apart, across the width of the Atlantic. The planes would follow this line of ships, which at night would regularly send up flares to light the route. Byrd was assigned to help organise the attempt, and again his organisational skills combined with his Navy and political contacts to get things done. He wrote:

> Red tape was cut at every opportunity. Bureaus of Ordnance, Navigation, Construction and Repair, and Operations were all subordinated at times to help us get ready.
>
> As the weeks flew by a thousand new details of preparation seemed to crop up every day. There were complications with the State Department in getting permission to land on foreign soil. Navigational instruments we had evolved had to be given special tests. We made flights for measurement of fuel consumption. Careful plans were laid for communication with the ships that would cover our course. Fuel depots and repair stations were prepared up the coast. Radio tests were a matter of routine.

Three flying boats, the *NC-1*, *NC-3* and *NC-4*, commenced the flight on 8 May 1919. To assist with navigation, Byrd was permitted aboard the *NC-3* for the first two legs from Long Island to Halifax and Trepassey, Newfoundland. The *NC-3*'s pilot, Commander Towers, wrote a description of Byrd during the first legs which gives a clue, as will be seen later, to what happened on the North Pole flight:

Byrd spent the afternoon vibrating between the forward
and after cockpits, trying smoke bombs, sextants, etc. My
cockpit was not very large, and with all the charts, chart
desk, sextants, drift indicator, binoculars, chronometers,
etc., stacked in there, very little room was left. As I wore
a telephone at all times, wires were trailing all about me,
and Byrd and I were continually getting all mixed up like a
couple of puppies on leashes. Occasionally one of the pilots
would come forward for a cup of coffee or a sandwich, or to
take a look at the chart to find out how we were progressing.
All these little festivities were rudely broken up about the
middle of the afternoon when a squall hit us.

The three flying boats reached Trepassey on 9 May and Byrd
was involved in the first air race of his life: the race to fly the
Atlantic. He wrote:

The situation was pretty critical due to the presence of the
foreign contestants for first Trans-Atlantic air honours.
British Captains John Alcock and Arthur Brown, R.A.F., were
there with their little plane all ready to start. Lieutenant
Commander Grieve, R.N. and H.B. Hawker were also
grooming to hop off for Ireland or England. As both had
rather small planes we felt they were taking big chances.

While the US Navy flying boats and the other teams waited
at Trepassey, Byrd learnt that a small US Navy airship, *C5*, had
arrived at nearby St John's and was also preparing to make the
crossing. Byrd quickly switched his allegiance:

I grasped at this straw. Perhaps I would fly the Atlantic after
all! Now began a brief but exciting period for me while I

nursed my last thin hope that I might still be in one of the aircraft to cross the ocean. If I got away and aboard her, and she flew, there was still a chance that the miracle for which I hoped might happen.

Byrd was ready to travel to St John's to plead his case for a place on the *C5* when he learnt the airship had broken away from its mooring and blown out to sea with no one on board. At Trepassey the three US Navy flying boats, along with the teams of Alcock and Brown, and Hawker and Grieve, waited for the weather to clear sufficiently to permit flying.

The three Navy flying boats were first away, on 16 May. They took off at 7.30 pm and became separated during the night. The next morning the *NC-3* was unable to locate any of the fifty US warships strung out across the ocean, so the crew landed on the water and attempted to establish their position. They spent two nights on the water before they drifted to San Miguel, one of the islands of the Azores. Their damaged plane could fly no further. The *NC-1* had a similar experience. It landed in rough seas and the crew bailed out water for six hours, before being picked up by a passing Greek merchant ship. Only the *NC-4* made it unscathed to the Azores after fifteen hours and eighteen minutes of flying. Here the crew waited nine days for the weather to clear.

In the meantime, one of the other teams at Trepassey began its flight. Hawker and Grieve took off on 18 May and, after flying for over fourteen hours and passing the Azores, were forced to ditch in the ocean to be picked up by a Danish steamer.

On 27 May the *NC-4* took off again, and after flying a further nine hours and forty-three minutes, landed at Lisbon, Portugal. Byrd had not been on the first flight across the

Atlantic, which had taken three flying boats and fifty warships to accomplish, but he wrote that:

> ... the American Navy – bless her – had once more won the admiration of the world; and the stars and stripes had been the first across the Atlantic through the air.

Byrd returned to Washington, where he continued to work at widening his influence and power within the Navy. He led the drive to create a Department of Aeronautics and opposed the famous Colonel Billy Mitchell and his efforts to create an independent air force, even to the point of testifying at Mitchell's court martial.

Byrd joined the Freemasons in March 1921. The organisation appealed to him because it cultivated the twin values of secrecy and loyalty, just as Byrd's mother had done. (Byrd would later form the first masonic lodge in Antarctica.) His membership delivered immediate results and within weeks he was selected for a task of responsibility and prestige. He was sent to England to join the crew of the airship *ZR-2* (which the British designated *R38*) and to use his navigational skills to help pilot it back to America.

The British had built the *R38* for the US Navy, based on the Zeppelin technology secured from Germany at the end of the war. At the time it was the largest airship yet built and the eyes of the aeronautical world looked keenly upon it. To be the navigator aboard the airship's first crossing of the Atlantic was a responsibility Byrd could relish. He arrived in England on 20 August and learnt that a final trial flight would take place within days. When he telephoned the commander of the airship and asked to be taken along, he was told places were limited. If he wanted to be included he should come to Howden Airfield immediately to have his name put on a list. The next morning Byrd missed the train to Howden, and when he finally arrived his place had been taken. As the airship took off on its trial flight Byrd could only stand and watch and curse his luck.

While flying over the city of Hull, a tight turn was ordered to test the massive airship at low altitude. Part-way through the turn, the frame snapped and split in two. The front section burst into flames and plunged into the Humber River, while the rear section floated to the ground. Of the forty-nine men on board only five survived.

By coincidence, George Hubert Wilkins also missed the flight because of a late telegram. Wilkins had wanted to be on board because, at the time, he was interested in an airship for exploring the Arctic. Thus, fate determined that the two men, whose future paths were intertwined, were not to meet on the *R38*. Both Byrd and Wilkins would later write that they believed missing the airship was a result of some divine intervention – and a sign that they were destined for greater things.

In the aftermath of the disaster, Byrd returned to America to undertake a series of administrative appointments. In 1924 he was thirty-six years old. He had a solid, but not outstanding career in the Navy. He had achieved a good deal, but not fame. Still, he had influential friends.

During this period the US Navy and Army were competing for the attention of Congress, and the funding it could bestow. Both the Army and the Navy were aware of the importance of aviation and, in the days before the US Air Force, both were keen to be seen as at the forefront of aviation development. Army and Navy fliers were competing for headlines. US Army fliers flew from coast to coast in 1922. They flew nonstop from New York to San Diego in 1923. In 1924 US Army fliers made the first around-the-world flight using seaplanes.

William A. Moffett, the head of the US Navy's Bureau of Aeronautics, wanted similar headlines focusing on the achievements of the Navy. In January 1924 the Navy announced it would fly its rigid airship *Shenandoah* from Nome, Alaska, to Spitsbergen, crossing the Arctic Sea and possibly landing at the North Pole en route. It was a plan that would upstage anything that had gone before it. According to Moffett, the planned flight would explore unknown areas and demonstrate the practicality of a trans-polar air route. It would also claim any newly discovered land for the United States. Four weeks after the Navy's announcement of the flight, Byrd was assigned to temporary duty with Moffett and attached to the 'Shenandoah Arctic flight'. However, President Coolidge stepped in and ordered it be postponed until such time as Congress could investigate further. Later in the year the *Shenandoah* was damaged in an electrical storm, putting the flight on hold indefinitely.

The stalled plans again left Byrd searching for a focus for his ambition. The North Pole flight had begun to crystallise in his mind and the importance of discovering any new land in the Arctic Ocean was known to American political powers. Byrd decided to organise his own expedition, to take place in the coming summer of 1925, and cleverly enlisted the support of both the US Navy and private enterprise. Edsel Ford and John D. Rockefeller Jr both subscribed $15,000 to the venture.

At this point Byrd became aware that the National Geographic Society was sponsoring an expedition, led by Donald MacMillan, to explore north of Greenland. This expedition's second-in-command was Eugene F. McDonald, a Chicagoan millionaire, head of the Zenith radio manufacturing company and himself a lieutenant commander in the Naval Reserve. MacMillan's plans were further advanced than Byrd's and had some serious support. The National Geographic Society had induced President Coolidge to throw his weight behind the idea, while McDonald was testing radio communications in the Arctic, something in which the US Navy were vitally interested.

Byrd asked the Navy for the use of three seaplanes. MacMillan and McDonald had already approached it for ships, men and logistical support. Unable to decide which group should receive its support, the Navy offered a deal. It would lend three planes and crews to Byrd, but his expedition would form part of MacMillan's.

This would prove to be an unhappy compromise. The overall expedition would be under the command of MacMillan, an explorer with his snowshoes firmly planted in the dogsled era, and a man who believed that planes were unsuitable for work in the Arctic. Furthermore, MacMillan's agenda for the expedition was purely scientific. Byrd, on the other hand, saw planes as the future and was interested in their military potential, Arctic air routes being strategically important to America's defence. Byrd had orders drawn up that allowed him to make decisions independently of MacMillan but, as events would prove, making a decision and receiving the support to carry it out were two different things.

Shortly before the expedition was about to leave, news came that Amundsen and Ellsworth had taken off from Spitsbergen and had not been heard from for two weeks. Byrd announced that his priority would be to look for the lost explorers.

The MacMillan Arctic Expedition left Wiscassett, Maine, on 20 June 1925. Byrd realised there were difficulties in the chain of command almost immediately. He had expected to be appointed second-in-command but MacMillan had chosen Eugene McDonald instead. McDonald's agenda seemed to be to promote his radio sets, and throughout the expedition America received daily radio reports. Byrd, his aeroplanes, his pilots, support crew and indeed his very ideas were reduced to the status of unwelcome guests.

As the expedition's two ships ploughed north, a small compensation came Byrd's way. News was received that Amundsen, Ellsworth and the four others had returned safely to Kings Bay; thus Byrd was relieved of the obligation of searching for them. He could now fly where he chose. On 1 August the expedition reached Etah, a small settlement on the north-west coast of Greenland, approximately 700 miles from the Pole.

The US Navy had loaned Byrd amphibian aeroplanes, which were built by the Loening Aircraft Company in America. The Loenings were a relatively new design and didn't use a boat-shaped hull to land on water, as earlier amphibians had. They were also light and manoeuvrable, which made them ideal for taking off and landing on small waterways. They were powered by a four-cylinder inline water-cooled engine, which could take them to a top speed of 112 miles per hour. In every way but one they were ideal for Byrd's purpose. Their drawback was that their size meant limited carrying and fuel capacity. With full tanks they had a range of only 500 miles: not enough to get Byrd to the North Pole and back from Etah. To do serious exploring and possibly reach the Pole, Byrd would have to find an advance base and stock it with fuel. This plan was further frustrated when the planes were test-flown and found to be tail-heavy. Cargo carried in the tail would have to be moved forward, and this meant removing some of the forward fuel tanks, reducing the flying range even more.

The expedition had planned to get coal for the ships from the settlement at Etah but found the locals had only limited supplies and, with winter coming, wouldn't give any away.

Byrd had been hoping that MacMillan would use one of the ships to help him establish a fuel base farther north but, citing the shortage of coal, MacMillan refused to do so. Meanwhile, McDonald was being completely unhelpful with the radio sets, refusing to allow Byrd to use them when he needed to.

When the first extended flights got into the air on 8 August Byrd realised the magnetic compasses were inaccurate. The only compass on which he could rely was the clockwork sun compass, and that was only of value when the fliers could actually see the sun. After the initial flights poor weather kept the planes on the ground for three days, then Byrd led a flight north-west in an attempt to establish an advance base. They were unable to locate suitable open water so Byrd returned to Etah and waited for more clear weather. He wrote in his diary on 13 August:

> Good weather has come at last. The *NA-2* and *3* are out of commission. Bennett and I are going tonight for the blessed old navy. We must make a showing for her. Everything went wrong today. *NA-1* lost cowling overboard. *NA-2* went down by nose. Almost lost her. *NA-3* nearly sunk by icebergs and injured lower wing on raft. Later MacMillan wouldn't let me go. He seems to have given up. MacMillan seems to be in a great hurry to pack up and go back. Wonder what is on his mind.

The *NA-2*, which had partially sunk, was hoisted out of the water but did not fly again during the expedition. The next day *NA-1* and *NA-3* were flown to a fjord on Ellesmere Land, where open water had been spotted on an earlier flight. The pilots were able to land the two planes and wade to the beach to stock 100 gallons of fuel, as well as food and supplies. Byrd now had his advance base and was ready for his exploratory flights north. But when he returned the next day the water was already beginning to freeze over and a landing was impossible. The problems of an expedition trying to work so late in the season were becoming obvious, and, despite a thorough search, the crews were unable to find another suitable landing place. Back at Etah the *NA-3* caught fire, and over the next few days the fjord began to freeze over. Byrd got in one last flight, over the Greenland ice cap, before he had to admit that the flying season was finished. MacMillan, eager to get his ships south before they were frozen in, ordered everything to be loaded back on board.

For Byrd it had been a frustrating and disappointing time, yet after returning from the five-week expedition he wrote in the National Geographic Society's magazine: 'Aviation will conquer the Arctic – and the Antarctic too. But it will be difficult and hazardous.'

Despite his frustrations Byrd had learnt a good deal. Etah, on the north-west coast of Greenland, was not a suitable base from which to launch an aerial assault on the North Pole. It was too remote, the summer season when the fjords were free of ice too brief, while the shortage of coal added further difficulties. A better base would be the coalmining settlement of Kings Bay, Spitsbergen. And he would need a plane or airship capable of flying to the Pole and back, a distance of some 1500 miles, without refuelling. He would need to be in charge of the expedition and to have men under him that he could trust to follow his orders.

Byrd's plans for his next expedition began to formalise in his mind. He would take an expedition to Kings Bay in the summer of 1926 and, using a long-range plane or an airship, fly to the North Pole.

4

The Ice Queen

At the time he died, Sir Hubert Wilkins believed he was one of the few earthly mortals chosen to host a 'thought adjuster', a kind of messenger of God who would 'indwell' in a mortal and, by influencing their thought, influence mankind and raise humanity to a higher state of civilisation, closer to God. According to the *Urantia Book*, which Wilkins believed to be divinely inspired, thought adjusters travelled from 'Divinington':

> Adjusters reach their human subjects on Urantia (planet Earth) on average, just prior to the sixth birthday. In present generation it is running five years, ten months and four days; that is, on the 2,134th day of terrestrial life.

If we are to believe this, then Wilkins' thought adjuster would have begun to indwell in him in mid–1894, when he was a child on his parents' farm.

George Hubert Wilkins was born on 31 October 1888 – six days after Richard Evelyn Byrd. His family lived in a remote farming area of the young colony of South Australia. He was the youngest of thirteen children in a family with neither wealth nor influence. When he was born his father was already fifty-two and his mother forty-nine; the next youngest sibling was twelve years his senior. Curiously, unlike his brothers and sisters, there is no record of Wilkins' birth. The first written record we have of his existence is a school certificate he received shortly before his sixth birthday.

Wilkins' childhood was lonely and remote, and was made more so by the fact his ageing parents were strict Methodists. The only singing allowed was church hymns. Organ music was acceptable, whereas pianos were the instruments of ungodly music halls. To the highly creative and imaginative Wilkins, it was an upbringing he could not wait to escape. In a speech many years later, he told the audience:

> My youth was spent on a large ranch in Australia and there I saw the devastating results of unexpected droughts and famines. Hundreds of sheep and thousands of cattle and horses died of starvation during a long and sustained drought that lasted from 1900 to 1903. It was the pitiful state of those starving animals that first awakened my thoughts to the possibility and potentialities of meteorological forecasting – forecasting that would tell us in advance when to expect droughts and their duration. Surely it might be possible to foretell climate sufficiently well to enable us to lay up a supply for the period of drought . . . [and] to tell us when to prepare for rainy days.

There are few independent records of Wilkins' early life. He attended the Mount Bryan East Primary School, and while the building, like the Wilkins' homestead, still stands, the school records for the period in question were destroyed by a teacher in 1926. One independent view of Wilkins as a child comes from a school friend, 'Buzz' Simmons:

George was always very aggressive. I don't mean quarrelsome, but he would always have a go at anything. We were always having foot races. We were pretty even but one day I beat him a couple of times so he took his boots and shirt off. I beat him again, so off came everything – he was left in his birthday suit. We had a draw. 'Now I've got no clothes on,' he said, 'will you go down to the dam and I will swim against you?' So down we go but he could always beat me at swimming.

He finished school about 14, and of course like the rest of us, he had to go on the plough. A double furrow set plough. Three horses. He would walk alongside them all day, reading. He told me he intended to be an engineer. He kept studying from then on.

Wilkins' family moved to the state's capital, Adelaide, in 1905. There he enrolled in, but failed to complete, a course in engineering, preferring to sing and play musical instruments. Two years later he commenced an engineering apprenticeship but this only lasted a few months. Young George could stand it no longer. He left Adelaide, stowing away on a ship, and arrived in Sydney. Here, twenty years old and free of family influence, he joined the fledgling film industry. He used the engineering skills he had acquired to work, firstly as a projectionist, and then as a cinematographer. For three years he projected films, shot films and sometimes acted in them. It was a life he loved, and for the next fifty years, whenever he was not exploring, he would immerse himself in the company of singers, artists, writers and actors.

In 1911 Wilkins made his way to England to work as a cameraman. He quickly established a reputation as a newsreel cinematographer willing to do almost anything. He straddled the fuselage of a plane to take aerial shots. He went aloft in a balloon. He filmed the Balkans War. In 1913 he accepted the position of official photographer on an Arctic expedition led by Vilhamjur Stefansson, who was planning to explore the largely unknown area between Canada and the North Pole. The expedition would become one of the biggest shambles in polar exploration. Wilkins wrote to his parents:

> Three years is a long time to spend from civilisation, especially if one expects to be climbing the ladder of fame and fortune just as we reach the age that I am now.
>
> Well, one does not get an opportunity to join an expedition to the polar regions every day of the week, and although they have been numerous there is still a spice of adventure left in the work, especially with this one where we expect to find, not a new race of people, but a section of a race, a few tribes as yet uncontaminated by contact with even the most primitive civilisation.

Stefansson preached the theory of the 'friendly Arctic' – that it was a place where a man with a gun, a knife and the right knowledge could live indefinitely. Loading three ships with supplies and surrounding himself with willing, adventurous young men, Stefansson led his expedition through the Bering Strait and into the Arctic Sea in July 1913. The men, many of them fresh out of university, were dressed in tweed suits as they crossed the Arctic Circle for the first time. Wilkins also sported a bowler hat. As they sailed east along the coast of Alaska, the main expedition ship, the *Karluk*, became stuck in the ice and began to drift back westwards. Stefansson decided that this was the time, despite the ship being fully provisioned, to hunt caribou.

The incident is curious and deserves a short digression, because it put events in motion that would later lead to Wilkins leaving his homeland, Australia, vowing never to return. Stefansson's critics have always argued that he was thoughtless or irresponsible in leaving the *Karluk* to go hunting at such a time. Stefansson, in his defence, maintained that it was an opportunity to secure more meat. But on closer examination it becomes obvious that this was not his motive. In one of his books, Stefansson details the technique for stalking and shooting a herd of caribou, impressing on the reader the importance of doing so alone. Stefansson wrote: 'My general rule was well understood, that two men must never go after the same band of caribou.'

Why, then, did he take along two Eskimo and three Arctic novices? The answer is that Stefansson was not seeking caribou but the race of 'Blonde Eskimo' that he sought to cement his reputation. He knew, or must have had suspicions, that the *Karluk* was doomed and he did not want to jeopardise his primary objective. And if he did find his Blonde Eskimo – which, by the way, never existed – he wanted the right people to record the find. So he took his photographer, Wilkins, to capture the pictures, his anthropologist, Diamond Jenness, to prove they were a new race, and his secretary, Burt McConnell, to record the details, along with two Eskimo guides. Wilkins, Jenness and McConnell were still dressed in their tweed suits.

The others on the ship, including one woman and two children, were left to their own devices in the 'friendly Arctic'; eleven of them died before the rest finally managed to reach Siberia. What is significant is that among the men who died was a Scottish explorer and surgeon of some renown, Alister Forbes Mackay. Mackay had been the surgeon on Shackleton's *Nimrod* expedition to Antarctica in 1907. On that trip he had made friends with a young Australian geologist, also on his first trip to Antarctica, Douglas Mawson. With Shackleton's blessing, Mackay, Mawson and Edgeworth David trekked to the South Magnetic Pole, reaching it on 16 January 1909, and forming a bond that only men who undergo such extreme journeys can form. Five years later Mackay died in the Arctic as a result of Stefansson's selfishness and disregard for the welfare of the people he led. Douglas Mawson (later Sir Douglas) went on to lead his own Antarctic expeditions and become Australia's most celebrated explorer. But the tragedy of the *Karluk* poisoned Mawson against Stefansson and, by association, his countryman Wilkins. Exploration, as practised by Stefansson and Wilkins, was not science, Mawson believed, but simply self-promotional stunts, and he was never afraid to say so. His dislike of Wilkins simmered for years and would eventually erupt into outright hostility in the 1930s.

But that lay in the future. In the Arctic in 1913, Wilkins, Stefansson and the men who had got off the doomed *Karluk* eventually met up with the men from the other ships, redistributed supplies and then went in different directions. Wilkins later estimated that he walked some 5000 miles during the following three years, exploring the islands north of Canada.

Reaching a small trading post at Herschell Island in 1916, Wilkins received mail from his family telling him that his father had died and urging him to return home. He also learnt that Europe had been at war for more than two years. He would cross the Arctic Circle again, this time travelling south as an experienced Arctic survivor. Stefansson, for all his faults, poor organisation and disregard for the safety of his men, rivalled Amundsen in his ability to learn from the Eskimo and adapt to living in the polar regions. Wilkins learnt from a master. The expedition also changed the direction of his life.

Years later Wilkins would write children's stories. One of them was called 'An Antarctic Fairy Story' and described an 'Ice Queen' who, when she saw her first 'Explorer Man', fell in love with him. But she was unable to make him see her because she was made entirely of ice. The wise 'Old Man Penguin' told her that the only way the Explorer Man would see her was if she became human by feeling emotion. To do that she had to produce tears. And the only way to do that was to allow her heart of ice to melt. The story reaches its climax with the Explorer Man leaving, still not having seen the Ice Queen:

> All the time the Explorer Man stood on deck and watched and at last . . . he was so sad at parting he came and stood on the ice and stretched out his arms to all the beauty and a tear stole softly down his cheek.
>
> Suddenly her heart gave a big crack and something melted in it and a tear rolled down her cheek also. And in that moment he saw her swaying in the sunset with her arms outstretched to him, and he said, 'Little Queen, how beautiful you are and how wonderful you dance. I love you. I shall never forget you and some day I'll come back.'
>
> And then the ship began to move so he hastily got on board and waved a sad farewell to her.

Wilkins, in a sense, had seen his Ice Queen. He would spend the rest of his life going back to see her again.

Wilkins returned to Australia and applied for a commission in the Australian Royal Flying Corps (RFC), the forerunner of the Royal Australian Air Force. On his application, under 'trade or calling' he wrote 'Explorer'. On 1 May 1917 he was officially accepted into the 9th Reinforcements, RFC, as a 2nd Lieutenant, and ten days later he left Sydney by ship for England, arriving in mid-July. As a photographer/cinematographer, he could not have arrived at a more opportune time.

Until July 1917 the few official photographs of Australians in the war had been taken by a British officer. Now the Australian War Records Office, under the guidance of C. E. W. Bean, wanted more professional photographs; by chance, the two most qualified Australians of the era were about to land on his doorstep. One was Wilkins, and the other was J. F. (Frank) Hurley, who had just returned from the Antarctic, where he had been the photographer on Shackleton's *Endurance* expedition. Hurley and Bean, however, did not get along and within months Hurley went to Palestine to head the photographic section that would record Australians fighting in the Middle East. From that time until the end of the war, Wilkins was responsible for the film and photographs of Australians taken at the Western Front.

Within weeks of arriving, Wilkins' work ethic and complete disregard for his personal safety had seen him cited for the Military Cross:

> During the five battles before Ypres from September 20th to October 12th and in the fighting between those dates and since, Lieut. G. H. Wilkins acted as Australian Records Photographer. On September 20th, early in the fight forward of our old trenches, a shell bursting from beneath a tank from which he was operating broke some of the gear he was carrying. In spite of this he continued to obtain records of every subject of value for Australian history, providing invaluable pictures of the front line during the period of fighting in Polygon Wood. In subsequent fighting he again had the gear he was carrying broken by a shell but persisted without relief during the period almost all other officers

engaged in work of equal danger were relieved. He was
round the front line during the Battle of Broadseinde Ridge
on October 4th, obtaining records beyond our furthest
objectives and valuable pictures of consolidation. Later in
the month he was blown from the Zonnebecke Duckboards
by a shell and picked up by a passing party of Canadians;
but he has continued his work during the winter without
relaxation. This work has been imposed on Lieut. Wilkins
by his own sense of duty, the results being invaluable as
records while he rarely obtains the credit of publication. His
demeanour has been remarkably gallant and has noticeably
brought credit upon his office amongst the troops.

By the end of the war Wilkins had been wounded some
fifteen times and twice awarded the Military Cross, the second
time for rallying troops and leading them into battle: a remarkable
effort, considering he refused to carry a gun. He became, and
remains, the only official Australian photographer, in any war,
to receive a combat decoration. He would later write:

Even amid all this destruction my thoughts often went back
to my wanderings in the Arctic, and I was more than ever
convinced that the aeroplane was the answer to exploring
the unmapped regions with speed and safety. Someday,
when the world returned to normal, I hoped to sail through
the polar skies in pursuit, not of an enemy, but of the secrets
of nature that would help conquer the natural enemies of all
mankind.

Three years in the Arctic, followed by time at the Western
Front seeing the mass slaughter of humanity in World War
One, focused Wilkins' future ambition. Mankind could only

move forward when the people of all nations were fed and felt secure enough so as not to go to war. Only when they were free of their concern for physical survival could people devote their mental energies to higher cultural and theological pursuits. To achieve this freedom from anxiety the world needed to produce enough food to feed everyone. This in turn could only be achieved if scientists and farmers had a better understanding of the weather, and this understanding could only happen when weather stations were established in the Arctic and Antarctic. Wilkins would later say in a speech:

> The greatest advantage we can gain from the polar regions today is information in relation to the movement of air masses. Those huge volumes of air which sweep from region to region and upon which we gain moisture, temperature and which, as primary forces of climate, affect mankind in every inhabited part of the world. Droughts and famine, floods and frosts, which now quite unpredictably control the provision of our physical and material requirements, have a heavy bearing on the social development of every country. Long-range forecasts, in predetermining periods of drought and plenty, would be of inestimable value in respect to the economic outlook of the world.

Immediately after the war, Wilkins worked in London, cataloguing the film and photographs that had been collected by the Australian War Records Office. While there he submitted a plan for polar weather stations to the Royal Meteorological Society. The Society replied that such weather stations, although useful, could not be established until both the Arctic and the Antarctic had been sufficiently explored. No one knew if there was land in the vicinity of the North Pole. No one knew the size of the Antarctic continent, or even if it was a continent and not a series of large islands.

Wilkins decided that he should assist by filling in the blanks on the map of the world. He threw his lot in with John Lachlan Cope, a veteran of Shackleton's *Endurance* expedition. Cope's grandly named Imperial Antarctic Expedition planned to take ten planes to Antarctica and, by criss-crossing the continent, to map it thoroughly.

While he was waiting for Cope to organise the expedition, Wilkins wanted to increase his navigation and flying experience by competing in the England–Australia Air Race. He was accepted as a member of the four-person team entered by the Blackburn Aircraft Company, which successfully left England on 21 November 1919. After repeated engine problems the team's plane crash-landed on Crete and their race was over.

Wilkins then made his way by ship to South America, the stepping-off point for the Imperial Antarctic Expedition, where he discovered that John Lachlan Cope's ideas had far outreached his abilities. There was no expedition ship, no planes and no money. There was virtually no expedition at all. Just Cope and two companions. Cope's plan was to hitch a ride south with the whalers, winter over in Antarctica, then when the whalers returned for the following summer season, hitch a ride back. Against his better judgement, Wilkins went south and saw Antarctica for the first time.

On the trip he learnt that it was valuable to have the whalers onside, because they had been travelling to South Georgia and Graham Land for decades. Wilkins also saw Deception Island, where one of the main whaling stations was located, and studied the thick, flat ice in the bay. It would, he surmised, make an ideal runway for a plane. He noted it for future reference and returned north, refusing to waste his time wintering over.

On his return to South America Wilkins received two offers by telegram. One was from Stefansson, who was planning to explore north of Canada again. The other was from Sir Ernest Shackleton, who was also planning to explore this area. While pondering his options Wilkins became aware that Stefansson and Shackleton were competing for more than just his services: they had also both applied for funding from the Canadian government. Ultimately, so as not to offend either polar hero, Canada decided to fund neither. Shackleton switched his plans from an expedition in the Canadian Arctic to another one in the Antarctic. If Wilkins would wait, he could come south with Shackleton, who offered to take a plane on the expedition. Likewise, Stefansson had changed his plans and also offered Wilkins a position, but there were no planes in Stefansson's idea. Wilkins wrote his mother:

> I finally decided to go with Sir Ernest Shackleton, although I do not know if it would have been better for me to have gone back with Mr. Stefansson.
>
> It is also important from the point of view of establishing meteorological stations in a ring around Antarctica, from where we may be able to obtain information that would lead to the possibility of predicting the weather conditions in Australia, Africa and South America for many months ahead, thus letting the farmers know what sort of season to expect from year to year.

Shackleton's plans were almost as grand as John Lachlan Cope's had been – and the result was almost as dismal. After the expedition ship, the *Quest*, left England it had to put into Portugal for repairs. Originally, the plan had been to sail down the west coast of Africa to Cape Town, where the *Quest* could take on board the plane promised to Wilkins. With the whole expedition so far behind schedule, however, the idea of stopping at Cape Town to collect a plane was abandoned.

The *Quest* struggled out into the Atlantic and finally made the crossing to Rio de Janeiro, using its old-fashioned square sail. There it would be delayed for weeks while the engine was overhauled yet again. Wilkins went on ahead to South Georgia with the whalers, where he collected specimens of birds and waited for Shackleton's expedition to catch up. When it did arrive, Wilkins learned that Shackleton had died of a heart attack. Wilkins rejoined the rest of the expedition as it sailed south to touch Graham Land and meet Shackleton's obligations to his sponsor, before turning around and heading north.

By now Wilkins was running short of ideas. Stefansson had nothing on offer, Shackleton was dead and Amundsen was broke. Wilkins' only option was to organise and lead his own expedition. He decided to return to the Antarctic and explore the coast between the Ross Sea and Graham Land, with a view to finding suitable sites for permanent weather stations. But by 1923 the enthusiasm for Antarctic expeditions had waned and sponsors were difficult to find. After several unsuccessful attempts to drum up support for his ideas, Wilkins returned to cinematography. He travelled to Russia to film the effects of poverty on behalf of the Quakers, then he was asked by the British Museum of Natural History to collect specimens of flora and fauna in northern Australia. Sensing an opportunity to ingratiate himself with leading scientific bodies, and perhaps to get more backing for his Antarctic project, he accepted the position and returned to Australia in 1924.

Wilkins collected his specimens in the Australian outback while lobbying Australian societies and the government for support. He finally convinced the South Australian branch of the Royal Geographical Society to back his expedition to Antarctica, and left them to raise funds while he returned to Europe to purchase suitable aeroplanes. He left Australia in July 1925, announcing to the press that he would travel to Pisa, Italy, where he would purchase two Dornier-Wal flying boats of the type just used by Amundsen and Ellsworth to almost reach the North Pole.

His planned expedition would ship the planes to the Ross Sea, and from there fly them along the coast of King Edward VII Land to Graham Land. From there the expedition members would be picked up by the whalers and would sail to South America. It seemed a realistic undertaking, but sponsorship and support from Australia were not forthcoming. The South Australian branch of the Royal Geographical Society reported that very little money had been raised and that the purchase of two new Dornier-Wals was out of the question.

Wilkins travelled to Norway in an effort to convince Amundsen to loan him the *N-25*, which had been brought back from the Arctic a few weeks previously. But the wily and still-in-debt Amundsen wasn't loaning anyone anything. Without informing Ellsworth, who actually owned the plane, Amundsen agreed to sell it to Wilkins.

Wilkins then sent another impassioned plea to Australia. Here was the ideal plane, he announced, and he had consulted with Amundsen himself on the flying conditions in the Ross Sea. Further, as a newspaper report explained: 'Captain Wilkins has consulted Commander Prestud, one of the members of Captain Amundsen's Antarctic party, who journeyed 200 miles in King Edward's Land, and says an aeroplane can land almost anywhere.'

Wilkins had negotiated to purchase the plane, and the plan looked good on paper, but still the money from Australia was not forthcoming. And by this time, even had the money been available, it was getting too late for him to get his plane from Europe to the Antarctic in time for the southern summer of 1925.

At this point Wilkins' old Arctic mentor, Vilhamjur Stefansson, proposed an alternative. There was a great deal of enthusiasm in America for exploring the Arctic from the air, Stefansson explained. Amundsen and Ellsworth were mounting another expedition to reach the North Pole from Spitsbergen. Richard Byrd was also planning to fly from Spitsbergen to the North Pole. If Wilkins planned an expedition to fly to the Pole from the other side of the Arctic Sea, then Stefansson felt sure that the necessary support and sponsorship would be available in America. The idea, and the possibility of the financial support that had not been forthcoming from Australia, appealed to Wilkins.

Cook and Peary had walked north from Greenland. Amundsen and Ellsworth had flown north from Spitsbergen. As a result, the largest unexplored area of the Arctic was north of Alaska and, after being a member of Stefansson's expedition in 1913, Wilkins knew the northern Alaskan coast well. A plan began to crystallise in his mind. He would purchase a plane and take it by ship to Seward, Alaska, and from there by rail to Fairbanks. At Fairbanks he would assemble the plane and fly it north, over the Endicott Mountains, to Barrow on the coast. In fact, he would make a number of flights to Barrow to stockpile fuel before making the long flight, out over the unknown, to the North Pole.

5

The Men Who Took the Airship

After his return in June 1925 from the flight in the flying boats, Amundsen immediately began to plan his next expedition with his now-wealthy new best friend, Lincoln Ellsworth. While still at Kings Bay, Amundsen had convinced Ellsworth that they could make the 'big trip' in an airship. Airships had longer flying ranges than planes and, if an engine failed, they could often stay aloft until it was repaired. Airships also had greater payload capacities than the flimsy planes of the era, so Amundsen could carry more equipment and supplies.

For initial advice about where they would find a suitable airship, Amundsen turned to his Dornier-Wal pilot, Hjalmer Riiser-Larsen. Riiser-Larsen was a quiet giant of a man who had attached himself to Amundsen and had now become the ageing explorer's minder. He had flown in airships and completed a course in airship theory. Riiser-Larsen knew of a suitable airship for sale in Italy for $100,000. Ellsworth said that he would be willing to buy it. Amundsen returned home to continue his battles with creditors, Ellsworth returned to America, where he hoped to bathe in the glory of his fame as explorer-hero, and Riiser-Larsen went to Italy to investigate the possibility of buying the N-class airship.

Airship design has three categories: rigid, semi-rigid and non-rigid. The German Zeppelins were rigid. That is, their cigar shape was constructed using a framework of rings held together by girders running the length of the airship. Within this framework were multiple gas cells or lifting bags. The whole lot was covered by a large envelope or outer covering. The non-rigid airship, on the other hand, had no frame at all. The airbag was inflated and the fuselage slung underneath it. Deflated, it would lie flat on the ground. The semi-rigid airship, designed and built by Umberto Nobile, came somewhere between the two. It had a flexible keel running the length of the airbag, from which the gondola or fuselage could be slung, as well as a rigid nose cone. It had more strength than the non-rigid without the enormous weight of the rigid, making it the ideal compromise for polar flights, during which high winds might be experienced.

Umberto Nobile was born near Naples in 1885. He graduated from the University of Naples with diplomas in industrial and electrical engineering before turning his hand to aeronautical engineering – particularly the design of rigid airships. When Italy entered World War One, Nobile was turned down for military service on medical grounds. He decided his contribution would be in the area of engineering, and with three other engineers founded the Stabilmento di Construzioni Aeronautiche to design and build airships. At the end of the war the group split up, largely because the others believed that large rigid airships were the future of aviation, while Nobile believed smaller semi-rigids were more suited to the needs of Italy. In 1919 he became director of the military airship works near Rome; two years later he began designing the semi-rigid N-class. In October 1922 Benito Mussolini seized power after the 'March on Rome' and Italy became a fascist state ambitious for power and glory. Nobile, newly promoted to colonel in the Italian armed forces, built the first N-class airship, designated *N1*, in 1923.

On 15 July 1925 Nobile received an unexpected telegram from Amundsen, asking him to attend an important and secret meeting. The meeting took place ten days later at Amundsen's home in Oslo. Riiser-Larsen, who had just returned after inspecting Nobile's airship, and Rolf Thommessen, President of the Aero Club of Norway and the wealthy owner of Norway's daily newspaper, were also present. Lincoln Ellsworth was not, having already returned to America. Amundsen outlined his idea. The *N1* would be flown from Rome to Kings Bay, where it would be refuelled and prepared for an Arctic journey. From Kings Bay it would head directly for the North Pole, then continue to Barrow on the north coast of Alaska. Nobile agreed that the flight was possible but pointed out that the *N1* had been built with the materials available to him at the time and was heavier than he would have liked. He currently had a new airship under construction; if Amundsen could wait until the spring of 1927, the new airship would be far more suitable for the long Arctic voyage. But Amundsen was insistent. Others were planning flights to the North Pole. He had been beaten by Peary in 1909 and it wasn't going to happen again. They had to make the flight in the spring of 1926. Nobile had just eight months to get the *N1* ready and fly it to Spitsbergen.

From the outset, the expedition was a clash of agendas and egos. Ellsworth wanted to be co-leader and have his name as part of the expedition title because he had pledged $100,000 to buy the airship. Amundsen wanted to lead the expedition and discover any new land in the Arctic. Nobile, feeling the hot breath of Mussolini on his neck, wanted to demonstrate the superiority of Italian airships to the world.

And Rolf Thommessen wanted to promote the expedition on behalf of Norway.

After the initial discussions with Nobile, Amundsen cabled Ellsworth, asking him to up his contribution to $130,000. Ellsworth countered by asking for confirmation that he would be an expedition leader. He was also concerned that the expedition would be seen as predominantly Norwegian. So another of his conditions was that an American newspaper be given the rights to cover the story. Amundsen agreed.

The next step was to negotiate an agreement with the Italian government. Amundsen hurried to Rome, where the deal was signed by himself and Mussolini in September 1925. The semi-rigid airship *N1* would be provided for the purpose of making a flight from Spitsbergen to Alaska, across the North Pole. The airship would cost the expedition $75,000 and the Italian government would buy it back for $46,000 if it was returned in good condition. The Italian government also agreed to provide an officer to command the *N1*.

When he learnt of the deal, Ellsworth was still uneasy, feeling that his contribution would be overshadowed by that of Nobile, who had been nominated as airship commander. He cabled the Aero Club of Norway, asking for confirmation that the official title would be 'the Amundsen Ellsworth Transpolar Flight'. His contribution, he insisted, depended on it. He also insisted that this title be immediately announced to the press in Norway and America. Rolf Thommessen cabled back that the Aero Club of Norway had no objections, and that it had already been announced in the Norwegian press that Ellsworth was co-leader and navigator for the expedition. This immediately offended Leif Dietrichson, the pilot of Ellsworth's Dornier-Wal in their 1925 flight. Dietrichson understood he was to be navigator, and he also knew Ellsworth couldn't navigate with any certainty. He would be doing the work while Ellsworth would receive the credit. He flatly refused to participate in any flight where the incompetent Ellsworth had a sextant in his hands.

Amundsen stepped in to attempt to mend the rift but without success. Dietrichson's navigation skills could be replaced but Ellsworth's financial contribution could not, so Dietrichson left the expedition. Ellsworth promised to go to navigation school to brush up on his skills, but instead, while the airship was being made ready, used the time to go camping in the Grand Canyon.

With the agreements in place, Nobile began to work on the problem of making the airship, which was designed for passenger travel around the warm Mediterranean, suitable for a 2500-mile flight over the Arctic. The *N1* was 348 feet (106 metres) long and had a volume of 654,000 cubic feet (18,518 cubic metres). It was puny when compared with the Zeppelins being built at the time, which were roughly twice as long and had a gas volume seven times greater. To travel the long distance required of it, the *N1* would need to be made as light as possible, so Nobile began to make calculations for the proposed journey that few people outside his field of expertise would understand.

An airship begins each journey with an existing amount of hydrogen and ballast. Neither can be added during the flight. The hydrogen gives the airship its lift, while the ballast can be jettisoned to give further lift. But the calculations for this flight were more complicated. Hydrogen expands with higher temperatures. It also expands with increased altitude, as the surrounding air pressure decreases. The ideal time to get an airship in the air is at night when the temperature is cooler. More hydrogen can be pumped into the gas bags and maximum lift obtained. As an airship rises in the atmosphere, the hydrogen will expand, further increasing lift, and to stop the gas bags bursting hydrogen needs to be 'valved off'. During the day, as the temperature increases, the hydrogen expands, requiring the commander to valve off precious hydrogen as well. When the temperature drops or the airship loses altitude, the hydrogen contracts.

Even if he were to maintain a cruising speed of fifty miles per hour, Nobile knew the flight from Spitsbergen to Alaska would take fifty hours. Maintaining altitude while conserving ballast and hydrogen would be a very delicate balancing act. As events would show, these were principles of airship flight that neither Amundsen nor Ellsworth understood.

Nobile first had to get the *N1* from Italy to Spitsbergen. This in itself would be a feat. The nearest airship hangar to Spitsbergen, where he could take on more fuel and hydrogen, was a derelict airship base in Leningrad. Nobile decided to ask the Russian authorities if they would make it operable for him. To give himself an option in the event that they said no, he also asked the English to nominate a base at which he could refuel. The English offered Pulham. To complicate matters further, the Aero Club of Norway asked if Nobile would go via Norway so that the Norwegian people could see 'their' airship. Nobile agreed, and after the Russians showed great enthusiasm to prepare their base, he decided that the *N1* would travel to Kings Bay via England, Norway and Russia. The combined distance was 4500 miles.

With such an integral role, Nobile felt that he should co-author the official book to be written about the expedition, or at least contribute chapters on the technical aspects of the flight. He said as much to the Aero Club of Norway, which in turn asked the sensitive Ellsworth for his agreement. Ellsworth cabled his okay. When Amundsen, who was back on the lecture circuit in America trying to pay off debts, heard about this new agreement he was furious. His income depended on lectures and book sales and he would not, he insisted, share these with Nobile. Nobile now pushed further and insisted his name be included in the official expedition title. Cables continued to be sent between Italy, America and Norway until a compromise was reached. Nobile would not contribute to the official book, but his name would be included in the expedition title. Thus the 'Amundsen-Ellsworth-Nobile Transpolar Flight' staggered towards take-off.

Other negotiations continued. With the name in place, next came the problem of the chain of command. Nobile said that if conditions were unfavourable for the 'big trip', he would only take the airship as far as the North Pole and then return to Kings Bay. As the airship's designer, and the only person qualified to pilot it, he was the obvious person to make the decisions about what was possible – and what was not. Naturally, this upset Amundsen, who wanted to have the final say. Beyond the Pole was the only area where new land might be discovered, and Amundsen desperately wanted to go there. A written agreement was eventually signed. Amundsen and Ellsworth would be 'expedition leaders', and Nobile would be 'airship commander'. The three would vote on any major decisions to be made. Ellsworth wrote:

> This gave control to Amundsen and me. Nobile seemed to think this might constrict his powers as pilot and was emphatic in his insistence, but we would have it no other way. We went into the North under that arrangement; and when a difference of opinion did actually arise . . . Amundsen and I voted against Nobile.

The agreement also put in writing that the flight would be from Spitsbergen, across the North Pole to the north coast of Alaska. The composition of the crew was also clarified. Nobile wanted as many crew as possible to be Italian. They understood what was required to fly the airship and, more to the point, they spoke Italian. To maintain authenticity as a Norwegian expedition, the Aero Club of Norway wanted as many as possible to be Norwegian. The final agreement stipulated that a total crew of sixteen would be carried, with Nobile having the right to reduce the number if he needed to reduce weight, and that six of the members, including Nobile, would be Italian.

While these protracted negotiations were taking place, the Aero Club of Norway was busy trying to get an airship hangar built at Kings Bay. Some 2000 tons of equipment, including 21,189 cubic feet (600 cubic metres) of timber and fifty tons of iron, began to be shipped to Spitsbergen in October 1925. Twenty workers accompanied the supplies, with the task of working throughout the winter to get the hangar built. Despite the falling temperatures and almost impossible conditions, the frame of the hangar was erected by mid–February and the workmen covered it with 107,639 square feet (10,000 square metres) of canvas. On 24 March 1926 the mooring mast and 900 cylinders of hydrogen arrived by ship.

Three days later, back in Italy, the semi–rigid airship was officially handed over to the expedition. Nobile, Ellsworth and Amundsen were present. Mussolini turned up for the ceremony and, in the words of Nobile, 'the Italian flag, which for two years had proudly flown from [the *N1*'s] stern, was hauled down and replaced by that of Norway'. Mussolini gave the flag to Nobile to drop at the North Pole. The airship was officially renamed *Norge* (Norway). Twelve days later it lifted off from Ciampo Airfield near Rome to begin the long and hazardous journey north to Spitsbergen. Amundsen and Ellsworth didn't trouble themselves to make the trip in the airship. Their round of official dinners and engagements continued. Ellsworth, in particular, was enjoying the limelight and the opportunity to make speeches about the future of aviation and exploration, as well as his personal contribution to both.

Amundsen, Ellsworth and the Norwegian crew members arrived at Kings Bay by ship on 20 April, only to learn that the mooring mast was still not erected because poor weather had stopped work. By this time the *Norge* had reached Leningrad and was safely housed in the Russian airship hangar, awaiting the news that the mooring mast was ready. The weather cleared and construction of the mast continued. A telegram was sent to Nobile, telling him the mast would be ready on 2 May and to make the flight across as soon after that as the weather allowed.

At Kings Bay, on 29 April, Amundsen and Ellsworth were waiting for the completion of the mooring mast and for the arrival of their airship when sailors from the expedition ship, the *Heimdal*, spotted smoke on the horizon. The sailors called to the workers on shore, who shouted the news to the men bolting the mooring mast together. Quickly the word spread around the camp. Bernt Balchen, a young Norwegian pilot attached to the expedition, was in the machine shop when he heard his name called. He came outside and looked to the horizon in the direction that everyone was pointing. For the next few hours the men watched the smoke. Years later, Balchen described the scene:

> All morning long we have paused now and then in our
> work, and glanced at the smoking funnel on the horizon,
> and muttering uneasily to each other. We are not sure yet.
> It could be a supply ship for the mine, or a sealer headed

for the ice pack. We look over the tar paper roofs of the mining camp, toward the superintendent's house on the hill where Captain Amundsen is living. Has he heard yet, does he know? We shake our heads and look back again at the strange vessel, holding a straight course for Kings Bay.

The men continued to watch the ship get closer. At noon it revealed its identity with a radio message. It was the American vessel *Chantier*, and on board was Lieutenant Commander Richard Byrd and his party. He had fifty men and two planes and was anxious to get ashore. Would the Norwegians be so kind as to have the *Heimdal* moved away from the dock so that he could begin unloading? Balchen continued:

All work at our base has halted, and the men of the Amundsen expedition stand in silent groups along the bluff. We resent this foreign ship coming here to our country to snatch the prize, which we feel belongs to Captain Amundsen alone. We of his party are loyal to him to the point of worship, and any one of us would lay down our life without question for one of the greatest of all living explorers.

One of the men turns, and nudges another, and we all look up at a lone figure on the hill behind us. People always turn to look at Roald Amundsen, as their eyes would be drawn to the tallest mountain. He stands at rest on his ski poles, still very straight in his middle fifties, as hard muscled and vigorous as a young athlete. With his hand he slowly pushes back the visor of his ski cap to view the rival expedition.

His face is expressionless and we cannot read it. Beneath the thick tufts of his eyebrows, white as hoarfrost, his eyes in their deep sockets are hidden in shadow. His cheeks are leathery and folded in hard creases, with a fine network of wrinkles spreading out from the corners of his eyes like a map of all the dog trails he has run. The most prominent feature of his face is the thin and arched nose, which gives him the look of an eagle. It is a face carved in a cliff, the face of a Viking.

We wait for him to speak, but he pivots on his skis without a word and strides back to the headquarters building.

The *Chantier* steamed closer and Byrd repeated his request to have the *Heimdal* moved.

6

Let George Do It

Wilkins had been extremely disappointed that his Antarctic plans did not receive the publicity and support in Australia that he felt they deserved.

'I don't suppose the English papers will become interested until I start from Point Barrow, if they are even then,' he had written to a friend. 'If I manage to find land they might sit up and think about it for a moment.' At the time, he had been writing a book on his expedition in the Australian outback, and in it he had taken the opportunity to have a swipe at what he saw as the apathy of his countrymen:

> Most Australians are well off in regard to creature comforts and many of them soon reach independent means; yet the absence of the expressed desire for culture and for higher things, and their contentedness with the mediocre make them perhaps the poorest rich people in the world today.

When he arrived in America at the end of 1925, looking for a plane to explore the Arctic, he found that attitudes were markedly different. Almost as soon as he announced his plans, the North American Newspaper Alliance (NANA) pledged $25,000 for exclusive reports from his expedition. Importantly, the Alliance would guarantee national publicity, which would in turn lead to further sponsorship and pledges of support. Unfortunately, Wilkins was about to learn that boundless enthusiasm was almost as debilitating as apathy. In his words:

> I proposed to take only one machine, adequate spares, one pilot and a mechanic, and with the minimum of expense, to make two or three short flights into the unknown area . . . but they don't do things that way in America.

The editor of *The Detroit News*, which was a member of the NANA, introduced Wilkins to the Detroit Aviation Society. A leading member of the society was Edsel Ford, son of the pioneering carmaker Henry Ford. To his father's bewilderment, the younger Ford was trying to assert his dominance over the Ford Motor Company and expand it into new areas, such as aviation. Edsel Ford had joined the Detroit Aviation Society in 1921 and had purchased the Stout Metal Airplane Company in 1925. He was currently building an all-metal body, three-engine monoplane. If it could be ready in time, Wilkins' expedition and the resulting publicity would be the ideal place to showcase the Ford Motor Company's new venture.

There were also many wealthy businessmen within the ranks of the Detroit Aviation Society who, along with Edsel Ford, wanted the city of Detroit to be seen not only as the centre of the American automobile industry, but the centre of the growing American aviation industry as well. The society threw its full weight behind Wilkins' plans. A board was appointed to manage the expedition, a committee of engineers to select equipment and a finance committee to raise funds. In addition, managers, secretaries, treasurers and publicists were brought on board. It became what Wilkins described as 'a hopeless muddle'.

Edsel Ford had also been approached by Richard Byrd to sponsor his planned flight to the North Pole. Ford put Wilkins and Byrd in touch with one another and they met. Wilkins offered Byrd a position in his upcoming expedition, and Byrd, playing his cards close to his chest, agreed to think about it. A few weeks later he wrote to Wilkins:

> I want to say to you very sincerely that I am distressed that I won't have the opportunity to serve under you. I know it would be very enjoyable and instructive. I have enjoyed knowing you and I hope we may see more of each other in the future. I hope to call on you in New York before you leave and I will tell you the whole story.

Wilkins also wanted to get to the Arctic early in the summer season. Writing of Amundsen and Ellsworth's previous flight, Wilkins noted that:

> [Amundsen's] aerial experience must have shown, even to him, that the greatest requirements for a successful polar flight are clear visibility and good navigation. On his flight during May toward the Pole and back he had been hampered with fog and low visibility. Adequate polar meteorological records show that earlier in the year good visibility and steadier winds can be relied upon. Had Amundsen taken into consideration his previous experience and the records of polar meteorology he would have planned to start earlier in the year and would probably have added much to the scientific knowledge of the Arctic.

When it became obvious that the Ford Trimotor would not be built in time for his early start, Wilkins turned to Anthony

Fokker. Fokker had built planes for the Germans in World War One, the most famous being the triplane flown by the 'Red Baron', Manfred von Richthofen. After the war Fokker moved to America, where he established a manufacturing business. Seeing a future in aviation for carrying passengers and mail, he developed large-bodied aircraft capable of carrying a pilot, co-pilot and passengers. Fokker designated each new model FI, FII, FIII, and so on. By 1925 he had developed a large plane designated the FVII, which was capable of carrying six passengers. The first models were a disappointment. The high cantilevered wing design was good, but the engine was not powerful enough to make the plane of commercial value. Fokker increased the engine size and designated the model FVIIA. Airlines of the era were looking for a safe passenger plane that could fly in the event that an engine failed. Fokker's answer was to hang two additional engines from the high wing and create the Fokker FVIIA-3m, which became known as the Fokker Trimotor. With this plane Fokker had immediate success.

Wilkins believed the new Fokker Trimotor would be ideal. He later wrote:

> Not having ridden in, or flown in his three-engined machine
> which at the time was creating a great deal of interest
> in American flying circles, I was happy on the afternoon
> we first met to fly in the trimotored monoplane with Mr.
> Fokker. He expressed great interest in my project.

Fokker saw the opportunity to upstage the Ford Motor Company and confided in Wilkins that he was currently building a new, larger-wing FVIIA-3m in his factory in Holland. 'With that machine I believe you will do all you want in the Arctic Ocean and then fly to Spitsbergen,' he told Wilkins. 'If those Detroit men don't stand behind you I will provide the machine.' Wilkins bought the Fokker and convinced the Detroit Aviation Society that it was a suitable plane for his purposes.

The expedition was named the Detroit Arctic Expedition. The influential businessmen of the society had the American President, Calvin Coolidge, write a letter of support. In part it read:

> ... the Detroit Aviation Society is planning to organize and
> privately finance an expedition to explore the land west
> of the North Pole. It has aroused the keenest personal
> interest. America has always been at the forefront of Arctic
> exploration and it is fitting that we should strive to be the
> first to open the unknown lands ...

The letter was reproduced in a promotional brochure that also stated the aims of the expedition as:

> ... to explore that area of the polar ice pack which has never
> been seen by man [and] claim for the United States any
> lands that may be found ...

At the time it was widely believed that a large land mass, even another continent, lay between Alaska and the North Pole. While Wilkins' preparations were underway, *The New York Times* reported:

> A few years ago the Federal tide expert, Dr R. A. Harris
> of Washington D.C., set to work on what he aptly termed
> 'discovery by deduction'. Astronomers use this method in
> predicting new stars. Chemists have used it in predicting
> new elements. Both schools have proved the theories time

and again. Dr Harris gathered all available tidal data taken
by various expeditions on the shores of the Polar Sea. Then
by piecing his figures together, he was able to tell whether
there was an unobstructed flow of the ocean current in
each part of the polar basin. He soon decided that either a
vast shoal or a land mass of nearly continental size must be
north of Alaska in order to account for tidal aberrations on
known adjacent shores ... In a few weeks the schoolroom
globe may boast another continent.

The idea of Wilkins claiming this land for the United States,
as the Detroit Aviation Society's brochure proposed, raised
an interesting issue. Wilkins was the leader of the expedition
and an Australian citizen. Tradition stated he had the right to
claim any new land found for his own country, regardless of
the nationality of his sponsors. The Detroit Aviation Society
was aware of this and imposed another condition: Major
Tom Lanphier of the United States Army Air Service would
be loaned to the expedition, and Wilkins instructed to make
him the chief pilot and second-in-command. Any flights of
discovery were to include Lanphier, who would then claim the
land for the United States. Another issue had been added to
the 'hopeless muddle'.

Wilkins' plan was to explore the area between the north
coast of Alaska and the North Pole and, if possible, to fly over
the Pole and continue on to Spitsbergen. He knew the north
coast of Alaska well and believed that if he could get a reliable
plane and fuel supplies to Barrow, he would be able to make
the flight to the North Pole. The plane would be taken by train
to Fairbanks, then flown over the Endicott Mountains. At the
same time, the heavy load of fuel would be taken to Barrow
by a combination of dogsled teams and Fordson snow tractors.

Edsel Ford and the other business interests of the Detroit Aviation Society were going to get maximum publicity from every aspect of the expedition.

In addition to Tom Lanphier, Wilkins also wanted pilots with experience in flying in the Arctic. He turned to his old mentor, Vilhamjur Stefansson, who nominated Carl 'Ben' Eielson. Eielson was born in Hatton, North Dakota, on 20 July 1897. He was the grandson of Norwegian immigrants. As a boy growing up in Hatton he'd been interested in flying, and when America entered World War One Eielson had enlisted in the Air Service of the United States Army. He had just completed his training when the war came to an end. Returning home, he'd organised an aero club in Hatton and bought an ex-army training plane, in which he put on exhibition flights and gave joy flights before going to Fairbanks to work as a school teacher. In Alaska he ordered another plane and soon found he was doing more flying than teaching. He was awarded the first airmail contract in Alaska in February 1924, but at the end of the season was unable to renew the contract so he returned to Hatton to study law. He was in Hatton when he received a telegram from Stefansson, asking him to come to New York because a George Wilkins had arrived from Australia and wanted pilots who had previously flown in Alaska.

The new Fokker Trimotor arrived from Holland in crates, still untested. Wilkins purchased a second single-engine Fokker as a support plane. Then his planes and his team went by train to Seattle, by ship to Seward, Alaska, and then by train to Fairbanks, where the unassembled planes were hauled by draught horses to their hangars on the outskirts of town. A makeshift runway was bulldozed in the snow.

When the planes were assembled on 11 March 1926, Palmer Hutchinson, a *Detroit News* journalist, encouraged Wilkins to hold a christening ceremony. Wilkins was reluctant at first, but finally agreed, in order to satisfy his sponsors. The two planes were taken out of their hangars and the people of Fairbanks gathered to witness the ceremony. The Fokker Trimotor was christened the *Detroiter* and the single-engine Fokker the *Alaskan*.

After the formalities Wilkins dispersed the crowd, telling them that the events were over for the day. Then he spoke to Palmer Hutchinson privately, telling him of his plan to test the big Fokker. If he waited, Wilkins explained, Hutchinson would get an exclusive for *The Detroit News*. Wilkins chose Lanphier to be the pilot for the trial flight even though it had become an open secret that the two men had little respect for each other. The engines of the *Detroiter* were started and, with Lanphier at the controls and Wilkins in the co-pilot's seat, the big Fokker made its way down the makeshift runway. The controls had not been balanced correctly and the plane slewed to one side, hitting a snow bank. The mechanics ran forward to push the plane back onto the runway, and in his eagerness Hutchinson also ran forward to help. He began pushing the wheel strut then, oblivious to the invisible spinning propeller, changed position to pull. As the plane moved forward he stood straight and stepped back, only to be killed instantly by the spinning blade. His body was carried from the field and the *Detroiter* solemnly wheeled back to its hangar.

A mood of gloom settled over the expedition. As Wilkins wrote, 'No one felt the same about the big Fokker after that.'

At the same time, word came that the Fordson snow tractor and dogsled section of the expedition had become bogged down on the trails. Sandy Smith, the leader of the group, had abandoned the heavy fuel supplies and was continuing on to Barrow using only the dogsleds. Wilkins would have to get the fuel supplies to Barrow himself.

A few days later Wilkins decided to leave the *Detroiter* in its hangar and take the single-engine *Alaskan* up for a test flight. This time, with Eielson at the controls and Wilkins again in the co-pilot's seat, the single-engine Fokker bounced along the runway and took to the air. It successfully circled Fairbanks for forty minutes before Wilkins instructed Eielson to set it down. Everything was fine until the plane had almost touched down. The engine stalled, and with no time to restart it, Eielson landed the plane heavily. It skidded along on its belly before ploughing into a fence at the end of the runway, finally stopping with a twisted propeller and smashed undercarriage. The *Alaskan* was hauled back to the hangar to be repaired.

Wilkins needed to send his sponsors some positive news. The following day he decided to give the *Detroiter* a test flight, despite the fact that many of the crew now considered it to be jinxed. With Wilkins on board, Lanphier got the big plane airborne and circled Fairbanks several times. Then, as they were coming in to land, the engines stalled and the *Detroiter* crashed in almost the same place as the *Alaskan*. The undercarriage and the engine mounts were smashed.

The Detroit Aviation Society was not getting the publicity it had hoped for. Part of the strategy of the expedition had been to raise funds from public donations. A weekly radio broadcast was made on Monday evenings, telling the citizens of Detroit how proud they should be of their expedition. Now, with one man dead, the snow tractors given up, both planes damaged and the expedition still only in Fairbanks, H. G. McCarroll, who gave the weekly broadcasts, had to work hard to raise enthusiasm to keep the public donations coming in:

A brave man has gone out to fight the bitter battle of the far north, many thousands of miles away from home and

it just seems as if Detroit has forgotten about him . . . The
world is just waiting to laugh at Detroit – to smile cynically
at our selfishness – in our lack of interest in the most heroic
undertaking since the war ended. We not only stand a good
chance of having to give up the expedition, but there is
every possibility that Amundsen is going to get up there
before Captain Wilkins. For some reason or other the
whole attitude of this town seems to be 'let George do it'.
Friends, I would hate in years to come to face my children
and to tell them that I was living in Detroit when the Detroit
Arctic Expedition was going on and didn't support it. School
children in generations to come will know of the Detroit
Arctic Expedition, of its glorious achievements and will
either be ashamed of their parents for not having supported
it or will be proud of them.

Despite the setbacks Wilkins pressed on with dogged
determination. It took three weeks to have the *Alaskan*
repaired. When it was ready Wilkins announced that he and
Eielson were going to attempt to fly to Barrow. He had no
weather reports from Barrow, because the dogsled section had
still not arrived with the radio, but he was confident he could
clear the Endicott Mountains and make the first flight to the
north coast of Alaska.

At 7.30 am on 31 March 1926 the heavily laden single-
engine Fokker took off and headed north for the 500-mile
journey to Barrow. Eielson was at the controls and Wilkins
navigated from the co-pilot's seat. Wilkins wrote:

We climbed steadily and steadily upwards, knowing we
would have to reach five thousand feet to cross the first
range of hills with safety. We thought that an altitude of six

thousand feet would see us through because the peaks of
the Endicott Range barring our course were shown on the
very latest maps procurable as five thousand feet . . .

Soon we could see that the mountain peaks ahead
were above our altitude. Our vision was not clear because
the glycerin from the boiling radiator was blowing back on
our windshields and fouling them. The sides of the cockpit
were open. We looked around and saw that surely enough
we were approaching at great speed the mountains that
towered above us . . .

Eielson nosed the machine upward. She climbed fairly
well, but at nine thousand feet she seemed to have reached
her ceiling with the load she carried. We were amazed at
first at the height of the mountains; five thousand feet on
the chart, and here we were at nine thousand feet and the
mountain tops still higher than we were . . .

Although we were not above the mountain peaks,
we could see between them, and by carefully threading
our way, we managed to pass to a broad white plain on
the other side. At this point our map was a blank. On it
nothing appeared between the mountains and the coast.

They continued until Wilkins estimated that they had
reached the end of the land. Unable to see the coast because of
the fog, he decided to keep flying north, out over an unexplored
area, to see if he could sight land.

I leaned over to Eielson and suggested, 'If you look ahead
you will see a hundred miles further north than any man has
seen until today. We are a hundred miles out over the Arctic
Sea. What do you say to going half an hour longer, just to
make it good measure?'

I could see that he was not anxious to go or quite
positive that I knew where we were. And to be sure I
was not, but I was certain that we were out over new
territory, and the joy that this feeling gave me must
have influenced Eielson.

'Whatever you think best,' he consented.

Approximately 125 miles north of the coast they had used
two-thirds of their fuel and were flying at 7000 feet (2386
metres). The weather had cleared and Wilkins looked ahead,
estimating that he could see for another seventy-five miles.
There was no land in sight – no new continent, as had been
predicted. Wilkins ordered Eielson to turn the plane around.

As they approached the land they flew lower, and Wilkins,
by identifying coastal features, was able to locate Barrow. Charlie
Brower, a trader at the small settlement at Barrow, had met
Wilkins when he had been there with Stefansson in 1913. Early
in 1926 Brower had received a telegram, arriving overland with
his supplies, that he could expect a plane to land at Barrow in late
February. The telegram had been signed by Wilkins. Brower had
been asked to map out an airfield on a flat area of ground, which
he had done. February had come and gone and there had been
no sign of a plane. Now, on the last day of March, the *Alaskan*
appeared from the sky and landed.

Wilkins set up the radio he had brought with him from
Fairbanks and sent news that he and Eielson had landed safely.
It was relayed to the Detroit Aviation Society, which finally
had something positive to report. McCarroll began his weekly
radio broadcast:

Hello folks. Here I am again. By this time I am bubbling over
with enthusiasm. Our courageous Captain Wilkins has done

what no man has done before him ... [He] flew 730 miles over dangerous mountain peaks and deep ravines and frozen rivers to Point Barrow and then without landing ... made ... a dash out over the frozen wastes of the Arctic Ocean.

I am thinking tonight of the boys and girls who opened their little banks and took all their funds and sent them in to further the progress of this expedition, and my heart is full of happiness for their sakes that Captain Wilkins, the man whom they believed in, has so nobly fulfilled their every hope. Detroit is making history and it is you, my friends, who have done it ...

McCarroll went on to call for more contributions. Amundsen and Ellsworth were still getting their airship to Norway. Byrd and his Fokker were still sailing to Spitsbergen. For the moment, it seemed to the world that Wilkins might win the air race to the North Pole.

At Barrow there was still no sign of the dogsled party that had left six weeks earlier, and Wilkins was concerned that they may have died on the trail. Meanwhile a storm settled in and it was 6 April before Wilkins and Eielson could make the return flight to Fairbanks. Leaving their equipment, including the radio, at Barrow, and with a lighter load of fuel, they were able to cross the Endicott Mountains at a height of 11,000 feet. With the exception of a landing when the engine began to misfire, they made the return journey safely.

Wilkins loaded the *Alaskan* with more drums of fuel and, two days after returning, he and Eielson made a second flight to Barrow. Shortly after they landed, the dogsled party arrived, tired, hungry and snow-blind. They had left most of the supplies, including the radio, back on the trail and had barely managed to reach Barrow. The ground party had taken six weeks to make the journey that Wilkins and Eielson were now making in six hours. The usefulness of aviation in Alaska had been proven beyond any doubt.

Wilkins and Eielson made a third flight to Barrow in the *Alaskan*, this time carrying 4750 pounds (2154 kilograms) of fuel. They now had stockpiled sufficient fuel to make the 2200-mile flight over the North Pole to Spitsbergen. But fate still had stumbling blocks to put in Wilkins' path.

Whenever the plane came to a stop in sub-zero temperatures the engine oil and radiator fluid had to be drained. Before starting the plane, the oil had to be heated and poured back into the engine. At the same time, if the temperature was very cold the engine itself had to be kept warm to stop it freezing solid. This was done by putting a heavy canvas covering over the engine to form a kind of tent, inside which a small fire could be lit on the ground. The fire was usually a blubber stove. The third time they were at Barrow, an Eskimo was tending the blubber stove when Wilkins and Eielson heard cries of 'The plane's on fire!' They ran outside to discover the canvas covering and sections of the nose ablaze. The fire was soon put out; the damage was minor, except that the heat had caused the laminations on the wooden propeller to separate.

Wilkins considered the propeller dangerous and any immediate plans for a long-distance flight over the Arctic Sea were put on hold. He radioed Fairbanks, where the *Detroiter* had just finished being repaired, and instructed Lanphier to fly it to Barrow, bringing a spare propeller for the *Alaskan*. Lanphier took the *Detroiter* up for a test flight then radioed back that it was unsuitable to fly to Barrow. The test flight had shown that, according to Lanphier, the plane's top speed was only ninety miles per hour, that its fuel consumption was fifty-two gallons per hour, and therefore that the plane could not carry sufficient fuel to get to Barrow and back. He also said that the centre engine, after the repairs, was out of alignment, which meant the plane could scarcely reach 5000 feet and would not be able to get over the mountains.

Wilkins was furious. The Fokker Trimotor had been bought to Alaska specifically to fly fuel and supplies to Barrow. And Lanphier had come along as chief pilot of the expedition, as well as its second-in-command. Now he was telling Wilkins he wouldn't make a flight that Wilkins and Eielson had already made three times. At Barrow they had no choice but to see whether the *Alaskan* would fly with its damaged propeller. They made a short test flight, considered that it was vibrating too much and landed again.

Wilkins stormed to the radio to demand that Lanphier fly the *Detroiter* to Barrow. But the small generator that powered the radio had burnt out and there was no way of making further contact. Wilkins and Eielson had no choice. They taped up the damaged propeller with copper wire, then spent three days balancing it as best they could, before flying the *Alaskan* back to Fairbanks.

A new propeller was put on the *Alaskan* and Wilkins was ready to return to Barrow, again with Eielson as pilot. This time as they taxied down the runway at Fairbanks there was a loud crack and the right wing of the plane broke clean off. Closer inspection showed that the wing had been damaged for some time, most likely since the plane's previous crash. How it had made the three flights over the mountains to Barrow was beyond anyone's comprehension.

Now face to face, rather than over a radio from 500 miles away, Wilkins ordered that the *Detroiter* be made ready for the flight to Barrow and Lanphier was told that he would be pilot. His co-pilot would be Sergeant Wisely, also on loan to the expedition from the Army Air Service, with Wilkins joining them as a passenger. Lanphier got the *Detroiter* into the air and headed north to Barrow with a load of over 700 gallons (2650 litres) of fuel and 45 gallons (170 litres) of oil. Wilkins wrote:

> We soon came to clouds and turned right and left looking for a clearing through which to pass. In this manner we got into the centre of the cloud mass, from which it would be difficult to escape. It was just as safe to attempt to continue the journey, as to attempt to return to Fairbanks. So we kept on flying one way and another; climbing as much as possible and edging further and further north until at last at an altitude of 11,000 feet we crossed the mountains, came out of the cloud and found ourselves over a low fog-bank which covered the tundra.
>
> So far we had experienced no difficulty with the machine. As a matter of fact this one, with its three engines and its ability to climb to 11,000 feet with a load was safer than the single engined machine.

The *Detroiter* landed safely at Barrow. Almost two months after the two Fokkers were wheeled out of their hangars at Fairbanks to be christened – and despite a fatal accident, three crashes, the tractor and dogsled section of the expedition abandoning their supplies on the trail, one plane catching fire and his chief pilot flatly refusing to fly his plane – Wilkins had finally managed to get the Fokker Trimotor and his fuel supply to Barrow. 'We filled the tanks with gasoline and hoped that on the next day we would be able to set out on a flight across the Arctic ice,' he wrote.

It was 8 May 1926. On the same day at Spitsbergen, on the other side of the Arctic, Richard Byrd was also preparing a Fokker Trimotor for a flight to the Pole. And Amundsen, Ellsworth and Nobile were getting their airship ready with the same goal.

On 7 March that year, under a headline reading 'Massed Attack on Polar Regions Begins Soon', *The New York Times* had reported:

> The greatest polar drive in history begins this month. Men, money, effort will be poured into Arctic expeditions this Spring and Summer in almost greater volume than were expended during man's 400 years of struggle to reach the North Pole.
>
> Think of it! Amundsen, Ellsworth, Byrd, Stefansson, Rasmussen, Wilkins and a dozen others are entered. All brave men; daring aviators, astute campaigners; steel fibred by years of experience with the ice-pack's harshness.

Now, eight weeks after the article had been published, three competitors were in the starting blocks.

7

Everything Was Staked on One Card

In the same edition of *The New York Times* that ran the article 'Massed Attack on Polar Regions Begins Soon', Byrd announced the plans for his flight to the North Pole. After debating the idea of using an airship, he had finally settled on a Fokker Trimotor. The *Times* reported:

> Lieut. Commander Richard E. Byrd U.S.N., who will lead one of the three major Arctic expeditions this summer, is pinning his faith to a heavier-than-air machine. The failure of Roald Amundsen last year to successfully negotiate the ice packs of the Arctic Circle with a heavier-than-air machine has not deterred Commander Byrd.

Byrd wrote in the paper:

> Captain Amundsen, after his attempt last year to fly from Spitsbergen to the North Pole, made up his mind that the airplane was not well fitted for Arctic work. Lieut. Commander MacMillan, Naval Reservist, came to the same conclusion.

Stefansson and Captain Wilkins, however, still believe that the airplane will prove itself valuable in Arctic exploration, and I agree with them . . .

[My] objects are to explore the unknown stretch of about 400 miles from Peary Land to the Pole and possibly to accomplish the sporting feat of reaching the Pole from the air.

The sporting element appeals strongly to me, but I am deeply interested in proving that the airplane can do the job. I want to see it done for the prestige of aircraft.

All three of us – Amundsen, Wilkins and myself – are seeking to discover new land and also to conquer the Arctic from the air. It is not exactly a race, but there is an element of competition in there.

The second-hand Fokker available to Byrd had been the first model FVIIA-3m built. It had already flown 20,000 miles and its wingspan was three feet narrower than Wilkins' plane, giving it slightly less payload capacity. It had two 100-gallon fuel tanks in the fuselage and two 110-gallon tanks incorporated in the main wing, giving it a total fuel capacity of 420 gallons. It would burn twenty-seven to twenty-eight gallons per hour. At a cruising speed of eighty-five miles per hour, therefore, it would need to be in the air for approximately seventeen and a half hours to fly the 1500 miles from Kings Bay to the North Pole and back, and would need almost 500 gallons of fuel. Byrd planned to carry the additional fuel in five-gallon drums. Despite basing his calculations on a cruising speed of eighty-five miles per hour, Byrd was careful to point out in his book *Skyward* that 'it was capable of speeds as high as 120 miles per hour'.

A contractual stipulation with the sale of any Fokker Trimotor was that the word Fokker appeared in large letters on both sides of the fuselage and beneath the wing. However, Byrd's main sponsor was Edsel Ford, who was trying to compete against Fokker with his own large trimotor plane. Byrd found himself in the awkward position of having to use one manufacturer's product while being sponsored by another. He compromised by naming his plane the *Josephine Ford*, after his sponsor's three-year-old daughter, and he had these words painted as large as was practical above 'Byrd Arctic Expedition' on the side of the fuselage.

For an expedition ship Byrd leased the USS *Chantier* from the Federal War Shipping Board, the agency given the responsibility of disposing of ships from World War One. To crew the ship he called for volunteers and was inundated with replies. Among them was Floyd Bennett, the pilot who had flown with him a year earlier in Greenland. Eventually, the Byrd Arctic Expedition sailed from New York on 5 April 1926 with fifty volunteers and all the fanfare Byrd could muster. John D. Rockefeller Jr gave a speech to the assembled crowd, and Byrd's older brother, the Governor of Virginia, attended. The enormous show of public support caused Byrd to reflect, 'I must keep the expedition on a high plane in every particular.' He must have felt that he was, at last, bringing honour and distinction to his family name.

He also sailed knowing that more than just his reputation was at stake. Contracts he had signed with media organisations meant he would personally receive additional money if he was the first to fly to the North Pole.

'The least Byrd would receive from his attempt, even if it failed, was $18,000,' Dr Raimund Goerler of the Byrd Polar Research Center has written. 'A successful flight would earn as much as $30,000 if Byrd wrote enough firsthand accounts.' Byrd's recent biographer, Lisle Rose, is more emphatic, saying that Byrd faced financial success if he flew to the North Pole and financial ruin if he did not.

For twenty-three days the *Chantier* lurched its way towards Spitsbergen, the entire crew ever mindful that the fragile plane, disassembled and stored in the hold, was the reason for their trip. Byrd wrote on 16 April 1926:

> Spent last night weighing equipment to be taken on planes and also deciding what is to be taken. The weight has to be kept down to a minimum and yet there are so many things we should have to add to our safety. We find that we should carry 1,400 lbs of equipment, food etc. That counts [pilot Floyd] Bennett and myself. We think this may leave us 1,800 miles cruising radius but as to that we can't tell until we reach Spitsbergen and actually try out the plane.

On 28 April Byrd was approaching Kings Bay in the *Chantier*. He radioed to Amundsen:

> Please arrange for our ship *Chantier* to go alongside dock at Kings Bay immediately upon arrival tomorrow night, Thursday about 6 pm. I wish to offer you any help we are capable of. We have fifty men aboard. Kindest and best regards to you and all members of your expedition from all members of our expedition and my personal greetings to you.

There was space for only one ship at the dock at Kings Bay, and Amundsen's and Ellsworth's ship, the *Heimdal*, was occupying it. Byrd would need the *Heimdal* moved if he was going to unload his plane. In the official book of their expedition, Amundsen and Ellsworth would later write:

The *Heimdal* . . . was busy taking on coal and water when the *Chantier* arrived. She had to do this so as to be ready for the time when the *Norge* left Leningrad, so that in case anything happened she could go out and offer assistance. There was also something wrong with one of the boilers, and this made it still further necessary for Captain Tank-Nielsen to refuse Byrd, when he asked for the place at the quay.

Byrd came ashore to meet with Amundsen. Bernt Balchen has left a detailed description of the meeting in his book, *Come North With Me*:

I watch the party work its way around the bay to the dock. A few curious families from the coal-mining village have hurried down to the water's edge, and they step back as the strangers pass. The barking of several sled dogs chained behind the houses is the only sound of greeting. They start across the long flat toward our camp, and the workers hauling supplies give them hostile glances and make way in sullen silence. I step out of the machine shop as they approach, and the leader of the group calls: 'I'm Commander Byrd. Can you tell me where I'll find Captain Amundsen?'

I am full of interest at meeting this explorer of whom we have heard so much. He is in navy uniform, every button of his blue overcoat carefully fastened, the bottoms of his trouser legs stuffed into sturdy buckled galoshes. Commander Byrd is in his late thirties. His face is clean-shaven and very handsome, with small regular features and a firm mouth. He reminds me at first of a young high school principal, but there is an unquestioned air of authority as well as competence about him. He is in

command, and the three other men in the party stand
respectfully in his shadow.

I wipe the grease from my hands with a ball of waste,
and lead the way up the hill, over the thawing snow.
Commander Byrd's eyes are darting from left to right as
we cross the camp area, and he is taking in every detail.
He observes the commissary and the hospital and distant
hangar, loaded with equipment, and his quick glance
climbs the framework of the mooring mast to the gin pole
at the top, ready to hoist the cone into place. A couple of
cooks peer out of the mess hall and mutter something
in Norwegian as we pass, but if he is aware of tension he
shows no sign.

I am always a fast walker, but he lengthens his stride
and keeps up with me, and I can see he is in fine physical
trim. We halt before the manager's building, and I knock
on the door. Amundsen answers: 'Come in.'

Captain Amundsen rises from behind a table strewn
with charts, and holds out his hand to Commander Byrd.
'Glad you're here safe, Commander,' he says. 'Welcome to
Spitsbergen.'

Byrd's manner is at first reserved. The *Heimdal*'s
refusal is still not forgotten, I suspect, and he is politely
formal as he introduces the other members of his
party. 'Lieutenant George Noville, my executive officer,
and Lieutenant Robb Oertell, who is handling the fuel
supplies.' He indicates a rawboned reticent figure lingering
in the doorway. 'And my pilot, Floyd Bennett.'

Lincoln Ellsworth edges unobtrusively in from the
kitchen. He and Amundsen had met Byrd in New York
three months earlier, and they shake hands briefly. I am
curious to see how these fellow countrymen greet each

other. They are courteous, of course, but there is no real
warmth in their greeting; and a couple of times, glancing
at Ellsworth as he slips into the background, I detect a
trace of annoyance in his face, as though he is piqued
at the fact he is no longer the only American explorer in
Kings Bay.

Amundsen remarks genially that he is sorry he could
not keep the promise he made to Byrd in New York: 'I told
you the bay would still be frozen over in May,' he says,
'and you would have an ice surface to take off on skis.
But there's one thing we should never say up here – that
a certain thing will happen at a certain time in the polar
regions. This has been an early spring, so I have not been
able to keep my word.'

I cannot help but notice the striking contrast between
the two leaders: Amundsen, shaggy-haired and rugged
and seasoned as an oak mast; Byrd immaculately groomed
and slender and every inch the cultured gentleman. He
is half a head shorter than Amundsen, and must look
up as they talk. Amundsen senses that this makes him
uncomfortable, and motions to everybody to be seated.

Noville and Oertell move over to the sofa and talk
together in low tones, so as not to disturb the heads of the
two expeditions, and I borrow a chair from the kitchen and
straddle it, while Amundsen and Byrd unroll maps and
discuss their mutual problems.

A short time later:

Commander Byrd pushes back the maps on the table, and
shakes his head. 'That's the route, yes, but how will I ever get
my plane in the air?'

'There is a flat area in front of this house,' Amundsen
says, running north through the centre of the camp to the
very edge of the fjord. 'You can tramp it level and use it for
your take-off strip.'

Byrd looks at him curiously. 'You are being very
generous to a rival.'

'But we are not competitors,' Amundsen corrects
him. 'We are collaborators in a joint assault on the polar
regions, an attack by two vehicles, one lighter and one
heavier than air.'

He stands up and faces Byrd across the table. 'We are
partners in this venture together.'

Byrd then went to the captain of the *Heimdal* and asked him
when the *Chantier* could get alongside the dock to get his plane
ashore. Captain Tank-Nielsen replied Monday. Byrd wrote a
note in his diary: 'I then requested that he let us get alongside
when he is not coaling at night and put the plane ashore. He
would not do that.'

Byrd was furious. He could not wait four days before
getting his plane unloaded. He still had to assemble and test it,
while the *Norge* airship, which was waiting at Leningrad for fine
weather, could be expected at any time. Byrd hit upon a bold
but dangerous idea to get his plane ashore. He wrote:

The only thing for us to do was to anchor as close as possible
to the shore and send our plane through the ice drift by
means of some sort of raft. When the Norwegians heard
what we planned to do they sent word urging us to desist.
'You know nothing about ice,' was the gist of their message,
'or you would not attempt such a thing. The ice is almost
certain to start moving before you can get ashore.'

By laying heavy planks across the gunwhales of our four whaleboats the crew constructed a big raft. Of course that left the *Chantier* without boats, which I did not like on account of the dangers from the ice. It began to snow; and the air was cold and raw as all hands worked at top speed to meet the emergency of a landing that was far from safe.

We were taking a tremendous chance in doing this, for had a wind sprung up the pontoon would have been crushed and blown out to sea. It was either get our personnel and equipment ashore this way or come back to the States ignominious failures. My men were anxious to take the risk with their lives.

'Involuntarily we all held our breath,' the watching Amundsen wrote. 'It sounds so easy, but it must be borne in mind that every inch meant imminent danger to the whole transport. Everything was staked on one card, and – they won.'

A cheer went up from both camps when the raft reached the beach. For the moment it seemed as if nothing was going to stop the Americans being first to the Pole. But as soon as they had the plane unloaded a new obstacle presented itself. Byrd wrote:

When the plane was pulled over planking from the ice foot the wheels sank deep down in the snow. We replaced them immediately with skis. Little did I realize then how soon those great looking skis which I had made with a tremendous factor of safety would be broken like paper in the rough snow.

We had much to learn.

Now Byrd's crew worked around the clock to get the Fokker assembled and tested. By Sunday morning (2 May) the plane stood ready for its first flight. The flat area of ground behind the airship hangar, suggested by Amundsen, was selected as a runway and for the next twenty-four hours the crew worked in shifts to trample the snow flat. On 3 May, with Floyd Bennett at the controls and Byrd in the co-pilot's seat, the *Josephine Ford* attempted to take off. Balchen had been watching the preparation:

Earlier this morning, as I crossed the landing strip on my way to the coal dock, I noticed the *Josephine Ford* parked ready for its initial flight, and Lieutenant Oertell on his knees with a can of wax and a brush, polishing the skis. I asked him what in the world he was doing. He explained that he was waxing the bottoms so that they would slide on the snow surface. Now, in the Arctic if there is one thing that we know it is this: that the hard crystalline snow, at this time of the year, acts like sandpaper, and even if wax gave a sliding surface, it wouldn't last long. Our experience in Norway with both racing skis and airplane skis has taught us to use an entirely different preparation, a mixture of pine tar and resin burned into the wood with a blowtorch. I described this to Oertell, but he said there was no time to change, because the test hop was due at noon.

Byrd described what happened on the first attempt to get the *Josephine Ford* airborne:

The plane's first attempt to take off for a trial flight ended in a snowdrift and nearly upset - which not only would have hurt us, but would have upset the expedition as well! A ski was broken to bits and the landing gear bent and broken.

Things then looked black, but the men refused to lose heart. Then twice again we broke our ski in pretty much the same way. We were having difficulties – that would never be experienced in the States – in getting off the snow with the lightest possible load. What would happen when we tried our total load of about 10,000 pounds?

Balchen continued to watch the proceeding with interest and, not a little sympathy:

In the back of my mind, all morning long, my hunch about the undersized skis on the *Josephine Ford* has kept nagging me. Back in the naval aircraft factory in Horten, I had experimented with various types of ski landing gear, and I know what is required in both strength and in flexibility to stand up under a heavy trimotor plane. I realize that any delay to Byrd will better Amundsen's own chances, but at the same time I feel a kinship with the American party that is hard to explain . . . Deep inside me today as I watched these spirited youngsters of the rival camp double-timing up and down the landing strip to pack the snow flat with their feet, roughhousing as they worked and making fun of every new hardship, I knew I should be happy to belong to such a team myself. If Captain Amundsen is not first over the Pole, I shall be glad to see the honor go to these Americans.

Another reason for Balchen's sympathy with the Americans can probably be traced to the closeness he felt to Byrd's pilot, Floyd Bennett. In his description of the first meeting at Kings Bay between Amundsen and Byrd, Balchen wrote:

Of all the men in the room I think I understand Bennett
best. He is, like me, a flier, who is at home anywhere behind
the controls of an airplane. He earned his wings in the
United States Navy, he tells me quietly while the leaders are
talking, and last year he flew Commander Byrd from Etah
in northwest Greenland on the Donald MacMillan Arctic
Expedition – the first flying, in fact, that had ever been done
in the high Canadian arctic. It does not matter where he
flies, so long as he is flying. We are almost the same age, and
he impresses me as simple and straightforward and direct.
I have a feeling that some day we shall be flying together.

Watching the failed take-off attempts, Balchen understood
the nature of the trouble: the waxed skis were simply not strong
enough to support the plane. After another broken ski, Balchen
decided to help the Americans. Whether he did so with
Amundsen's blessing is uncertain. Balchen wrote:

At noon, in the machine shop making a new drive shaft for
the tractor, I hear above the sputter of my welding torch
the full throttled roar of an airplane's motors. In the next
second all three engines snarl and choke off abruptly, and
there is dead silence. I yank off my dark goggles and run to
the window, but cannot see the landing strip. As I head for
the door, it is flung open and Captain Amundsen shoulders
his way in: 'Balchen, there's been an accident. The Fokker's
broken a ski. Go see what you can do to help'.

Balchen's version was written in his autobiography,
many years later, and may have served to give Amundsen's
endorsement to his actions. Byrd, on the other hand, wrote in
his personal diary at the time:

> Took lunch with Amundsen who professes great friendship
> but gave Lt. Balchen (who is a peach and wanted to help us
> and has helped us) orders not to come near us again.

Nevertheless, Balchen discussed the problem with Floyd Bennett
and suggested a solution. Although spare skis were aboard
the *Chantier*, Balchen explained that they would not endure
unless they were strengthened with wood that was both strong
and flexible. Nothing suitable could be found at Kings Bay, so
Balchen suggested the oars from the *Chantier*'s lifeboats. The
oars were brought ashore and the ship's carpenter cut them into
strips and attached them to the new skis. Balchen then showed
Byrd's crew how to burn in a mixture of pine tar and resin.

While the Americans began building new skis to fit to
the Fokker, the Norwegians completed their mooring mast.
Amundsen radioed Nobile, who was waiting with the *Norge* in
Leningrad, that he should fly to Kings Bay as soon as the weather
permitted. An anxious Ellsworth sent Riiser-Larsen, also on the
Norge, a separate message: 'For heavens sake hurry.' At five am
the next morning (5 May) the *Norge* lifted off and began its
journey to Spitsbergen. Forty-eight hours later it gently floated
over Kings Bay, where it had barely been moored to its mast
and walked into its hangar before Amundsen asked Nobile
how soon it could be ready for its flight. Nobile replied that
he needed time to replace a port engine, which had damaged
its crankshaft, as well as repair a torn rudder. In explaining to
Amundsen that he would have the repairs completed as quickly
as possible in order to get away before Byrd, Nobile wrote that
'Amundsen was not worried about it, thinking that the thick
snow would delay him [Byrd] for quite a while'.

A day later, with new wood-strengthened skis fitted to
the Fokker, Byrd's crew got the plane ready for a trial flight.

All the while, the Italians and Norwegians worked steadily to repair the *Norge*. Then news came that would spur Byrd on to hurry even more. That morning Wilkins, with Lanphier and Wisely as pilots, had got his Fokker Trimotor, the *Detroiter*, to Barrow. Wilkins had radioed Kings Bay, saying he was ready to commence his long flight across the Arctic, via the North Pole. He asked if the weather at Spitsbergen was suitable for flying. As Balchen put it, 'Now it is a three-way contest.'

By noon Byrd was ready. With Floyd Bennett at the controls, the *Josephine Ford*'s engines were started again and warmed up. This time the Fokker was fully laden with all the supplies and fuel it could carry. There would be no more trial flights. The plane was perched at the top of a small ramp at the beginning of the airstrip and secured by a rope from the rear of its tail to a pole in the ground. Bennett opened the throttles and the three massive engines surged towards full power. The plane was straining at the rope. At the precise point of maximum revolutions, a ground crew member cut the rope with an axe to release the plane from its 'starting gate' on the preciously short runway. Amid a deafening roar of the engines, a wildly excited ground crew and the sheets of blinding snow thrown up by the propellers, the Fokker lurched forward.

Just a few metres. Then stopped. Bennett increased and decreased the engine speed, trying to rock the plane free, but it wouldn't budge. Byrd's frustration must have been palpable as he climbed from the plane that was going nowhere. They had strengthened the skis and coated them with pine tar and resin. Now what?

Byrd called Balchen over and asked him why the plane wouldn't move. Balchen explained that they were trying to take off at the wrong time of the day. By midday the temperature had risen and the snow had become sticky. To get such a heavy plane off the ground, they would need to wait until night when the snow freezes over again and becomes icy.

That night, at midnight, the *Josephine Ford*'s engines were started again. They were warmed up, and this time the big Fokker moved forward easily. It gathered speed and lifted into the air. Watching it, Bernt Balchen took out his notebook and wrote: '9 May. Jo Ford, B and B, depart Kings Bay, 0037.' Byrd was away.

Balchen wrote:

All the rest of the night and the following day we try to carry on our duties as usual around the camp, but there is only one thought on our minds. We do not mention it to each other, but the anxiety of every man is apparent in the strange silence as we work, and the occasional pauses to scan the empty northern sky.

And later that day:

We are in the middle of dinner when we hear shouts outside, and one of the Italian soldiers comes bounding into the mess hall, out of breath. He chatters in broken English, 'She come – a motor!'

It was a little over fifteen hours since Byrd had taken off. The Norwegians and Italians rushed out of the mess hall and searched the skies to see a tiny speck in the distance. The Americans, still aboard the *Chantier*, were caught unawares and immediately lowered their lifeboats and rowed furiously towards the shore. The Fokker landed and Amundsen, followed by Ellsworth, was the first to step forward and greet Byrd. Balchen observed:

The men of the Byrd expedition are charging up over the hill, and Amundsen steps back as they surround their leader, yelling and cheering, pounding each other on the back, wild with victory. Two pairs of husky lads hoist Byrd and Bennett onto their shoulders, and the others follow as if in a football snake dance as they carry the conquering heroes down the hill to the *Chantier*. In all the excitement no one has asked about the operational difficulties and details of the flight. Tonight the waiting world will hear in Byrd's own words that he has done what no man in history has ever done before. He has flown over the North Pole.

In his diary, Balchen jotted: '9 May. Jo. Ford returns Kings Bay 1607.'

8

The Big Trip

Three days after arriving at Kings Bay, and one day after Byrd's return from the Pole, the *Norge* was ready. Now it was Amundsen who began to drag his feet. The explorer who had pushed and urged Nobile to make haste was in no hurry to leave.

Noting that the evening of 10 May was calm, Nobile announced his intention of leaving during the night, when the air was coolest and he could fill the gas bags with the maximum amount of hydrogen, and therefore lift off with the maximum amount of fuel for the engines. But by eleven pm the wind began to increase in intensity and Nobile stood the crew down to await orders. The Norwegians and Italians went to get a few hours sleep. At one am the wind was dropping again, so Nobile instructed the mechanics to be roused and the engines tested. Departure would be at five am. The hour arrived with the Italians aboard the airship but no sign of the Norwegians – not even the ground crew. The temperature began to rise and Nobile was forced to valve off hydrogen. Six o'clock arrived and still no Norwegians. Nobile valved off more precious hydrogen and had to unload petrol as a result.

At seven am the Norwegian ground crew began to straggle out. Nobile had valved off hydrogen three times and unloaded

400 pounds (181 kilograms) of petrol to compensate. It was close to eight am when Amundsen, Ellsworth, Riiser-Larsen and the Norwegian air crew, all of whom had enjoyed a full night's sleep followed by a hearty breakfast, finally arrived.

The *Norge* would carry sixteen people. These would consist of eight Norwegians, six Italians, one Swede and one American (Ellsworth). Three of the sixteen men had no hands-on role in running the airship. These were Amundsen and Ellsworth, who had installed velvet-covered aluminium chairs for themselves in the centre of the control cabin, and Fredrik Ramm, a Norwegian journalist. This left six Italians, six Norwegians and one Swede actually responsible for operating the airship. Because the Italians could not speak Norwegian and vice versa, the chosen 'language of command' in the control cabin was English, which neither group spoke fluently. Further complicating matters, Amundsen, who had no active role and no knowledge of airships, was the expedition leader. Nobile was officially 'airship commander'. Riiser-Larsen, who was the only Norwegian with even limited airship experience, was second-in-command of the airship under Nobile.

The order to let go the ropes was given at 9.50 am, 11 May 1926. The first attempt to cross the Arctic Sea had begun. Nobile wrote:

> How light I felt. A few hours previously I had been shivering with cold. Now I would have liked to take off my furs. We flew towards the mouth of the bay. The last stage of our journey had finally started. Our lovely ship was sailing along at nearly 50 miles and hour towards the Pole – and beyond the Pole into the unknown . . .
>
> . . . what would happen beyond the Pole, in the unexplored zone, nobody could say. What the weather

would be like, whether or not we should find a mountain
range which Peary thought he had glimpsed, where, when
and how we should land, and what would happen to us
after the landing: all these were questions which could
only be answered by guesswork.

Nobile ordered an adjustment to the elevators to bring the
nose up between three and six degrees and, using the engine
and propellers, took the airship up to 1350 feet (411 metres).
By late morning they were cruising over the pack ice, but a
check of their ground speed showed them travelling at only
thirty-three miles per hour. Figuring he had a strong headwind,
Nobile ordered the elevators back to bring the airship level
and, slightly overloaded as it was, it began to lose height. At
600 feet (182 metres) the elevators were adjusted again and the
altitude maintained. The manoeuvre worked. There was less
headwind and the airship was travelling at forty-three miles per
hour. A few hours later, hoping the wind at a higher altitude
had changed direction, Nobile took the airship to 3650 feet
(1112 metres). He was right. The speed increased to over fifty
miles per hour.

For the next eight hours they moved steadily towards the
North Pole. The crew functioned smoothly, and Amundsen
and Ellsworth sat contentedly in their chairs. The only
technical problem encountered between Kings Bay and the
North Pole happened when water vapour in a fuel line froze,
blocking the line and stopping the port engine. It was cleared
and the engine restarted.

By late evening the weather had begun to change and they
flew into dense cloud. It cleared briefly, to be replaced by
snow and fog. Within minutes of entering the fog the outer
metal parts of the airship began to ice up, the windows became

covered and vision obscured. Nobile took the airship higher, until it was above the deadly fog and out of danger.

Then at one am on 12 May 1926, Nobile took the airship down to 1000 feet, where Riiser-Larsen, crouched at a port hole with a sextant, shot the sun's altitude. Everyone waited silently. The sun was appearing and disappearing in the cloud. Nobile ordered the engines stopped and the airship down to 600 feet.

Watching the sun's reflected image sink slowly to sit on the artificial horizon, Riiser-Larsen quietly declared, 'We are there.'

They had reached at the North Pole on 12 May 1926, at 1.30 am.

Amundsen and Oscar Wisting shook hands quietly. Fifteen years earlier Wisting had stood with Amundsen at the South Pole. Now the two Norwegians were the only men in the world to have been to both Poles.

Three previous expeditions had claimed to have reached the North Pole. Frederick A. Cook's claim has never been taken seriously, except by his supporters, who see conspiracies hatched by Peary's followers. More recently, Peary's claim has come under scrutiny and most experts now agree that he did not fully take into account the drift of the ice pack, while he also allowed himself generous margins of error in his dead reckoning. An impartial reading of all the evidence shows that neither man can fairly be credited with having reached the exact North Pole. Richard Byrd claimed to have reached it three days before the *Norge*, but his assertion would soon be surrounded by controversy. Ultimately, the crew of the *Norge* should go into the history books as having been the first men to reach the exact North Pole, whether by air or on foot. Certainly they were the first men whose claim cannot be disputed.

On board the *Norge* it was a significant occasion but there
was little celebration because the occupants were divided into
rival camps. Amundsen and Ellsworth took out their small
Norwegian and American flags and dropped them through a
porthole. The large Italian flag, which had been struck from
the *N1* when it had been renamed the *Norge*, and which
Mussolini had told Nobile to drop at the Pole, was brought
out. With great celebration the Italians released it through
a porthole. Amundsen laughed within their hearing, while
Nobile recorded in the airship's logbook: 'Planted the Italian
flag at the Pole.'

Nobile was now enduring his second night without sleep,
and the *Norge* was heading into unknown territory. He took the
airship up to 2000 feet and their journey continued. Just over
seven hours later, at 85° north latitude, the fog returned and
totally obscured their view of the ice below. If there was land
in this unexplored territory, they could not see it. Amundsen
would not be setting foot on Roald Amundsen Land.

The fog brought more immediate concerns for Nobile. The
exposed metal sections of the exterior began to ice up. At first
this meant extra weight, but it was counteracted by the reduced
weight of the consumed fuel. Then, as the ice began to fall off
under its own weight, shards began to hit the propellers and
be flung against the gas bags. The first damage took place at
1.40 pm, twelve hours and 540 miles past the Pole. To the crew
it sounded like an explosion. Nobile wrote:

Soon they came to tell me that the covering of the metal
framework of the ship had been holed by a piece of ice flung
from a propeller . . . I was really worried by the pieces of ice
which flung off from the airscrews as if from a sling, [and]
kept violently striking against the hull of the ship. One of

them might pierce the walls of the gas-chamber and cause an irreparable loss of hydrogen.

Between 80° and 79° north, the fog cleared briefly to give them a glimpse of open sea. They could not be sure there was no land north of Alaska, but they could say reasonably safely that there was no large continent. They had been in the air over thirty-two hours. For the next few hours they would drift in and out of fog. According to Nobile:

> In this brief respite I had time to look around. The cabin was horribly dirty. The dozens of thermos flasks heaped on the floor ... presented a particularly sad spectacle: some of them empty, others overturned, others broken. Coffee and tea had been spilt everywhere, and all over the place were the remains of food. In the midst of all this mess there stuck out picturesquely Amundsen's enormous feet, with his grass stuffed shoes, his diver's gaiters and red and white gloves.

At 6.45 am, after the airship had been aloft for forty-five hours, Riiser-Larsen, peering out a window, called out, 'Land ahead to starboard.' Nobile knew he was on the north coast of Alaska and was now faced with a dilemma. He could fly roughly straight ahead, cross the mountains and reach Fairbanks. But the mountains had not been properly mapped and no one knew their exact heights. As Wilkins had found out a few weeks earlier, they exceeded the accepted estimates. Nobile's other choice was to turn right and follow the coast around the Seward Peninsula, alongside the Bering Strait, and continue down to Nome. 'Rome to Nome' had been a catch cry before he had left Italy, and Nobile liked the sound of it. The coast would also be a safer option than trying to get the altitude to cross the mountains. Nobile ordered the crew to turn the airship to starboard and follow the coast.

The last leg of the journey should perhaps have been the easiest but it turned out to be the most difficult. This was accentuated by the fact that the relief of reaching Alaska released the level of tension that had kept the crew alert, and they all began to feel the affects of fatigue. Nobile himself had had no more than two or three hours' sleep in the last seventy-two hours. But there was no one to whom he could hand over the controls of the airship. The fog began again soon after noon, making it impossible to see the coast. Nobile took the airship as high as possible but could not escape it. When it did clear enough for them to see below, they were over the Bering Strait and heading for Siberia. Working against a wind intent on blowing them south-west towards Japan, Nobile turned the airship around. It was 9.30 pm before he again found the coast of Alaska. He would write:

> I cannot attempt to give any details of this breathless race
> under the implacable fog, among the hills, over the ice
> of Kotzbue Bay, over frozen lagoons. Who can tell what
> route we followed, or how we wound in and out of the fog?
> Even today I can still live through the emotions of this wild
> flight under the fog, without knowing where we were or
> where we were going; but the recollection is confused,
> as in a nightmare.

This time, when they found the coast, they followed it south. Nobile handed the controls to Riiser-Larsen and catnapped. Before long he was roused from his sleep and told there was a village below. As he looked out the porthole he realised the settlement consisted of only a few huts and was too small to be

Nome. But he decided to land anyway. The airship floated gently to the ground and Amundsen was the first to step off, followed by Ellsworth. Nobile was the last to leave the airship, opening the valves to release the hydrogen as he did so. He recalled:

> The *Norge* was lying lifeless, destroyed, on the white snowfield. She had brought us safe and sound, for thousands of miles, to our goal, always obedient to commands, untiring, almost as if she realised the magnitude of the task I had set her ... without her strong, elastic framework giving way; she had withstood wind, snow, frost, rain and fog.

The *Norge* had landed at the small settlement of Teller, 100 miles north of Nome. An epic flight had ended, but acrimony was about to begin.

9

Beyond a Reasonable Doubt

On 8 May 1926, while Byrd was preparing to take off for the North Pole, and while Amundsen, Ellsworth and Nobile were waiting for the *Norge* to be repaired at Kings Bay, Wilkins had landed at Barrow with his Fokker, the *Detroiter*. He had the fuel tanks filled and hoped to get away on his trans–Arctic flight the next day. But the morning brought fog, and while it might have been possible to fly above it, Wilkins felt it would defeat the purpose of looking for new land. So he waited:

> We were in constant touch with the outside world by wireless, and learned that Byrd and Amundsen were ready at Spitsbergen to make a polar flight. Shortly after we learned that Byrd had flown to the Pole and back, and that Amundsen was about to start. Then came the news that the *Norge* was on its way. We calculated the time and on the evening of the thirteenth of May we set our watches, hoping to see the airship as she passed. The weather had been very dull early in the day, but toward evening the clouds broke up just a little, and in the distance we saw a small dark object threading its way between them. We recognised it at once as the airship.
>
> Since my earliest experience in the Arctic, I had believed that it would be possible to use both airplanes

and airships for polar flying, and as I stood on the coast at Point Barrow watching Amundsen, Ellsworth and Nobile pass, it was the realization of my plan. That perhaps was the greatest thrill of my life.

Wilkins now waited for the weather to clear. He waited and watched from Barrow but thick fog continued. Finally, at the beginning of June he cabled the Detroit Aviation Society, explaining that it was no longer possible to do any useful work that season. He asked whether the society would support him the following year. It replied that it would continue its support and that Wilkins was to do what he thought best. He left the fuel supply at Barrow, flew back to Fairbanks and stored the *Detroiter* and the wrecked *Alaskan*.

* * *

Byrd made no more flights in the Arctic after the North Pole. The grand plans for exploration he had announced to the world before the expedition set sail came to naught. His one flight had flown the same route as Amundsen and Ellsworth the year before, and nothing new had been added to the knowledge of the Arctic. Byrd simply watched Amundsen, Nobile and Ellsworth take off, waited until they were safely past the Pole lest he was needed for a rescue mission, then busied himself with the important job of getting back to America to reap the fruits of his success.

In the days after the flight, Bernt Balchen, who had not gone along on the *Norge*, and Floyd Bennett became close friends. At Bennett's suggestion, Byrd invited the Norwegian to come back to America on the *Chantier*. Byrd was already discussing the possibility of flying to the South Pole and felt that Balchen's practical skills with aeroplanes fitted with skis could be an asset. Balchen jumped at the chance. Here was an opportunity to go to the 'new world' and fly the very latest aircraft with his new friend.

The *Chantier* returned to New York on 18 June 1926, but was ordered by Byrd to remain offshore for two days. It was Thursday and Byrd's publicity people had arranged parades for the Saturday, when the most people would be able to attend. Byrd was orchestrating his rise to celebrity and carefully managing what he called the 'hero business'. A huge crowd greeted the ship at the docks. The members of the expedition, with Byrd and Floyd Bennett prominent at the front, were given a ticker-tape parade down Broadway. It was the biggest celebration since the victory parade for troops returning from World War One. Byrd ordered Balchen to remain on the *Chantier* because he was not an official member of the expedition and therefore couldn't participate in the celebration, despite the fact that Balchen had helped make the North Pole flight possible.

While he was taking his bows in front of his public and enjoying his new celebrity, Byrd submitted the navigational findings for his flight to the National Geographic Society. The society's board of trustees then appointed a committee to examine the records and determine if Byrd had actually reached the North Pole. Among others, the society president, Dr Gilbert Grosvenor, was a member of the committee.

In 1926 Byrd had various means of navigating his way to the North Pole. He had to fly directly north from Spitsbergen, but he could not use a magnetic compass because magnetic north was to the west of him. He could, however, use the newly invented sun compass, which was designed specifically for navigation in high latitudes. The sun compass relies on the fact that the sun is a fixed point in space and that the Earth revolves on its axis every twenty-four hours. Before leaving on a flight, the navigator determines in which direction he wants to fly and aligns the sun compass to point in that direction. He points a second indicator at the sun and winds a clockwork mechanism, which moves to compensate for the earth's rotation, so that the first indicator stays pointed in the direction chosen.

With the sun compass Byrd could keep his plane headed north, but he could not use it to measure whether he was drifting to the left or the right of the line (meridian) of longitude he was following. To measure and compensate for this, Byrd used a drift indicator. This device, installed in the floor of a plane, allowed the navigator to look ahead to a specific point on the ground (or the ice). Using a thin line down the centre of the indicator, the navigator watched that point, in relation to the line, to see if the plane was drifting. He could then direct the pilot to steer left or right to compensate.

So, Byrd could keep his plane pointing north with a sun compass and stay on the meridian of longitude with a drift indicator. But neither would tell him when he had actually reached the North Pole. There were only two ways he could do this – by dead reckoning or with a sextant.

Dead reckoning was based on speed, time and direction. For example, if a person wanted to reach a point 200 miles to the west, and travelled in that direction at a speed of fifty miles per hour for four hours, then they would be at that point – providing the measurements of speed, direction and time were accurate. For Byrd, the most difficult measurement to take in an aeroplane was speed. Or more precisely, 'ground speed' as opposed to 'air speed'. A plane, at certain engine revolutions, might pass through the air at eighty miles per hour. But with a headwind of twenty miles per hour its speed over the ground might only be sixty miles per hour.

In 1926 ground speed indicators were often incorporated into the drift indicator in the floor of the plane. If one looked forward at an angle of forty-five degrees to a point on the ground, then that point would be the same distance ahead of the plane as the plane was above the ground. One could start a stopwatch when the sight was taken and stop it when the plane was directly above the point sighted. The distance travelled, being equal to the altitude, could then be compared to the time elapsed and the ground speed calculated.

Such calculations needed the plane to be travelling over level ground and the plane's altitude to be known accurately. But the committee of the National Geographic Society was not about to accept dead reckoning as proof Byrd had reached the North Pole, writing that:

> The distances depend on estimates of speed, and estimates of speed depend on the altitude of the plane obtained with an aneroid barometer.
>
> The barometer readings of altitude depend on the assumption that the sea-level atmospheric pressure remains constant over the whole route of the flight, something which in ordinary latitudes rarely happens between points so widely separated. We do not know if these conditions are better in the Polar Regions. It is our belief, therefore, that estimates of speed may be subject to large errors.

This meant Byrd's only way of accurately determining if he was at the North Pole was to use a sextant.

After the magnetic compass, the sextant (with its predecessors, the astrolabe, backstaff, sea quadrant and octant) is the oldest instrument of navigation. So named because the shape of its arc is roughly one-sixth of a circle, the sextant uses two mirrors to measure the angle between two objects a long distance away. Most often the sextant is used to measure the angle between the horizon and the sun. As one travels north or south to different latitudes, so the angle of the sun in relation to the horizon changes.

One of the mirrors, the 'index mirror', is mounted on the moveable index arm. The index arm is moved to reflect the sun, or another heavenly body, onto the 'horizon mirror'. This lower mirror is designed so that the reflected image of the sun is superimposed on the horizon. The navigator looks through a small telescope towards the horizon. Then the index arm is moved until the reflected sun is 'sitting' on the horizon. The angle of the sun is then read off the arc.

Knowing the angle of the sun alone does not mean the navigator will immediately know his latitude. The sun's height in the sky changes throughout the day. Nor will it be the same height at the same time every day. The angle or height increases in summer and decreases in winter. It also changes from year to year. Navigators use almanacs produced for each year by the British Admiralty and the United States Hydrographic Office, which give the movements for the sun and other heavenly bodies throughout the year.

Navigators take the angle of the sun, noting the time of the day and their longitude, then consult the almanac to determine their latitude. When he set off for the North Pole, Byrd was not travelling to a particular landmark, such as an island or a hilltop, from which he could take a sextant reading and then return to announce at what latitude that landmark lay. Instead he was flying north to reach a particular point of latitude. In other words, he had to fly north until he reached a point that gave him a certain sextant reading: a reading that he knew before he commenced the flight. He could not plant a flag, build a rock cairn or identify some feature that proved he had been to the North Pole. He could only come back and say, 'My sextant reading was X at this time, therefore I was at the North Pole.' Of course, the desired sextant reading could be known by anyone with an almanac for 1926.

Sextants are delicate instruments. The index mirror only needs to move a small amount to change the reading. At a time when navigators' lives, and the lives of their fellow crew members, often depended on their sextant readings, navigators handled their sextants with extreme care. They were carefully checked before setting out, and fine adjustments would be made to the mirrors with micrometer screws. During the voyages they would be laid, right side down, in specially constructed boxes so that the index and horizon mirrors were not bumped or jarred.

Byrd's sextant was a 'bubble sextant', which was different to the traditional mariners' sextant and designed specifically for aviators. In fact, Byrd had helped develop the bubble sextant during his time in the Navy. Instead of looking through a small telescope to sight the horizon and therefore ensure one side of the angle was parallel with the surface of the earth, the bubble sextant used the principal of the spirit level to ensure the sextant was held level.

Elaborating on its findings to its readers, the committee of the National Geographic Society explained that any inaccuracy in Byrd knowing his location would be:

> . . . wholly due to errors in the observed elevation of the sun.
> These elevations were determined with a sextant, in which

the bubble supplies the horizon of reference, an instrument developed by Commander Byrd and in the use of which he is most skillful.

Byrd supplied the sextant readings that he claimed to have taken. The National Geographic Society had no choice but to conclude that he had reached the North Pole:

At 8 hours 58 minutes, 55 seconds (GCT) an observation of the altitude of the sun gave a latitude of 89 degrees 55.3 on the meridian of flight. This point is 4.7 miles from the Pole.

Continuing his flight on the same course and at the speed of 74 miles per hour, which he had averaged since 8 hours 18 minutes, would bring Commander Byrd close to the Pole in 3 minutes 49 seconds, making the probable time of his arrival at the Pole 9 hours 3 minutes Greenwich Civil Time.

Byrd claimed that he then flew around the Pole, taking four sextant readings to confirm his position. The committee observed:

These four observations confirmed his dead reckoning position of the Pole. He then attempted to fly his plane in a circle several miles in diameter, with his Pole position as a center.

After taking his four sightings, Byrd claimed, he then instructed Bennett to head back to Spitsbergen following the fifteenth east meridian. At the time they turned to head back, the sun was directly ahead, crossing the said meridian. The National Geographic Society's committee noted:

At the moment when the sun would be crossing the 15th meridian, along which he had laid his course, he had the plane steadied, pointed directly towards the sun, and observed at the same instant that the shadow of the sun compass was down the middle of the band, thus verifying his position as being on that meridian.

Soon after leaving the Pole the sextant which Commander Byrd was using slid off the chart table, breaking the horizon glass. This made it necessary to navigate the return trip wholly by dead reckoning.

This navigation by dead reckoning:

... had an even more satisfactory verification when, at about 14 hours 30 minutes GCT, he sighted land dead ahead and soon identified Grey Point (Grey Hook), Spitsbergen, just west of the 15th meridian.

It is unfortunate that no sextant observations could be made on the return trip; but the successful landfall at Grey Hook demonstrates Commander Byrd's skill in navigating along a predetermined course, and in our opinion is one of the strongest evidences that he was equally successful in his flight northward.

The feat of flying a plane 600 miles from land and returning directly to the point aimed for is a remarkable exhibition of skillful navigation and shows beyond a reasonable doubt that he knew where he was at all times during the flight.

It is the opinion of your committee that at very close to 9 hours 3 minutes Greenwich Civil Time, May 9, 1926, Lieutenant Commander Richard Evelyn Byrd was at the North Pole, in so far as an observer in an airplane, using the most accurate instruments and methods available for determining his position, could ascertain.

The National Geographic Society's report is remarkable for its trust in Byrd's claims to have taken the necessary sextant readings. The '600 miles from land' that Byrd flew are the longer nautical miles, although the article never says so.

Byrd left Kings Bay at 12.37 am and supposedly reached the North Pole at 9.03 am. Therefore he flew 770 statute miles in eight hours and twenty-six minutes, demanding an average speed of over ninety miles per hour. For some reason, according to the National Geographic Society's committee, he only covered the last forty minutes at seventy-four miles per hour. Byrd claimed he circled the Pole for twelve or thirteen minutes, taking his sextant readings, then left at 9.16 am. He arrived back at Kings Bay at 4.07 pm. His return flight had taken 6 hours 51 minutes, so his average speed would have to have been almost 113 miles per hour. At a time when Wilkins, on the other side of the Arctic Ocean, was discovering that the maximum speed he could coax out of his Fokker Trimotor was ninety miles per hour, Byrd was flying his at 113 miles per hour. As Byrd later wrote in *Skyward*:

The wind began to freshen and change direction soon after we left the Pole, and soon we were making over 100 miles an hour.

The elements were surely smiling that day on us, two insignificant specks of mortality flying there over that great, vast white area in a small plane with only one companion, speechless and deaf from the motors, just a dot in the center of 10,000 square miles of visible desolation.

The committee that examined Byrd's records had been appointed soon after his return to New York, but Byrd's supporters did not wait for its verdict. Three days after he arrived home, President Calvin Coolidge presented Byrd with the National Geographic Society's Hubbard Medal. Later in the year, when Congress convened, it conferred the nation's highest award, the Medal of Honor, on both Byrd and Floyd Bennett. President Coolidge personally signed the citation that was awarded for 'conspicuous courage and intrepidity in demonstrating that it is possible for aircraft to travel in continuous flight from a now inhabited portion of the earth over the North Pole and return'. Byrd was promoted from Lieutenant-Commander to Commander in the Naval Reserve and awarded the Distinguished Service Medal and the Distinguished Flying Cross.

Byrd was astute enough to know that he could not rest forever on this one laurel. He also realised that fame, and the fortune that followed, came from firsts. Further flights in the Arctic, as he had previously said he was going to make, would be a waste of time. No first in that area could match his North Pole flight. Byrd began to focus his efforts on becoming the first person to fly to the South Pole. But while he was preparing for what was obviously a major expedition south, he also began to consider the possibility of flying nonstop across the Atlantic to claim the Orteig Prize. Raymond Orteig, a New York hotel owner, had offered $25,000 to the first person, or persons, to fly nonstop, in either direction, between Paris and New York. The prize had remained uncollected for seven years.

While Byrd was travelling about the country receiving his accolades, it was arranged for the *Josephine Ford* to tour America on a promotional tour. Floyd Bennett would be the pilot and Bernt Balchen the co-pilot. During the flight around the country the two friends learnt about each other's flying capabilities. The only change made to the Fokker was that the skis had been removed and replaced with wheels, which, if anything, would make the plane fly faster. On the tour of America it also carried a much lighter load.

Bennett was a pilot who would navigate visually. He would fly low, following railway tracks, roads and known landmarks. He freely admitted that he had no experience in flying by instruments and explained to Balchen that the best way to know where you were was to fly low enough to read the sign on a railway station. Balchen, on the other hand, was trained in Norway, where low cloud made visibility poor. This meant flying by dead reckoning. Using a stopwatch and compass to navigate, Balchen had become proficient at observing wind drift. He also knew that the crucial element of dead reckoning was to know the plane's speed.

The forty-city, two-month tour began on 7 October 1926. After a few stops, where Bennett was called upon to make a speech, the pair discussed the possibility of flying to Paris and claiming the Orteig Prize. But would Byrd be willing to lend them the *Josephine Ford*? If he was, could the plane make the distance nonstop? Balchen resolved to keep an accurate log of the plane's flying capabilities, including speed and fuel consumption, to find out. The pair continued the national tour, through the midwest to Los Angeles, then swinging south through Texas, across to Florida then back up the east coast. When they reached Washington they announced their idea for the transatlantic flight. Learning of the idea, Byrd instructed them to deliver the *Josephine Ford* to the Ford Museum in Dearborn, Michigan, where it would become a permanent exhibit. Balchen wrote in *Come North With Me*:

We circle the Detroit air strip, and come around for the final approach. I think back to the first time I saw the big Fokker rafted ashore on lifeboats through the churning ice of Kings Bay. It has come a long way to end its brave life here in a dusty museum. The tires screech, and the *Josephine Ford* settles on the grass and rolls to a stop for the last time . . .

My eye runs over the instrument gauges, and automatically I note down the speed and fuel consumption for the last time. Still figuring, though it looks like an academic question now, I run over the data I have compiled on the tour. 'Tell me,' I ask Bennett, 'what do you get for our average cruising speed?'

Bennett takes his own log out of the leg pocket of his coveralls. 'Let's see. About 70 miles an hour.'

'So do I.'

Eighty years later the *Josephine Ford* still sits in the Henry Ford Museum in Dearborn, a silent witness to what really happened on the North Pole flight.

10

Tempting Fate a Second Time

Whatever Amundsen might have expected from the flight of the *Norge*, he should hardly have been displeased. Ellsworth had paid for it. The Aero Club of Norway had organised the ground crew and hangar at Kings Bay. The Italian government had supplied the main operational members of the air crew. And Nobile had taken his brilliantly designed airship and piloted it over 4500 miles from Rome to Spitsbergen, then another 3000 miles over the largely unexplored Arctic Ocean. Amundsen had spent nothing and done little. In his own words, he had 'the easiest task of all'. Nobile would write:

> Together we had crossed the Arctic, together our flags had dropped upon the Pole. Each of us had contributed his own share to the success of the enterprise. Amundsen, who first thought of it, had brought to it the prestige of his past exploits; Ellsworth had made it a practical possibility by putting up his share of the expenses; I had borne the responsibility of preparing the ship and superintending the flight from Rome to America. Our widely divergent life-paths had run together for a while; but now at Seattle they branched off again, each following his own course.

I was never to see Amundsen again, though once more his name was to be linked with mine . . .

Amundsen may have been disappointed that Byrd had beaten him to the North Pole, or disappointed that he had found no new land to claim and name. More likely, he was upset that Nobile was sharing the fame and kudos resulting from the flight, thereby detracting from Amundsen's own ability to draw crowds to the all-important money-making lecture circuit. Whatever his motive, Amundsen launched an ongoing personal attack against Nobile. It was an attack that even Amundsen's admirers said was beneath him. Had there been a major mishap he may have had justification. But because Nobile had pulled off the whole flight so brilliantly, Amundsen was reduced to nit-picking the most trivial things. Nobile had 'lost his head' and was in tears when giving orders. Nobile endangered the airship and only the quick actions of Riiser-Larsen had saved them. Often Riiser-Larsen would be in control of the airship while Nobile stood around doing nothing, seemingly bewildered. Worst of all, Nobile had taken his Italian Air Force uniform and, when the expedition returned to populated cities, proudly wore it and gave the Fascist salute at every opportunity.

Most people saw Amundsen's outbursts as the ramblings of a bitter, broke and lonely man, but the more they continued, the more the proud Italian was forced into a position where he had to save face – both for himself and the Fascist government he represented. Nobile chose to answer the criticisms, not with words but by undertaking further flights in the Arctic. And this time the crew and support staff would all be Italian.

With hindsight, it was not Nobile's best decision. There were no major 'firsts' that the Italians could achieve to impress the newspapers; they had already flown an airship over the top of the world. Even Mussolini warned him, 'Perhaps it would be better not to tempt fate a second time.' Despite having minimal backing from his government and no truly original objective, Nobile continued to push his plans for a return to the Arctic. And like so many polar explorers before him, he veiled his personal ambition with the cloak of scientific discovery. The Italian expedition to the Arctic would be, in Nobile's words, 'the first scientific aerial exploration of the Arctic'. In fact, it would become one of the Arctic's most famous disasters.

* * *

At the end of Wilkins' 1926 expedition, the Detroit Aviation Society had one Fokker Trimotor, one single-engine Fokker with an irreparably damaged wing, 3500 gallons of aviation fuel at Barrow and a $30,000 debt. Yet Wilkins still had a strong desire to continue his work. In his view, he needed two lighter planes capable of taking off on the makeshift runway at Barrow and, he hoped, capable of landing and taking off on the polar ice. He decided that the ideal planes for him were Stinson biplanes: not only could they take off and land easily with loads of up to 1500 pounds, but also because they were made in Detroit, which Wilkins hoped would be attractive to the men charged with promoting the city's aviation manufacturing industry. Wilkins met the directors of the Detroit Aviation Society on 22 November 1926. He brought Eddie Stinson with him to help pitch his idea.

Wilkins' plan was to purchase one Stinson biplane without an engine (costing $7000). He would have one of the Wright J4 Whirlwind engines taken from the *Detroiter*, overhauled and fitted to the Stinson (costing $5000). The Stinson would be test-flown at Detroit, then crated and shipped to Fairbanks (costing $3500). Allowing $10,000 for the cost of personnel and other related expenses, the Detroit Aviation Society could have a second year's expedition for just $25,500, a long way short of the first year, which had cost $155,849. The board of directors was not impressed. They still had to recoup the $30,000 they were out of pocket for the first year, and there seemed little news value to be gained in having an Australian explorer fly to a remote area of the Arctic. The board decided not to sponsor Wilkins for another year. Instead, it was agreed that he would own the equipment from the expedition, including the two Fokkers and the fuel at Barrow. He would be responsible for funding his expeditions in future, and he also agreed to pay the society twenty per cent of the earnings from any such expeditions until the $30,000 debt had been paid back.

While his relationship with the Detroit Aviation Society was effectively over, Wilkins still had supporters at *The Detroit News*. The paper was currently paying him $5000 to show his films from the expedition at the ninety public schools in Detroit, which he was doing at a rate of four schools a day. *The Detroit News* decided to sponsor Wilkins for a second year, with the new venture being named the Detroit News Expedition.

The new crew was decidedly smaller than in 1926. Ben Eielson was the pilot. Wilkins hired a second pilot, Alger Graham, who was experienced with Stinson planes. Also on the team were Arthur Smith, representing *The Detroit News*, Orval Porter, a mechanic, and two radio operators, Howard Mason and Walter Hemrick. Mason was to be stationed at Barrow, and Hemrick at Fairbanks, to relay messages back to *The Detroit News*.

Wilkins bought two Stinson biplanes, named them *Detroit News 1* and *Detroit News 2*, and shipped them to Fairbanks. He also still had faith in the single-engine Fokker, the *Alaskan*, which was stored with the *Detroiter* at Fairbanks, except that its wing had been smashed beyond repair. The fuselages of the Fokkers were similar and Wilkins was able to remove the engines from the wing of the Trimotor and fit the wing to the *Alaskan*. Unlike the Stinsons, which had open cockpits, this 'composite' plane would be more comfortable in the Arctic conditions. Unfortunately, it crashed while being tested at Fairbanks and Wilkins gave up all hope of using it.

On 29 March 1927 the two open-cockpit Stinsons, each carrying three men, were successfully flown to Barrow, where the temperature was forty-two degrees Fahrenheit below zero. Wilkins and Eielson were now ready to pick up where they had left off a year before and discover if there was any land between Alaska and the North Pole. Wilkins wrote:

> I went carefully over the possibilities and considered proposed routes . . . We intended to follow a course towards 78 degrees North Latitude, 180 degrees Longitude. Should we reach that point we intended to land and take soundings. If the soundings were shallow and indicated land not far ahead, we would continue on the same course, but if the soundings were deep, showing that we had gone well beyond the Continental Shelf, we would turn straight south for two hours or about two hundred miles and take another sounding. From the southerly position, no matter what the soundings indicated, it would be necessary, because of the reduced gas supply, to return direct to Barrow.

It was Wilkins' plan to fly to the blind spot on the map and, if possible, land the Stinson on the ice. Once on the ice, he intended to cut a hole in it and take depth soundings. This was done by lowering a small explosive charge a few metres below

133

the surface of the water. The charge would be detonated, the sound would travel down, bounce off the seabed and then return to the surface as an echo. The elapsed time between the charge being detonated and the echo being heard would be timed with a stopwatch. The longer the time, obviously, the deeper the ocean. One second of elapsed time equated to 2460 feet (750 metres) of ocean depth.

Wilkins and Eielson took off for the unknown in *Detroit News 1* at six am on 31 March 1927. As the small Stinson flew north, Howard Mason sat by his radio, waiting for the signals Wilkins was to send every half hour. Mason would later write his own account of what he called his *Arctic Adventure*:

> They were soon lost to sight, but the OK signal, cranked out on the hand generator, came though fine every half hour telling us that they were still going. That is for the first two hours. Then signals became weaker. That gave me a sinking feeling because I knew the old set was not kicking out like it should and that with them putting 100 miles between us every hour we should soon lose their signals altogether, which we did.

Approximately four hours and fifty minutes and 450 miles north of Barrow, the engine of the Stinson began to splutter. Wilkins looked out of the plane at the ice and, as it was impossible to be heard above the noise of the engine, he scribbled a note and handed it to Eielson. The note read: 'That's good ice to land on.'

Two years earlier Ellsworth and Amundsen had crash-landed on the ice, spent four weeks getting off, then returned to say publicly that safe landings and take-offs on the Arctic ice were impossible. Yet here were Wilkins and Eielson, about to attempt the first planned landing on the Arctic ice, and even with the spluttering engine, Eielson managed to set the Stinson down on its metal skis. Wilkins climbed out of the plane and, using his sextant, estimated their position was 77° 45' north, 175° west. The spluttering engine stopped and Eielson, fearing they would never get off the ice again, immediately began working to get it started. Wilkins lowered a detonating device through a gap in the ice and readied his stopwatch. He detonated the device and waited for the echo. He heard it, pressed his stopwatch and read 7.3 seconds. It meant the depth of the ocean was almost 18,000 feet (5500 metres). That seemed incredibly deep to Wilkins – particularly if there might be land in the area. He thought perhaps he hadn't heard it right:

> I was much astonished to find that my calculations indicated an ocean more than three miles deep. I doubted the correctness of the reading and prepared to try again. Just about that time Eielson got the engine started – the noise of it would interfere with my work so I shouted, 'Stop that engine and come over here to see what readings you get on this instrument.' Eielson gave me a look of surprise, but he stopped the engine. Ben took three soundings, heard echo on two. He was not sure when he pressed the watch on one; on the other he read 7.25. He did not hear the third. I was much impressed and said, 'We have made a great discovery. This Arctic Deep is unique and probably, just as important, if not more important to science, than the discovery of an island.'
>
> 'Yes,' said Eielson, 'it may be an important discovery for science, but since you made me stop the engine we will never get it started again, and we'll freeze to death here and we will be the only ones to know about the deep.'

Satisfied they had a correct reading, Wilkins and Eielson managed to start the engine and made three attempts to take off on the ice. But the engine would not rev above 1400 rpm. They stopped it again, cleaned the carburettor and fuel lines, then took off successfully. The time was two pm. They had flown where they wanted to fly and learnt what they had wanted to learn. Now they headed back to Barrow. Again the engine began misfiring and Eielson landed the plane on the ice. This time, however, he froze four fingers touching the metal cowling as he worked on the engine. For a second time they got the plane successfully off the ice and continued towards Barrow. Their concern now was petrol. The repeated attempts to get the plane into the air had used more fuel than Wilkins had anticipated, and they doubted they had enough to return.

Just after nine pm the engine stopped completely. This time Eielson had to glide down to land on the ice for a third time. Wilkins and Eielson sat in the plane overnight and rested. In the morning Wilkins took their bearings. They were approximately 125 miles from Barrow. The skis on the plane were broken, but without fuel they would not be taking off anyway. More than once during this and the previous expedition, Wilkins had stated that if the plane crashed or he was otherwise stranded on the ice, then he would simply walk back to land. As Stefansson had said, the Arctic was 'friendly', and a man trained to build an icehouse, catch fish and kill game could live there indefinitely. Many, including Amundsen, did not subscribe to the theory. Wilkins did, and now was his chance to prove it.

Back at Barrow, Wilkins and Eielson had not been heard from since their initial radio signals. The waiting Howard Mason would write:

Along the afternoon it clouded up quite suddenly and by
evening there was a howling gale and blizzard blowing . . .
We at Barrow hoped for the best and hoped the *Detroit
News 1* had completed its long flight and had at least
reached the coast on its return before running into the
storm. But with no radio signals after two days, and the
storm continuing unabated, things looked serious.

Then the next afternoon some dashes were heard,
right on the plane's wavelength, that told us they had
weathered the storm and were trying to get the set going.
That was good news, but not enough of it. The dashes
ceased. It was over an hour later when we heard them
again; pretty good signal, about R4 this time. Then the
slow even sending of the automatic contactor on the hand
generator started sending the two letter combinations
that stood for 'forced landing on sea ice', 'out of gas',
'plane damaged'. This was followed by some jerky hand
sending a doubtful position about 100 miles from
Barrow.

After sending this last radio signal, Wilkins prepared to leave
the Stinson and walk with Eielson back to land. Needing to
reduce weight to a minimum, they decided to leave the radio
behind. Wilkins left details of their findings in the plane in case
it was found and they were not. He later wrote:

We were in no desperate hurry. I had come to know by
experience that is does not pay to hurry when you are facing
dangerous Arctic conditions. But in this instance we could
not afford to be long delayed, because I found that Eielson,
who was not accustomed to working outdoors in the cold,
had frozen the ends of every one of his fingers.

We started out, each dragging an improvised sled,
traveling over old ice and pressure ridges. At night we
built snow houses and slept, comfortable and warm. After
three days with reduced load, we both hauled one sled.
After three more days, with reduced load, we abandoned
the sled and packed our food and clothing. The Norwegian
chocolate and biscuits were satisfying food. We did not
stint ourselves. We saw many fresh bear and fox tracks
and many seal breathing holes in the young ice.

At Barrow, without word being heard, Alger Graham
began to make flights in the second Stinson, the *Detroit News 2*,
looking for the pair. But he only flew along the coast and
dropped messages to Eskimos to keep a look out for the
men. His instructions from Detroit were specific: 'Do not
go far enough from the shore to put yourself or the *DN2*
in jeopardy.'

Wilkins wrote:

We battled over rough broken packs, crawling on hands and
knees much of the way. We crossed many leads of young ice
and passed much open water. Saw several seals, but as we
had sufficient food in our packs we did not care to delay to
get more.

It was now two weeks since Wilkins and Eielson had abandoned
the Stinson, and since their last radio signal had been heard
at Barrow. *The Detroit News* contacted Arthur Smith, their
representative at Barrow: 'Any hope of locating Wilkins by
going out in number two? Any reason for not trying it other
than Wilkins' orders?'

Smith replied by telegram: 'Wilkins told me one chance in million locating anyone on ice pack without his position within ten miles. We cannot guess Wilkins' position.'

Two weeks after the forced landing there was still no search party, other than Alger Graham flying up and down the coast dropping notes to the Eskimo. On some expeditions a message saying that men were stranded on the ice approximately 100 miles from a settlement would have brought waves of international search and rescue efforts. On the 1927 Detroit News Expedition it seems to have brought little more than bewilderment as to what to do. Howard Mason would write:

> So we at Barrow sat around helpless for all of three weeks waiting for more word . . . and with hope dwindling that the two men out on the ice would be able to get ashore safely. Searching flights were made up and down the coast and as far out to sea as it was safe to venture.
>
> One night about 1.00 am . . . there was a racket outside . . . of more dogs than usual. In came Takpuk, an Eskimo who had just arrived from the eastward after six day's travel, bringing a letter from Wilkins. They were safe.

Wilkins and Eielson had reached Beechey Point. The letter, addressed to Smith and Mason, explained what had happened:

> I am sending this by Eskimo with a fast dog team and would be glad if you would ask [Alger] Graham to come over for us when the weather is suitable . . . [After explaining the details of their walk] two more sights gave us our position and we headed for Beechey Point where we arrived sunburnt and tired. Eielson's fingertips black and blistered, but not dangerously frozen.

Their calculations showed that they had walked eighty miles in twelve days across the shifting ice. Before being flown back to Barrow, and then Fairbanks, the persistent Wilkins was already planning his next flight over the Arctic.

* * *

At the end of the promotional flight, when the *Josephine Ford* had been delivered to the Henry Ford Museum, Bernt Balchen got work as a test pilot for Anthony Fokker and was sent to Canada to teach flying in Arctic conditions.

Meanwhile, Byrd was proceeding with his plan to be the first to fly nonstop between New York and Paris. Floyd Bennett would be pilot, Bert Acosta co-pilot, Byrd the navigator and George Noville the radio operator. Edsel Ford was unable to build a special Ford Trimotor quickly enough, so Byrd again turned to Anthony Fokker, who immediately began building a new, larger Fokker Trimotor.

During the test flights, however, a rift developed between Anthony Fokker and Byrd that time would only widen. Fokker had planned to make the first test flights of the new plane himself. Byrd insisted that Floyd Bennett and George Noville go along also. Then, at the last minute, Byrd climbed aboard and crawled forward into the cabin. The untried plane was now nose-heavy and crashed on landing. Fokker blamed Byrd and Byrd implied that Fokker's actions immediately after the crash were cowardly and endangered the others. Whatever the cause of the crash, Floyd Bennett was seriously injured. He sustained a fractured right leg, a fractured skull and a punctured lung.

Byrd needed a replacement pilot; Balchen, still flying in Canada, received a letter asking him to join the transatlantic attempt. He agreed and returned to make several test flights in the new Fokker before flying it to Roosevelt Field on Long Island, from where it would leave on its attempt to fly to France. At the adjacent Curtiss Field, two other planes were also being prepared to fly the Atlantic. One was a Bellanca to be flown by Clarence Chamberlain. The other was a single-engine Ryan monoplane to be flown by an unknown pilot named Charles Lindbergh. Public interest began to focus on which of the three flights would get away first.

Meanwhile, the dispute between Byrd and Fokker worsened. Byrd now wanted Bert Acosta to pilot the plane. Fokker wanted Balchen, because he had proven that he was competent flying by dead reckoning, whereas Acosta, like Floyd Bennett, flew by following the ground. He freely admitted he knew little about instrument flying and proved it when he nearly crashed the plane after flying into cloud. If Byrd was going to fly the Atlantic with Acosta as pilot, he would have to wait until clear weather was forecast all the way. Balchen, however, wasn't an American. And Rodman Wanamaker, the department store owner who was sponsoring Byrd's flight, and who had named Byrd's plane *America*, also insisted all the crew be Americans. Anthony Fokker's frustration at Byrd's delay built until he exploded at Balchen, 'You must go on this flight and fly the aeroplane on instruments. As you can see, Acosta will get them killed. If they have to wait for good weather so Acosta can fly all the way, the plane will sit here all summer. I will be laughed at by the whole world!' Balchen applied for American citizenship so that he could be part of the crew.

On 20 May at Roosevelt Field, Balchen was awakened in his bunk in a hangar at five am. Anthony Fokker rushed in, shouting in German and calling him outside. A light rain was falling and, through the morning mist, Balchen could make out the Ryan monoplane, the *Spirit of St Louis*, at its take-off point.

The lanky figure of Charles Lindbergh, carrying sandwiches and a thermos of coffee, was climbing aboard. Fokker and Balchen joined a small group of people to watch the plane take off and wondered what Byrd's reaction would be. As always, it was reserved and diplomatic. He explained he was not interested in racing and was only making the flight to further the interests of aviation.

Charles Lindbergh landed at Le Bourget Airport near Paris after flying for thirty-three hours and thirty-nine minutes. Many other fliers had crossed the Atlantic before him. No lesser an authority than the *National Geographic* magazine stated that he was the ninety-second person to make the crossing. But he was the first to fly nonstop from America to the European mainland. And he had flown solo. More importantly, he was a quiet, unassuming, working-class boy. These qualities, which endeared him to the media and the American public – especially compared to the aloof, privileged Byrd – immediately made Lindbergh a popular American icon.

Byrd would not be the first to fly nonstop across the Atlantic. Nor would he be the second. On 4 June 1927 Clarence Chamberlain and Charles Levine took off, landing in Germany forty-two hours and thirty-one minutes later. Byrd finally took off, much to Anthony Fokker's disgust, at six am on 29 June, almost six weeks after Lindbergh. Balchen and Acosta shared the flying, Byrd navigated and George Noville was radio operator. Byrd described the take-off:

> Slowly the great ship gained altitude with its tremendous load. This was a critical time because, should any one of the engines stop or even falter until we could get to an altitude of 400 or 500 feet, the dump valves would be of no value, and the plane would crash.

I made notes in my log and remarks in my diary, the
same diary carried over the North Pole with me. I find this
entry made a few minutes after leaving Roosevelt Field:
'Altitude 300 feet, turning, after turn completed, altitude
400 feet.' The *America* had climbed on a turn and was
proving herself a very great plane.

Byrd and Balchen would leave different versions of the
flight across the Atlantic. Byrd highlighted his cool leadership,
navigation skills and calm control of the situation, while
Balchen claimed that Byrd didn't know where he was most of
the time and contributed little to the flight – except to frustrate
the pilots and endanger the plane with his irrational orders and
lack of knowledge.

Finally, heavy mist over France reduced visibility to almost
zero and made finding an airfield impossible. Balchen sought,
and found, a lighthouse on the coast and landed the plane in
shallow water just off the beach. The flight had lasted forty-two
hours and six minutes. Byrd and his crew inflated a raft and
paddled ashore. They walked along the beach, climbed the
hill and banged on the door of the lighthouse. It was five am
local time. The lighthouse keeper and his wife gave them dry
clothing and hot drinks, and the four men went to bed. After
sleeping a few hours they went back down the beach to find
that the *America* had floated ashore. Local villagers helped
salvage the engines and instruments, but as more people arrived
they began to cut pieces off the *America* for souvenirs.

The third successful nonstop flight from America to Europe
was still newsworthy, and Byrd began a round of engagements
and ceremonies. His star continued to rise, as did his sense
of self-importance. In his book *Skyward*, which tells of his
successful North Pole flight and the flight across the Atlantic,

one photograph shows Byrd and his crew with French pilots from World War One. The caption reads:

> The crew of the *America* visits the disabled French aviators. After Byrd's greeting one man, a cripple since the war, rose and walked!

Byrd, it seemed, was now able to work miracles. While he was in Paris he also publicly announced his next expedition: he would travel to Antarctica and fly to the South Pole.

11

Spitsbergen Bound

At the end of his 1927 expedition, where his ocean depth soundings had virtually proven that no land would be found northwest of Alaska, Wilkins was uncertain about what to attempt next. He was considering going south to explore the Antarctic and wrote to a friend:

> There was at one time a possibility that I might navigate a seaplane from Los Angeles to New Zealand via Tokyo and Australia, connect up with the Norwegian whalers at New Zealand, go south and fly from the Ross Sea to Graham Land.

But the area northeast of Alaska, which had been covered by fog when Amundsen, Ellsworth and Nobile had flown over it, remained unknown. Could land in this area possibly exist? If it did, it would be the closest land to the North Pole and the obvious choice for a meteorological base. A flight over this area became the focus of Wilkins' attention, and he developed his original plan to fly from Barrow to Greenland and either land and walk back to civilisation or, if the plane was still performing well, continue on to Spitsbergen. He outlined his plans:

[After taking off, I propose] making toward Greenland and
if we do not find any land make one or two descents to the
ice for soundings and then, from somewhere near the north
of Grant Land or Greenland, continue on to Spitsbergen. Of
course if we find land within 1,000 miles of Barrow I will
endeavor to return to Alaska. If land is not found and we
continue on to Spitsbergen I believe we will have completed
the main geographical exploration of the Arctic.

Wilkins had received a cable from *The Detroit News*, saying
that the paper would meet any outstanding expenses associated
with the 1927 expedition and that he could keep the remaining
Stinson. Wilkins sold the plane, leaving him with the two
Fokkers he had used in 1926, one of which didn't have a
wing. But he did not consider either of these planes suitable
for the long flight across the Arctic. Faced with the problem
of raising money to buy a suitable plane and mounting another
expedition, he turned again to *The Detroit News* for sponsorship.
He wrote:

[*The Detroit News*] were so disappointed I had not, during
my two years effort, reached the North Pole, that when I was
about to set out for the 1928 expedition, which had as its
purpose a flight across the Arctic Ocean, *The Detroit News*,
in a letter, forbade me to use their name ... and NANA [the
North American Newspaper Alliance] did not even answer
three written offers.

Wilkins also approached the Detroit Aviation Society, to
which he still owed $30,000 from his 1926 expedition, saying that
he proposed to use a new Stinson monoplane. Its performance
was superior to any of the planes he had used until then and,

importantly, it was built in Detroit. Wilkins hoped that if he could finally make a flight that would gain the city the publicity it had originally sought, then the society might be willing to forget about the money he owed them. But it was not interested in supporting him. After being rejected, Wilkins wrote: 'With one or two exceptions I could consider them friends no longer.'

But a breakthrough came from an unexpected source:

Then came a time when my girl friend, Lura B. Schreck, found a chance for the sale of one of the ... [Fokkers]: three Australians wished to fly from San Francisco to Hawaii and on to Fiji and Australia. They were trying to get a Ryan, similar to Lindbergh's *Spirit of St Louis*, but I was able to persuade them that what they really needed was my big three engine Fokker.

Wilkins sold them the *Detroiter* for $15,000, paid half of the money to the Detroit Aviation Society and kept the balance to buy a Stinson monoplane. While he was in San Francisco to deliver the Fokker, he saw a bright red monoplane, the first Lockheed Vega. He thought it the ideal plane for flying in the Arctic: streamlined, fast, light and capable of carrying enough fuel for over 2000 miles. He had to choose between the Stinson and the Lockheed. 'I gave the question much thought,' he wrote. 'The reasons for finally ordering a Lockheed are many and principally, in the first instance, financial.' The Stinson, fitted with the modifications he required, would have cost him over $15,000, ready to ship from Detroit. The Vega would cost $12,500, ready to ship from Los Angeles.

Despite the newspaper's request not to use its name, Wilkins went ahead and painted 'Detroit News–Wilkins Expedition' on the side of the Vega. The newspaper, paying small recognition to the proposed flight across the Arctic, wrote: 'If at first you don't succeed, Wilkins, fly, fly again.'

After ordering the Vega, Wilkins wrote to Eielson to ask if he would fly it. Eielson had taken a job as an inspector with the newly formed Bureau of Aeronautics and was travelling around America. By the time he received the letter, the first Lockheed Vega had disappeared without a trace over the Pacific. Nevertheless, the loyal Eielson agreed to join the expedition and travelled to California to inspect the new aircraft.

By the time Eielson had arrived, Lockheed had now built two more Vegas, one of which was for Wilkins. Eielson turned up on the day they were being tested and arrived in time to see one crash. Unperturbed, he climbed into the plane he would pilot, took it up for a test flight and almost flew into some electrical wires. He suggested to Wilkins they find a larger area to test the plane, and the next day he took it up again, with Wilkins aboard. After a few successful flights Eielson took Lura Schreck for a joy ride. The engine cut out and the undercarriage was damaged on the unplanned landing. The cause was an air lock in the fuel supply, so Wilkins had the system modified, as well as the landing gear made stronger.

After more test flights the Vega was crated and shipped to Fairbanks, arriving on 26 February 1928. Wilkins and Eielson spent three weeks testing their equipment in the cold weather and practising their morse code and navigation. On 19 March 1928 they flew to Barrow.

The previous year Howard Mason and Walter Hemrick had accompanied the expedition with a two-way radio to report for *The Detroit News*. This year there was no such communication with the outside world. Instead, Wilkins brought along a hand-generated radio transmitter and a separate receiver, which he gave to the schoolteacher at Barrow, asking him to listen for messages. But even if they had landed on the ice and been able to get a message to Barrow, they would have to wait weeks or months before the next dog team or ship carried the news to the rest of the world. Not that anyone was waiting for news. The world had stopped looking at Arctic aviators and no one but a few friends and Eielson's family knew they were going to attempt the flight.

Wilkins and Eielson dug out their runway and waited for favourable weather. They would clear the runway, it would snow again and they would clear the runway again. Finally, four weeks after arriving, the weather improved. Just after midday on 15 April 1928, the tiny red Lockheed Vega bumped down the narrow runway, its wings just two feet away from the snow piled up at the sides, before becoming airborne. Eielson sat at the controls in the single-seat cockpit. Behind him was a huge fuel tank, and behind the fuel tank Wilkins crouched ready to navigate them halfway around the world. Wilkins could see the top of Eielson's head over the fuel tank, but could not be heard over the roar of the engine. Their only means of communication was by tapping and passing notes.

> I put out my charts, tested both sextants for index error
> and put them in order ... set the wireless aerial, testing
> its note to get the best resonances; made sure the drift
> indicator was registering true and changed it from side
> to side. I discovered my stopwatch would not function if
> I left it in the cold cabin and had to keep it in my pocket.

The pair flew north-east from Barrow over a previously unseen area of the Arctic. They found no land. Wilkins navigated by a combination of sextant, dead reckoning (using his speed and drift indicator) and magnetic compass bearing. He later wrote about the difficulties of navigating by sextant from a plane in high latitudes:

> We had been in the air eleven hours. It was past midnight local time, but the sun – now almost due north – had been well above the horizon all of the time, yet for an hour or so it had been almost impossible to get even a reasonably accurate sextant observation, probably because of the refraction. My sights of the sun would differ so greatly as to vary its position by two degrees. It was almost beyond me as we sped along to keep the sun centered on the bubble of my sextant; I had to take many readings and take their mean. Around midnight from an altitude of three thousand feet we observed with the naked eye the dull red orb dance and skip like a mast-light of a distant ship rising and falling with the waves.

The pair were almost halfway through their intended journey and close to the area north of Grant Land, the northernmost part of the Canadian Archipelago, when Wilkins looked ahead and saw storm clouds. He also calculated that they had only just enough fuel to reach Spitsbergen. There would be none available to fly around looking for it if his navigation had been inaccurate.

> We were above a small local storm. There was the Greenland storm ahead on our right. If we kept on for an hour and the engine should give us trouble we could hardly expect to return to Grant Land. Could we, in that case, fly as a cripple through the storm to land on Greenland? On the other hand there was a fine landing field below. In case of accident we

knew we could support ourselves in Northern Grant Land.
If we could not rise into the air we could walk with more or
less ease and comfort to the Canadian Northwest Mounted
Police Station on Bache Peninsula, which lies opposite Etah.
We might then return to civilization in the Autumn with
some vessel, but a true flying man sticks to his ship as does
a sailor.

Wilkins handed a note to Eielson that read:

Down there we can land and wait until it is over. Can we get
off again? If we go on we will meet storm over Spitsbergen
and perhaps never find land. Do you wish to land now?

Within a minute Eielson handed a note back: 'I'm willing to go
on and chance it.'

The pair continued on. Three hours later Wilkins managed
a sun sight and reckoned their position to be about 200 miles
north-west of Spitsbergen. They flew south-east and, two
hours later, were rewarded by the sight of mountain peaks
poking through the tops of the clouds. They dropped down
to find a smooth patch of snow-covered land. Flying over it,
they realised it was the one suitable landing place on a small
mountainous island. Almost out of fuel, they had no choice but
to set the Vega down. Eielson skilfully brought the plane into
a headwind so strong that it came to a stop within thirty feet of
the skis touching the snow. They had been in the air for twenty
hours and twenty-two minutes. The first aeroplane flight across
the Arctic Ocean was over.

On their small landing field, in the shadow of the mountains,
there was no opportunity to take a sun sighting. They reckoned
themselves on the west coast of Spitsbergen, possibly near

Kings Bay or Green Harbour, the only other settlement on the islands. They had twenty gallons of fuel left: enough to fly about 100 miles. They slept, rested and sat in their plane for five days. When the weather cleared they prepared to take off, planning to get their bearings once out of the shadow of the mountains and to head for the nearest settlement, reaching it before their fuel ran out. They made two attempts to take off but Wilkins couldn't push the plane free and still get back on board. The third time he was forced to sit half out of the plane and push off with a long stick. It worked, and they were barely airborne before they spotted the radio masts of Green Harbour. They landed to be greeted by the small Norwegian population inhabiting the government radio station. Wilkins wrote:

> Then we learned how fortunate we were. At Green Harbour stands the Government Radio, communicating direct to Norway and operating at that time of year between eight in the morning and nine at night ... As it was we could have immediate communication. The whole radio station and its staff was at our convenience.

In an attempt to publicise the achievement, Wilkins wired *The New York Times*, which wired back: 'Send 500 words.' Wilkins wrote:

> I began sending the message from Spitsbergen station a hundred or so words at a time. There was some delay due to electronic interference and other business coming into Spitsbergen station and even before I had filed the full 500 words I received a message from *The New York Times* saying, 'send all you have'.

On 22 April 1928 *The New York Times* ran as its banner front-page headline: 'Wilkins Flies Arctic. No New Land Found.' George Hubert Wilkins was front-page news.

But while he and Eielson were suddenly celebrities in New York and around the world, they were also marooned at Green Harbour, where the ice-locked coast meant the nearest open water was twenty miles away. In any case, no ship was expected for nine months.

* * *

On the same day that Wilkins and Eielson lifted off from Barrow in their Lockheed Vega, Umberto Nobile lifted off from Milan, Italy, in his airship, *Italia*, to commence his own flight to Spitsbergen. At first he only got as far as Germany, where he had to set down for repairs. It was fifteen days before he got airborne again, this time flying to Vadso, Norway. Two days later, while Wilkins and Eielson were still stranded at Green Harbour, the *Italia* floated over Kings Bay to begin Nobile's second Arctic adventure.

On this expedition his objectives were unclear. His almost all-Italian crew were inexperienced in Arctic survival, while he had little support from the media and even less from the Italian government. Mussolini had refused outright to put his personal stamp of authority on the venture, and so the expedition flew under the banner of the Italian Geographic Society, which had previously shown no interest in polar exploration. The government had, however, sent a 'support ship' to Spitsbergen under Captain Giuseppe Romagna. The *Citta di Milano* (City of Milan) carried parts and supplies for the expedition but was not to be publicly associated with it. Officially, it had sailed to Spitsbergen on a 'training mission'.

This confused authority and purpose became evident when the *Italia* arrived over Kings Bay after the long flight from Vadso. Nobile radioed the *Citta di Milano* to have fifty men come out, take the lines of the airship and help guide it to the canvas-covered hangar, originally built for the *Norge* two years earlier. Captain Romagna refused to send the men, replying that they were sailors and not in Spitsbergen to work as ground crew for the airship. Nobile was left in a difficult position. Having just made the exhausting flight, and now being buffeted by winds, he had no ground crew to land his ship. His brother, Amedeo, who had travelled to Kings Bay separately, was waiting on the ground as Nobile circled. Nobile leant out a window and called to him through a megaphone, 'Get me the miners!' Amedeo immediately ran to the nearby coalmines and asked the manager for help. The Norwegian miners put down their tools and ran to assist the airship into its hangar while the Italian crew of the *Citta di Milano* watched in amusement.

On the ground Captain Romagna explained to Nobile that the *Citta di Milano* was in Spitsbergen primarily to take meteorological observations and not to help the *Italia* or its crew. Furthermore, direct support could only be given if he received approval from Rome. If Romagna was to allow his men to assist the *Italia*, he would first have to radio for permission.

Even after arriving at Kings Bay with his airship and crew, Nobile's plans were as confused as his authority. The expedition wasn't scientific. Only one Italian scientist, a professor of physics from the University of Milan, had been brought along. Nor, it seemed, was it an expedition of discovery. Nobile wanted to make one flight to the North Pole, to drop a wooden cross entrusted to him by Pope Pius XI and thus to 'consecrate the summit of the world'. After this his plan was to:

> ... leave ... without any prearranged route or goal, but
> simply with the idea of taking the best possible advantage
> of the wind ... whether we would travel towards the
> Severnya Zemlya or towards the American coast was
> something we would decide en route taking into account the
> meteorological situation.

So, with no plan, untrained men and no ground support, Nobile began the polar flights he hoped would upstage the flight of the *Norge*.

* * *

The arrival of the Italians at Spitsbergen was fortuitous for the stranded Wilkins and Eielson. The captain of the small Norwegian steamer, the *Hobby*, which had brought supplies to Kings Bay for Nobile, now radioed to say he would stop at the edge of the ice pack, twenty miles from Green Harbour, and that if Wilkins and Eielson could get their plane across the ice he would take them on board and back to Norway. On 10 May Wilkins and Eielson started the engine of their trusty Vega and taxied it to the edge of the ice pack. Five days later they arrived in Tromso to a heroes' welcome.

* * *

On 11 May, a day after Wilkins and Eielson boarded the *Hobby*, Nobile made his first flight from Kings Bay. He only went a short distance before bad weather and a frayed rudder cable forced him back. Four days later he took off again, this time for a flight of sixty-nine hours that didn't reach the North Pole and didn't discover anything of significance. Rome and the media took little interest. Then on 23 May the *Italia* lifted off from Kings Bay on a flight that would capture the attention of the world for all the wrong reasons.

First, Nobile flew directly to the North Pole, where he arrived at 12.24 am on 25 May. The crew dropped the heavy wooden cross entrusted to them by the Pope, sang the Fascist anthem and, two hours later, began the return journey to Kings Bay. Shortly after leaving the Pole, Nobile began radioing the *Citta di Milano* that they were in trouble, low on fuel and battling headwinds. Captain Romagna dutifully forwarded the radio signals on to Rome. Two hours later Nobile radioed that the *Italia* was heavy with ice and that the elevator wheels had frozen. Their position was still north-east of Spitsbergen.

* * *

In Norway huge crowds turned out to see Wilkins and Eielson, and at one point they were carried on men's shoulders through the streets of Oslo. Eielson, whose grandparents were Norwegian, still spoke the language and the crowds would erupt into joyous cheering whenever he stepped to the microphone. Here, everyone agreed, was another great Norwegian explorer in the mould of Nansen, Amundsen and Sverdup. The pair of aviators were introduced to the king and then, as if to signify the greatest honour Norway could bestow on them, they were taken to visit Amundsen.

For Wilkins it must have been an uncomfortable meeting. Polar exploration is riddled with factions and rivalries. Many explorers had been cool toward Amundsen since he had beaten Scott to the South Pole. They believed Amundsen had not played fair by keeping his plans secret from Scott. And the fact that Amundsen had eaten his sled dogs along the route had rankled many an Englishman. Better to die in your tracks, as Scott had done, than resort to eating the loyal companions who had laboured to haul you over the ice. Wilkins was Australian by birth and English by cultural loyalty. He sat squarely in the Scott-supporting camp. What's more, Amundsen had regularly criticised Wilkins' mentor, Stefansson. In the two years since he had returned from the *Norge* flight, Amundsen had published his autobiography. He had taken the opportunity not only to take a few swipes at Nobile, but at the rest of the exploring community as well, including Stefansson.

Wilkins, in a review of the book, had taken his own swipes back at Amundsen. On Amundsen's navigation of the Northwest Passage, Wilkins had written:

> It will be remembered that the British expeditions while in search of Sir John Franklin's party 'discovered' the northwest passage. Boats approaching from the west had overlapped the track of boats coming in from the east and men had actually made both the northeast and northwest passage through channel deep enough for navigation in large sailing vessels, while Amundsen – with bilked creditors in the offing – dragged and kedged the *Gjoa*, drawing only a few inches of water over the rock bottomed shallows between the Parry archipelago; it can hardly be claimed that he sailed the northwest passage.

On Amundsen's criticism of Stefansson's theory of the friendly Arctic, Wilkins managed a double-edged swipe: 'In all his polar travels Amundsen has shown little personal desire to kill anything for food more difficult to hunt than the dogs hitched to his sled.' Wilkins went on to criticise Amundsen's 1925 attempt to reach the North Pole in flying boats:

While the Amundsen–Ellsworth expedition did a great deal
to prove that air travel was possible in high latitudes, the
plans and results of that expedition showed that Amundsen
was not as well acquainted with Arctic conditions as one
would be inclined to believe ... All [his] difficulties and
dangers might well have been avoided if Amundsen's
knowledge of Arctic conditions and airplanes had been
greater.

Wilkins went on to point out, as many others had done, that
Amundsen really brought only his name and reputation to the
flight of the *Norge*. It was Nobile and his crew who had done
all the work.

Wilkins and Eielson were taken to meet Amundsen at his
house. Film of the meeting survives, but no first-hand account.
The three men are shown sitting in three separate chairs, apart
from each other, smiling and chatting in the forced manner that
people manage in front of cameras. No one could know that it
would be the last moving footage shot of Amundsen.

Amundsen capped off the visit with a formal dinner that
evening in their honour. During the after-dinner speeches, a
messenger arrived with the news that the *Italia* had crashed on
the ice and radio signals from its crew had ceased.

* * *

The last message from the *Italia* had been heard on the morning
of 25 May 1928. Minutes after the radio message had been
sent, the *Italia* hit the ice heavily, the gondola shearing away
from the main airbag with the impact. Without the weight
of the gondola the airbag lifted again and floated skyward.
Six crewmen in the airbag could only look down through

the gaping hole as the ground receded. Neither they, nor the airbag, were ever seen again. Of the ten crewmen left on the ground, one was already dead.

Nobile had survived, but felt himself to be dying. He later wrote:

> It seemed that death was very near – that maybe I had only two or three hours to live. I was glad of this. It meant that I should not have to watch the despair and slow death-agony of my comrades.

While the others looked for supplies and checked each other's injuries, Nobile spoke pessimistically about their chances. When one sleeping bag was found he ordered his men to put him in it so that he could 'die there in peace'. By his own admission, once inside the bag his main concerns were not for his men but for his dog, Titina. When the dog, which Nobile insisted on taking with him everywhere (once even to the White House, where it had urinated on the carpet), ran over Natale Cecioni's broken leg, causing him agony, Nobile chastised Cecioni for smacking the dog away. Thirty minutes after being put in the sleeping bag, Nobile had come back from death's door and watched while the fit men organised the campsite and gathered supplies. When informed that the men had found the body of Vincenzo Pomella, Nobile said that the news:

> ... left me indifferent. It was not hardness of heart, but involuntarily I reflected that it was better for him to have died then and there and escaped the lingering death reserved for us. For my part I envied him his lot.

Pomella may not have shared the thoughts of Nobile, who in fact would live to be ninety-three.

On the ice with a tent, radio and provisions for forty-five days, Nobile's ability to lead, give orders or make judgements based on known facts was practically nonexistent. The fit men continued to organise their small camp while Nobile dithered about what should be done. The radio operator, Giuseppe Biagi, repeatedly sent signals. But no messages came back and the men began to doubt their radio was working properly.

On waking three days after the crash, the survivors could see Charles XII Island on the horizon. They confirmed it was the island by taking their bearings; they discovered they were at 80° 49' north and 26° 20' east. Remarkably, the drift of the ice pack had brought them close to the island, which lay off the northeast coast of Spitsbergen.

The Swede, Finn Malmgren, whom Nobile described as his 'only ice expert', wanted to walk to land. Others wanted to go with him. Cecioni, who had a broken leg, began building a sled so that he could be taken too. Yet Nobile procrastinated, and by the next day they had drifted to the east and the coast was out of sight. Sextant bearings showed that they were drifting east at a rate of ten miles a day. Malmgren and the others begged Nobile to be allowed to walk to the land but, for no understandable reason, he insisted they wait to see what happened. Two more days passed before he finally told the men they could do as they wished.

Finn Malmgren, along with two Italian naval officers, Adalberto Mariano and Filippo Zappi, resolved to make a dash for the land in order to get help. Late on 30 May the trio said their goodbyes and left. There was no thought now of the entire party going and hauling the injured men, because the land was now at least thirty miles farther away than when they had crashed.

The remaining six survivors, including Nobile, continued to debate their future and send out messages on their radio every hour. Surprisingly, these radio messages were never picked up by the *Citta di Milano*. A likely explanation is that the messages were being ignored, in the hope that the men would perish and disappear. Had the airship returned from the North Pole successfully, Mussolini could have claimed the flight as a triumph for Fascist Italy. Now that it had crashed, it was an embarrassment best quickly forgotten.

But the men on the ice stubbornly refused to die. And Biagi, nursing his set with its fading batteries, continued to send out signals: 'SOS . . . Italia . . . SOS . . . Italia . . .'

* * *

During April, May and June of 1928, while Wilkins and Eielson were making their historic flight and returning to celebrity, and while the Italians were crashing their airship, Byrd's plans to fly to the South Pole were receiving continual setbacks. His original idea, outlined while he was still in Europe, was to fly to the South Pole, land there, then continue to the other side of the continent. It was an ambitious plan that had plenty of 'firsts'. Byrd would be the first to fly in Antarctica. The first to fly to the South Pole. The first to cross the continent. And there were ample opportunities to discover and claim new land.

Originally announced in July 1927, Byrd's plan had been to leave for the south a few months later and complete the crossing in the southern summer of 1927/28. He would not winter over in Antarctica, but rather would return immediately to America to claim the glory and financial rewards that would follow. But a few weeks after his initial announcement, Byrd said he would be postponing the expedition for twelve months to give himself the time to organise it properly. No one else was planning to take planes to the Antarctic so, unlike the North Pole and the Atlantic, Byrd had the luxury of not having to race.

Byrd was astute enough to keep Bernt Balchen on side. Balchen and Floyd Bennett were good friends and would make a good team. But Balchen had two other advantages: he could fly using instruments and he was Norwegian (or at least Norwegian by birth, having now applied for US citizenship). He would, therefore, be vital in communicating with, and perhaps getting assistance from, the Norwegian whalers who spent every southern summer plying the waters around Byrd's planned take-off and landing points, the Ross Ice Shelf and Graham Land. There was no question; Bernt Balchen would have to be included in the expedition.

Byrd corresponded with Amundsen, asking his advice on a ship and a place from which to launch his flight to the South Pole. Not surprisingly, the veteran explorer recommended a Norwegian ship to penetrate the ice pack, and that the best place would be his old base, Framheim, on the eastern side of the Ross Ice Shelf. He also recommended that Byrd take plenty of dogs. Ultimately, Byrd's plan would replicate Amundsen's successful Antarctic expedition – with the exception that the final dash to the Pole would be made in a plane rather than on foot with dogs and sledges. On Amundsen's advice, Byrd bought a wooden Norwegian sailing ship, the *Samson*, and ordered that it be sailed to New York.

Byrd's plan grew. He would take radio sets to the Antarctic and have contact with the outside world. In fact, the entire expedition began to adopt the 'can do' American spirit of the 1920s. By the beginning of 1928 the expedition was growing at a rate that was concerning even Byrd. Estimates of the cost were reaching $500,000 at a time when a fashionable New York house cost $20,000. Byrd was working hard to keep the money coming in. He sold exclusive film rights to Paramount, exclusive book rights to Putnam and exclusive newspaper rights to a syndicate that included *The New York Times*. He also began to modify his plans. The expedition would not cross Antarctica, a plan that required a base on each side of the continent. Instead, he would fly to the South Pole and back from a base on the Ross Ice Shelf.

Byrd Aviation Associates, consisting of wealthy businessmen and influential organisations, was formed to assist with the fundraising. Coming on board were Edsel Ford, John D. Rockefeller Jr and Harold Vanderbilt, as well as *The New York Times* and its associated newspapers.

Byrd had originally planned to take two Fokkers with him: one single-engine and one trimotor. After Edsel Ford donated a new Ford Trimotor, Byrd changed his plan to include the Ford and the single-engine Fokker. He also wanted a smaller, lighter plane as a backup. He ordered Balchen and Bennett to fly a new Bellanca to Canada and test it in cold weather.

Bennett was still recovering from the punctured lung sustained while testing the *America*, and he contracted pneumonia when he reached the cold climate of Canada. He was taken to a hospital in Quebec but died on 25 April 1928. Balchen was with him while he was ill and later claimed that Bennett had told him he would be shocked if he knew what had really happened on the North Pole flight. But Bennett said nothing more. The only witness to Byrd's actions on the flight was, like the *Josephine Ford*, now silent forever.

Whatever the long-term impact on Byrd and his reputation, at the time it would have been a crushing blow. Bennett was a close and trusted friend. He was also Byrd's first choice as pilot for the South Pole expedition. Now he had died at a time when Byrd's worries were beginning to pile up around him.

His expedition was short of funds. His ship had still not arrived from Norway. He had pilots to find, planes to test and equipment to get from New York to the other end of the world. And less than six months to do it.

Five weeks after Bennett's death, Byrd received more news that would deal him a severe blow. On 1 June 1928 the *New York Journal* announced that George Wilkins and Ben Eielson, the two popular heroes who had just returned from their epic flight across the Arctic Ocean, were planning a new expedition. This time Wilkins and Eielson would take their efficient Lockheed Vega south and fly across Antarctica via the Pole. Byrd was in a race again – against a competitor who was competent, cashed-up and capable of beating him to the South Pole.

12

The Hares and the Tortoise

On hearing that contact with the airship *Italia* had been lost, Wilkins and Eielson offered to return to Spitsbergen with their Lockheed Vega to commence searching for Nobile and his crew. A reply came from Rome that it was unnecessary: a search was being organised and everything was under control. On hearing this, Wilkins and Eielson travelled to Denmark and Germany, and were lauded at banquet after banquet. On 4 June they were in Holland when the King of England's birthday honours were announced: Captain George Wilkins was to be knighted and would be known as Captain Sir George Wilkins. Within a year, however, he would be insisting people simply call him Sir Hubert.

The two heroes continued on to France, and then crossed the channel to England, where Wilkins was presented to the king. They then travelled by liner to America, where a new round of celebrations awaited them.

In New York they were again greeted by crowds; Mayor Jimmy Walker knew just how to organise a public celebration. Wilkins and Eielson were given the keys to the city at the town hall. But Walker had an additional surprise. Hearing that Wilkins and Eielson were both bachelors and each had an eye for a pretty girl, Walker made sure there were plenty on hand.

For the forty-year-old Wilkins, Walker went to particular trouble, arranging for Suzanne Bennett, an Australian dancer working on Broadway, to come along. Bennett later admitted she had never heard of Sir George Wilkins but went along anyway. The pair hit it off and Wilkins invited her to dinner that evening. The explorer now had a girlfriend on the east coast, as well as on the west coast.

After his Barrow–Spitsbergen flight, Wilkins felt that there were two areas of polar exploration worth pursuing. In the south it would be to map Antarctica, most of which remained unseen. In the north, now that it was fairly certain there was no new land to be discovered, it was to be able to travel about the Arctic Ocean safely and take meteorological observations. Wilkins thought the best way to do this would be by submarine, an idea that he and Vilhamjur Stefansson had discussed during the 1913 Canadian Arctic Expedition.

Stefansson claimed to have seen whales break through the thin ice crust to get air. Wilkins' flights of 1927 and 1928 had indicated that the Arctic was a deep ocean. If this was so, and it was only covered by a thin layer of ice rarely more than two metres thick, then it would be feasible for a submarine to travel under the ice and surface at will. This was an idea some thirty years ahead of its time. Whether to take a submarine north or an aeroplane south was the decision Wilkins now had to make. The man who made it for him was William Randolph Hearst.

Hearst was an ambitious newspaperman whose influence on publishing, the media and indeed American life is now legendary. He received his journalistic training at the *New York World*, which was owned and operated by an equally famous name in newspapers, Joseph Pulitzer. In 1887 Hearst, aged twenty-three, moved to San Francisco to take control of a small newspaper owned by his father, the *San Francisco Examiner*. The younger Hearst introduced revolutionary changes that made the paper one for the people. He focused on human stories and championed the underdog. He lowered the cover price. He splashed big headlines on the front page. He ran stories about sex and murder. He took on corrupt politicians and public utilities. His readers lapped it up, and within four years he had trebled circulation. In 1895 he moved back to New York, ready to try his unique way of running a newspaper in the most competitive media market in the world. Hearst purchased the *New York Journal* and began a long running battle for circulation and advertising revenue with his former employer, Joseph Pulitzer.

The rivalry coined the phrase 'yellow journalism'. The term had its roots in a cartoon character called the Yellow Kid, who dressed in a flour sack and championed the rights of the underprivileged. Hearst hired the cartoonist, who was working for Pulitzer, to bring the popular character to the *New York Journal*. Pulitzer countered by hiring another cartoonist to draw *The Yellow Kid*. Yellow journalism became an expression for buying the news, making the news or doing whatever it took to get people to buy papers. William Randolph Hearst was the master of yellow journalism and built up a chain of newspapers across America.

In 1928, at the height of his power and ambition, Hearst was constantly seeking ways to challenge or embarrass his competitors and the establishment. Richard Byrd was mounting a large expedition to fly in Antarctica, and he had the backing of the establishment – the Fords, the Rockefellers, the Astors – and, more to the point, he had the backing of the rival *New York Times*. Every day the *Times* was calling for support and donations while promoting Byrd's expedition to Antarctica. What could Hearst do to put a spanner in the works? The answer flew into his lap: George Hubert Wilkins. The Australian had just flown his light, single-engine plane 2200 miles across the Arctic. Now, if Wilkins could hurry down to the Antarctic and fly across the continent via the South Pole before Byrd, then Byrd's ambitions would be destroyed and his backers embarrassed.

Hearst approached Wilkins through T. V. Ranck with an offer. After meeting Wilkins in Europe, Ranck cabled Hearst:

Wilkins willing accept total forty thousand dollars we offered for Antarctic exploration with ten thousand dollars additional should he chance go over the pole . . . he says if we will pay ten thousand on signing agreement and fifteen thousand addition before he leaves the country . . . this would leave us fifteen thousand to pay fulfillment his program provided he does not go over the pole.

At same time Wilkins intimated confidentially that he might attempt the pole flight . . . he could see no reason he said why he should not try it if he gets down there and finds Byrd hasn't gone over.

Additional ten thousand you offered figured in his thoughts this connection and of course would cover all required of us if he went across pole.

What did Byrd make of the announcement that Wilkins and Eielson were going to fly across Antarctica via the South Pole? What were his feelings toward Wilkins and, for that matter, Wilkins' feelings toward him? Neither man has left a record of his opinion of the other. Suzanne Bennett, in later life, would tell a story about how Byrd arrived at Wilkins' apartment in New York and, with tears in his eyes, begged the Australian not to go south. But like much of what Suzanne said, it should not be taken seriously.

However, the two men, who had met two years earlier when Wilkins had offered Byrd a position with the Detroit Arctic Expedition, certainly met again now. The weeks following the announcement in the *New York Journal* produced the only photograph of them together. It must have been taken late in the month and was organised by the publisher George Putnam's Sons, which was in the process of publishing both Wilkins' *Flying the Arctic* and Byrd's *Skyward*. The publicity photograph brought together some of the news-making flyers of the time and also tells us a little about the character of both Wilkins and Byrd, if not about their relationship.

The media-savvy Byrd did what he regularly did for photographs. He dressed in his white navy uniform and positioned himself in the centre of the group. In the black and white newspaper pictures of the era Byrd always stood out. He would write in *Skyward*:

> Now I discovered that the success of our flight from Spitzbergen touched some responsive public chord which loosed a torrent of attention upon me and my expedition. I wondered what it all meant. What I ultimately found out about 'being a hero' gave me as much of a 'kick' as did the sensation of circling the Pole.

Of the eight people in the photograph, Wilkins is the only one not looking at the camera. He stares off to the side, his mind seemingly elsewhere. In *Flying the Arctic* he would write:

> The greatest hardship I have ever suffered, and the most trying ordeal ever undertaken, was to address from time to time an audience ... and then stand while some raucous-voiced high pressure salesman sold my photograph or my

autograph for a hundred, fifty, twenty, five dollars, fifty
cents or what have you. I still shudder when I think of it.

Amelia Earhart also appears in the photograph. Indeed, June
1928 was a remarkable period in aviation history. It was a time
when the public's appetite for aviators was insatiable. Wilkins
and Eielson were being feted across Europe and America. The
world's attention was focusing on the drama unfolding with the
loss of the *Italia*. On 12 June 200,000 people greeted Charles
Kingsford Smith and his companions in Sydney, Australia, after
the first flight across the Pacific. A week later Amelia Earhart
became the first woman to fly the Atlantic and was an instant
celebrity. More than film stars, more than sports heroes, people
were clamouring to see and read about aviators. Now, the
announcement in the *New York Journal* fuelled the rampant
fascination. There was to be an air race to the South Pole
between Byrd and Wilkins.

* * *

On the evening of 3 June 1928, nine days after the *Italia* had hit
the ice, and four days after Malmgren and his two companions
had left to walk across the ice to land, an amateur radio operator,
Nicholas Schmidt, sitting by his wireless set in the tiny Russian
village of Wossenie-Wochma, 1200 miles from the crash site,
began to pick up a faint and broken message. Quickly he wrote
it down: 'Ital . . . Nobile . . . Fran . . . Josef . . . SOS . . . SOS
Terra . . . tengo . . . Eh H . . .', followed by a word he thought
might be 'Petermann'. In the Arctic, Petermann was a land
believed to be about 100 kilometres north of the Franz Josef
Archipelago.

Three days later Giuseppe Biagi was sitting by his radio set, listening – as he did almost constantly. Listening didn't drain the batteries the way sending messages did. As he transcribed the news bulletin from Rome, he suddenly shouted, 'They've heard us!' and kept on transcribing:

> The Soviet Union has informed the Italian Government that an SOS from the *Italia* has been picked up by a young Soviet farmer, Nicholas Schmidt, at Archangel, on the evening of June third . . .

If it had previously known *Italia* survivors were on the ice north-east of Spitsbergen, the Italian government could now no longer hide it from the world.

The news sparked an international rescue effort that had one major failing: it lacked coordination. The situation was made worse by the fact that, after the initial radio signal was heard by the Russian amateur, others also began to claim that they had heard the *Italia* crew's signals. As a result, the *Italia* was reported to be in various locations, some of them geographically impossible.

But for a brief time the world came to Spitsbergen. Journalists, thrill-seekers, photographers and would-be rescuers. Fame, and possibly fortune, awaited the aviator who could fly forth and rescue the downed Italians. Others flew or shipped their planes to Kings Bay purely out of a sense of responsibility. Among them was Hjalmer Riiser-Larsen, the pilot who had flown Amundsen on his 1925 attempt to reach the North Pole and who had subsequently been second-in-command of the *Norge*.

Meanwhile, Rome fiddled while Nobile froze. Ignoring international offers of help, the Italian government's response was to say that the rescue efforts from other countries were unnecessary.

One of Italy's leading pilots, Major Umberto Maddalena, in the latest and most powerful Italian-built Savoia-Marchetti S55 flying boat, would fly to Spitsbergen to effect the rescue. Aboard the *Citta di Milano*, Captain Romagna took the position that nothing would be done until Maddalena arrived.

In Norway, Roald Amundsen felt compelled to act. The old slanging match between him and Nobile had to be put aside; the 'White Eagle of Norway' announced he would fly north again. The only problem was that the Norwegian government would have none of it. Friction between Norway and Italy, caused by the Amundsen–Nobile feud, had caused a diplomatic row that was finally beginning to heal. Nobile had returned to the Arctic with the *Italia* largely to prove that he could fly airships in the region without Amundsen. Now that he had made a mess of it, the last thing the Italian government wanted was for Amundsen to go and rescue him. The Italians let this be known to the Norwegians, who in turn ordered the Norwegian Aero Club not to give Amundsen access to any planes. The Norwegian Aero Club, from which Amundsen had already resigned in a huff because it had forced him to include Nobile's name in the title of the 1926 expedition, readily complied.

With no money and no planes to mount his rescue attempt, Amundsen turned to Lincoln Ellsworth in America. Ellsworth, at the time, was in the middle of one of his chronic bouts of depression. Fearing for his welfare, friends encouraged him to become involved, but it was all beyond Ellsworth emotionally. He wired Amundsen some money.

But Amundsen still needed a plane. He went to the French, who were always looking for an opportunity to upstage Mussolini. The French government naturally wanted a French plane and a French crew to rescue the Italians. They arranged for a Latham 47, a biplane flying boat, to be made available to

Amundsen. It would be manned by a French pilot, Lieutenant Commander Rene Guillbaud, and three French crewmen. Amundsen insisted that Leif Dietrichson, the pilot who had flown Ellsworth's flying boat in 1925, also accompany him. On 16 June, Amundsen and Dietrichson travelled by train from Oslo to Tromso to meet the Frenchmen.

On 18 June, while waiting for suitable weather to make the flight from Tromso to Spitsbergen, Amundsen learnt that Major Maddalena had taken off from Vadso in his S55 flying boat and was already en route. The news spurred Amundsen on and he ordered the Frenchmen to get ready to take off immediately. He didn't want the Italians beating him to the glory. The four Frenchman, Amundsen and Dietrichson crowded into the dangerously underpowered flying boat and, with a last wave, took off. A day later they had still not arrived at Kings Bay and were reported as missing.

Maddalena, however, successfully reached Kings Bay and joined the other airmen already there.

Meanwhile the crew of the *Italia* struggled to survive on the ice. Flights were leaving Kings Bay and travelling north-east to search for them. On a number of occasions planes had flown so close that the stranded men had heard them, and sometimes even seen them. But the pilots had not seen the men. To assist in being located from the air, the Italians took glass balls of red dye, which they would use to measure the altitude of the airship over the ice, broke them and smeared the dye on their tent to make it more visible. 'We have dyed our tent red,' radio operator Biagi informed the *Citta di Milano*. Although the result was actually a faint, smeared brownish pink, their adventure was thereafter referred to as 'the Red Tent'.

A day after arriving at Kings Bay, Maddalena had refuelled his plane and made his first flight over the area. And while the

Italians on the ice could hear him, he could not see them. The following day Maddalena went out again, this time with a new radio on board and a civilian radio operator. Once they were in the vicinity of the Red Tent, Biagi, sitting on the ice with his radio, guided the plane towards them. Suddenly the plane was 300 feet above the frantically waving survivors. Maddalena turned around and on the second pass dropped supplies. The men scrambled over the ice to retrieve food, dry sleeping bags, new leather boots, smoke signals and more. To the Italians, who had been stranded on the ice for twenty-five days, it was welcome relief. Maddalena circled again and saw that there was no open water near the survivors to land a flying boat and few flat areas suitable for landing even a small plane on skis.

In the following days planes began to visit the Red Tent regularly, but none dared attempt a landing on the broken ice. Supplies, including food and clothing, were dropped, and cameramen leant from planes to film and photograph the men. It had been almost a month since the *Italia* had crashed. Seven crew members were dead. Three had left to walk to land. The remaining six were on the ice in the Red Tent. At first they had been ignored and forgotten. Now they had been found and fed, then filmed and made famous. If only someone would get them off the damn ice. To make matters worse, the search and rescue efforts had been divided; many of the planes and ships had to be diverted south to search for the missing Amundsen and his crew.

Into the centre ring of this circus of disorganisation stepped an adventurer and shameless self-promoter, Lieutenant Einar Lundborg of the Swedish Air Force. On 23 June Lundborg chanced his luck and landed his Fokker biplane on the ice near the Red Tent. The Italians were jubilant. Lundborg could, at maximum, take one person back. But which person?

Nobile later claimed that he argued for the other men to be taken off first but that Lundborg overruled him. Nobile had already worked out an order for evacuation, he said, and the first person on the list was the injured Cecioni. Lundborg said his orders were to take Nobile off first, but just who the Swede was taking orders from he never said. Why an Italian general should take orders from a Swedish lieutenant is also unclear. The upshot was that Nobile climbed aboard the plane to be rescued first. He also took along his dog, Titina. He would later argue that by being rescued first he would be in the best position to oversee the rescue of the rest of the men. He hoped, he explained, to get things happening aboard the *Citta di Milano*, which had hitherto not seemed too interested in rescuing them.

Exactly the opposite happened. Once returned to the *Citta di Milano*, Nobile was put under house arrest and kept from speaking to anyone, while the rescue effort was bogged down again in endless radio messages to Rome to ask for permission to undertake even the most minor tasks. Nobile, if nothing else, had played into their hands. By having himself rescued first they could accuse him of cowardice and incompetence. From this point on, the thrust of the Italian effort seems not to have been to get the remaining men off the ice but to build a strong case to show that Nobile was solely at fault for everything. And, naturally, that he was acting totally independently of the Italian government.

Meanwhile, five men still shivered on the ice and the three that had set off weeks earlier had not been sighted. Lundborg, having flown in and brought Nobile off the ice, now waited for the weather to clear to make another attempt.

By this time the Russian government had thrown its bearskin hat into the ring. It entered a tortoise into a race full of hare-brained ideas. Russia had a decommissioned icebreaker: a massive, thick-hulled coal-burning ship of 10,630 tons that could literally smash its way slowly though the ice pack. Previously used to smash the ice in harbours, the *Krasin* would now attempt to sail up the west coast of Spitsbergen and past Kings Bay, then enter the ice pack and sail around the top of the archipelago to reach the stranded survivors.

On 10 June, just one week after the amateur Russian radio operator had picked up the message from the Italians, workers had started preparing the *Krasin*, which had lain idle for years. Two weeks later, coaled and crewed, the Communist tortoise sailed from Bergen, Norway, to shouts of 'Save Amundsen!' On board was a full complement of international reporters, who would, the Russians hoped, show the world the superiority of the Communist way of working together. As if to demonstrate this comradeship, the captain of the *Krasin*, Karl Pavlovich, would take his meals at the common mess table, seated beside the ordinary seamen. On 27 June the *Krasin* crossed the Arctic Circle then continued to sail north past Spitsbergen. On 2 July it entered the ice pack.

Einar Lundborg, having rescued Nobile from the ice, had still not used up his fifteen minutes of fame. When the weather cleared he returned to the Red Tent. This time he was roaring drunk and his Fokker upended on landing, smashing the propeller. The five men in the tent now had to share their accommodation with their would-be rescuer, who quickly sank into depression.

On 6 July, forty-two days after the crash of the *Italia* and almost two weeks since Nobile had left, another plane landed at the Red Tent. But it was still not to bring salvation to the hapless crew of the airship. The plane was piloted by Lieutenant Schyberg, a friend of Lundborg and a fellow Swedish Air

Force officer. As the plane taxied successfully to a standstill, it might have been expected that what would follow would be a discussion as to who should leave the ice first. Cecioni, perhaps, who had been on the ice for six weeks with a broken leg? No such discussion took place. The ever resourceful Lundborg sprinted across the ice to the plane and climbed aboard before Schyberg had even stopped the engine. Lundborg shouted orders to the pilot and the Italians crawled out of their tent in time to see the plane pick up speed and take off. Now five again, they resumed their waiting.

Six days later the *Krasin* saw two men walking on the ice. They were Mariano and Zappi of the walking party. Malmgren, the Swedish meteorologist, had died and they had buried him on the ice. Weak and hungry, the two men were taken on board. The Russian tortoise resumed its plodding race and, three days later, reached the surviving crew of the *Italia*. Seven weeks after it had begun, the saga of the Red Tent was over.

Amundsen, Dietrichson and the French crew of the Latham 47 flying boat were never seen again. In August 1933 fishermen near Bear Island (between Norway and Spitsbergen) brought up something in their net that they described as 'part of a plane', but it was heavy, broke through the net and fell back to the ocean floor. In 1964 a fisherman on Edge Island (south-east of Spitsbergen) found a large piece of plywood from a plane. He used it for a wall of his hut until it was rediscovered and examined in 2003. It is considered to be from Amundsen's plane. Attempts to find Amundsen's remains, along with those of the crew, and the rest of the flying boat, continue to this day.

13

Opposite to the Bear

The word 'arctic' comes from the Greek *arktos*, meaning 'bear'. Early mariners would use the star constellation known as the Great Bear to tell them which direction was north. Heading north was heading towards the bear – arktos. Adding the prefix 'anti' meant they were going in the opposite direction.

Mariners heading away from the bear in the eighteenth century soon found themselves in cold, unforgiving waters and were content not to push their tiny wooden vessels any further. The intrepid British sailor Captain James Cook, on his second great voyage of discovery, sailed around the Antarctic continent in high southern latitudes and saw ice but no land. Following the publication of the details of Cook's voyage, British and American sailors headed south to kill thousands of fur and elephant seals. These hunters kept their discoveries secret, and no one can be certain if any of them saw the Antarctic continent. Captain Thaddeus Bellinghausen circumnavigated Antarctica in 1819–21 and pushed closer to the continent than Cook had done. He saw massive walls of ice at the edge of Greater Antarctica; opinion is divided as to whether seeing the ice that covers the land constitutes the first sighting of the continent. On 28 February 1831 Captain John Biscoe, working for the London sealing and whaling company of Enderby's, did see actual dirt and rock at what is now Enderby Land.

As with many polar firsts, there's a dispute about who was the first to set foot on Antarctica. In 1894 Carsten Borchgrevink, a Norwegian who had migrated to Australia, got work on a Norwegian whaling vessel that had stopped at Melbourne on its way south. On 24 January 1895 the vessel anchored off Cape Adare and four men rowed ashore in a longboat. The captain of the whaler, Leonard Kristensen, claimed to have been the first to step out of the longboat onto the land, whereas Borchgrevink declared that he jumped out while the boat was in the shallows and so touched land first.

The next 'first' was the first to winter over, and this honour goes – although not by intention – to the Belgian expedition ship *Belgica*. It got stuck in the ice west of the Antarctic Peninsula (Graham Land). The crew didn't reach land, but they did spend a winter in the Antarctic. On board were two men who were to become famous in polar exploration: Frederick A. Cook, who would claim to be the first person to reach the North Pole, and Roald Amundsen.

The man who said he got the jump on his captain from the longboat, Carsten Borchgrevink, went back to Cape Adare in 1898 and built a hut. He and nine others became the first men to winter over on the continent itself, although one man died during the ordeal. The hut still stands. Borchgrevink returned to Australia in January 1900 to usher in not only the twentieth century but also the heroic age of polar exploration. Robert Falcon Scott had a go at reaching the South Pole in 1901. Shackleton got within 100 miles in 1908. Then Amundsen and Scott had their famous race in 1911–1912. Others sent expeditions that reached one point or another, but the enormous continent remained largely unexplored.

Whalers weren't slow in chasing a dollar. At the beginning of the twentieth century whaling had evolved from the *Moby-Dick* days of men in longboats rowing after whales and throwing harpoons at them. To be of much economic value, whales had to be flensed soon after being killed and the flesh boiled down for its oil. In 1905 a Norwegian whaling captain, C. A. Larsen, introduced the first floating factory, while motorised 'catchers' went after the whales to kill them with harpoon guns. In the 1909–1910 season, seven floating factories, six shore stations and thirty-seven catchers killed over 6000 whales in Antarctic waters. Productivity, if that's the word for it, then almost doubled over the next five years. Whaling largely took place off Graham Land, when whalers sailed from South Georgia and the Falkland Islands. Between 1914 and 1918 the world was distracted by slaughter of another kind in Europe. At the end of World War One, the whalers were the first to be active in the Antarctic again.

Meanwhile, small expeditions by explorers achieved little, and nations – including Great Britain, Norway, Australia and New Zealand – talked about what should happen to the continent. Then in March 1924 France stung them into action. A French presidential decree claimed Adelie Land for France, based on the fact that its coast was sighted by Dumont D'Urville in 1840. As soon as one country had claimed a section of Antarctica, the scramble for territorial claims began in earnest. But journeying with dogs and sledges, trekking one exhausting painful step after another, was no way to explore and map a vast and inhospitable continent. By the mid-1920s Antarctica was waiting for the aeroplane.

* * *

On 16 June 1928 Byrd's expedition ship, the *Samson*, finally arrived in New York. The wooden Norwegian ship, which had been recommended by Amundsen, was a major disappointment to Byrd. It was not an issue Byrd could take up with his former rival, because two days after it arrived in New York, Amundsen left Norway in search of the Italians.

The *Samson* was powered by a combination of sail and a small coal-fired engine. It would need enormous amounts of coal to get down the coast of both North and South America, across the Pacific to New Zealand and then south to the Ross Ice Shelf. That wasn't its only problem. It was too small. Byrd's main aeroplane was no longer a Fokker Trimotor but a larger metal-body Ford Trimotor. Even disassembled, the big Ford would not fit in the hold of the *Samson*. So Byrd had to find a second expedition ship. He renamed the *Samson* the *City of New York*, while the second ship, a steel-hulled cargo steamer, was named *Eleanor Bolling*, after his mother.

On 25 August 1928 Byrd's expedition officially got underway when the *City of New York*, carrying 200 tons of hastily loaded supplies, sailed out of New York Harbour. A few weeks later another ship, the *Ross*, chartered to take crew and dogs as far as New Zealand, also left. Then on 26 September the *Eleanor Bolling* sailed for New Zealand with 300 tons of supplies. Byrd wasn't on any of the ships. Still needing financial support for the expedition, the budget for which had grown to $1 million, he began a promotional tour starting in Virginia. After travelling across America by train, stopping at major cities to speak and continue to raise funds, Byrd finally left Los Angeles on a whaler, the *C. A. Larsen*, bound for New Zealand, on 10 October 1928.

The expedition, sailing south on four ships, consisted of eighty-two men, but the number would fluctuate as stowaways were found, and in some cases retained, and as other crew members left for various reasons. In addition to the men, Byrd had the big Ford Trimotor, the single-engine Fokker and a smaller, single-engine Fairchild. Supplies, among other things, consisted of 1000 pounds of cigarettes, 1000 pounds of pipe tobacco, ten tons of sugar, five tons of flour, 500 pounds of chewing gum, 3500 chickens, 2500 turkeys, five tons of beef, three tons of bacon, six guitars, fifteen harmonicas, twelve ukuleles and an electric piano.

The *Ross* was the first ship to reach Dunedin, New Zealand, where it was found that five of the ninety dogs had died. Many more were close to death as a result of poor food. At Dunedin they were put into quarantine and their health improved after a change of diet. The *C. A. Larsen*, with Byrd on board, arrived on 5 November. Located at the bottom of the South Island, and often being the last stepping-off point for expeditions heading south, Dunedin has a proud association with Antarctic explorers. The city gave Byrd a warm welcome and Byrd, in turn, laid a wreath at the statue of Robert Falcon Scott.

Byrd now waited for the two ships carrying the bulk of his supplies to catch up. The *Eleanor Bolling* arrived on 18 November, with the overloaded *City of New York* finally arriving on 26 November. For the first time the Byrd Antarctic Expedition was all in the same place at the same time. What's more, the eighty-plus members of the expedition learnt to their joy that New Zealand had no prohibition. Alcohol could be bought on every day except Sunday, and the men took full advantage of their good fortune.

All vital stores for setting up the winter quarters were loaded onto the *City of New York* so that the *Eleanor Bolling* could tow it to the edge of the ice pack before returning to New Zealand to ferry more supplies south, including the two larger planes.

The *Ross*, having brought the dogs and dog handlers to New Zealand, played no further part in the expedition. Neither did the *C. A. Larsen*, which went off in search of whales.

The two remaining expedition ships left New Zealand on 2 December, and the *City of New York* reached the Ross Ice Shelf on 25 December. After following the edge of the ice for five days looking for a suitable site, Byrd gave the order to begin unloading. The location was near Amundsen's old base of Framheim.

Within days, T. V. Ranck of the Hearst Organisation was forwarding information to Wilkins, who, at the time, was on the other side of Antarctica:

> Byrd's main base Latitude 78° 40' South, Longitude
> 163° 20' West. That is Amundsen's old camp. He first
> touched Barrier at Latitude 78° 20' South, Longitude
> 177° 30' West. Held up only a few days by pack ice on
> voyage to base. Was towed by whaler *C. A. Larsen*.
>   Byrd's supply ship *Eleanor Bolling* which returned
> [to] New Zealand has just left there with two big planes
> mentioned my previous message. Must travel 2,700 miles
> to reach Byrd's base.

As Byrd was unloading, he was not to know that spies within his crew were secretly forwarding information to the Hearst Organisation.

* * *

The Wilkins–Hearst Antarctic Expedition left New York on 22 September 1928. Wilkins had conceived, planned, organised and got the expedition underway in just ten weeks. He had purchased a second Lockheed Vega to supplement the reliable plane that he and Ben Eielson had flown across the Arctic Ocean. No longer feeling he owed the city of Detroit a debt of gratitude, he had named his planes to honour his new friends in California. The original Vega he named *Los Angeles*; the new one he named *San Francisco*. On this expedition Eielson would again be the pilot. The supporting crew consisted of another pilot, Joe Crosson, a mechanic, Orval Porter, and wireless operator, William Gaston. Five men, two small planes, minimal equipment and a few months of preparation. If they could upstage the eighty-man, million-dollar Byrd Antarctic Expedition, then Hearst would have value for his $50,000.

It would be Wilkins' third trip to the Antarctic. The first, with Cope in 1920, had been a failure. The second, on Shackleton's final expedition, had also achieved little. But Wilkins had learnt from the experiences and he used the knowledge to formulate his plans quickly. He would get his planes and men to Montevideo, Uruguay, where they would board a Norwegian whaling ship bound for Deception Island, just off Graham Land. Wilkins had seen Deception Island with Cope and felt the flat ice of the frozen harbour would make an ideal runway. From Deception Island he would commence his exploring. From there it was 1800 miles to the South Pole and another 800 miles to where Byrd planned to set up his base at the Bay of Whales – a distance well within the range of the Lockheed Vegas. No one had yet explored Graham Land, so it was not known whether the land that pointed towards South America was a series of islands or a peninsula joined to the Antarctic mainland. For that matter, no one knew whether Antarctica was indeed one continent or two. And to the east and west of Graham Land lay thousands of miles of unexplored territory.

While planning his expedition, Wilkins had spoken with R. G. Casey, the Australian political liaison officer in London, who was on a committee discussing Australia's role in claiming Antarctic territory. Wilkins asked if his flights in the Antarctic would lend weight to the British and Australian claims to territory. After some deliberation, Casey wrote him a vague reply:

> Do you intend to drop British or Australian flags at intervals along the coastline from Edward VII Land to Graham Land? It would be a nice gesture – and perhaps would have its value in the future, especially if you made a record of the exact positions of the flags and if possible photographed them from the air. I understand that Byrd has no intentions of making his expedition other than scientific. It would add very considerable complications to the Antarctic complex if he were to scatter American flags about. But I don't suppose the Americans have any Antarctic aspirations. It is rather out of their line of country.

After formulating his plans, Wilkins arrived at Montevideo with his crew on 10 October 1928. It was the same day that Byrd left Los Angeles to sail for New Zealand. As with the air race to the North Pole, the race to the South Pole – in the early stages, at least – seemed to have Wilkins clearly in the lead.

At Montevideo Wilkins and his four crew members waited two weeks for the Norwegian whaler *Hectoria*, a 16,000-ton former White Star liner, to arrive. When it did the planes were put on board and the expedition headed for Deception Island. Surprisingly, 300 miles north of Deception Island, the *Hectoria* encountered pack ice. This was not a good sign so early in the season. When Wilkins was there with Cope and with Shackleton's *Quest* expedition, the sea had been open all the way to the island. Ice floating 300 miles from land meant that the harbour at Deception Island might not be frozen and Wilkins would not have his runway. The *Hectoria* reached Deception Island on 7 November. Wilkins wrote:

> Deception is a tiny dot on the Antarctic map, sheltered from the ocean by large members of the South Shetlands Islands group to the north and west, and by curving Palmer Peninsula (Graham Land) to the east. Geologically, the island is an extinct volcano, with the harbour lying in the ancient crater. The lofty peaks of the volcanic rim almost enclose it, like the letter C. The whalers established their station at the edge of this perfect natural harbour 120 years ago and it has been their base of operation ever since.
>
> We found little snow on the lower slopes of the island and the harbour ice was thin. In 1920 it had been six feet thick, but this time it was less than three feet thick at the same season of the year. The *Hectoria* easily broke through, and anchored so close to land that a gangway was put from her stern to the shore.

Quickly the small community came to life, as whalers settled into the camp for the summer and got their boats ready for hunting.

Four days after the *Hectoria* arrived, the Lockheed Vega *Los Angeles* was fitted with pontoons, swung over the side of the ship and lowered onto the water. Eielson made an attempt to get the plane airborne, but found it impossible due to the thousands of small birds that lived on the island and flocked to the water as soon as the ice was broken. They flew into the propeller at every attempt to take off. The *Los Angeles* and the *San Francisco* were towed to the beach and the men began looking for a suitable runway. They found a short flat area that sloped up a hillside, which they felt would be suitable for a take-off on wheels. Finally, after waiting eleven days for the weather to clear sufficiently, Eielson, with Wilkins in the navigator's seat, got the *Los Angeles* airborne and made a short test flight. The first plane to fly across the Arctic Ocean was now the first plane to fly in the Antarctic. The date was 22 November 1928.

A day later Joe Crosson took the *San Francisco* up for a trial flight. Shortly after, the thin layer of snow that had been covering the runway melted, exposing sharp lava rocks that would tear the tyres of the planes. The men looked around for another runway. Across the peninsula they found a promising spot. It involved taxiing up a sloping hill, making a turn, going down an incline, making another turn and then going up a slope. But it was the best available, so the men began removing the rocks and getting the surface as flat as possible. The work took weeks.

During this time a cold snap froze the harbour and Wilkins hoped it might now be thick enough to hold a plane. With wheels fitted to the *Los Angeles*, Eielson took off from the runway they had hacked out, flew around the island and came down to land on the harbour ice. The wheels hit the ice and the plane slid past the area Wilkins had marked out. The ice gave way and the plane sank down, nose-first, until only its wings stopped it going completely through and taking Eielson to the bottom of the harbour, which was some 400 metres deep. The men watching held their breath. Eielson clambered out of the plane and lay spreadeagled on the ice. The whalers left their work and came over to help. Carefully, very carefully, men crawled out over the ice to the plane and attached ropes to it. Then, in an eighteen-hour marathon of labour, they managed to haul the plane back over the ice to the beach.

Next they attached pontoons to the *San Francisco*, and Joe Crosson attempted to take off from the water. This time a motorboat preceded the plane to frighten the birds away. It was a valiant attempt but ultimately unsuccessful, with many birds still flying into the propellers.

Wilkins concluded that the only option was the winding, hilly runway they were building. It included two uphill sections, two turns and three ditches, but it was the best they were able to manage. It was 800 yards long and the Lockheed Vega needed 900 yards of flat runway to get into the air with a full load of fuel. Wilkins decided to load the *Los Angeles* with enough fuel for a round trip of 1400 miles and attempt to get airborne to follow the coast of Graham Land.

On 20 December Eielson and Wilkins bounced and bumped along the makeshift runway and lifted off, to the cheers of the whalers and their fellow expedition crew members. They climbed to 6000 feet, crossed the mountains to the eastern side of Graham Land and headed south. As they flew along the coast they were sighting land no one had seen before. It was the first time in history new land was being discovered from the air.

In his notebook Wilkins hastily drew the features he could see – features that, as he discovered them, he had the right to name. In the map he would draw, Wilkins would repay many debts. Cape McCarroll, after the publicist and broadcaster whose weekly radio program in 1926 had urged Detroiters to rally behind the 'courageous Captain Wilkins'. Evans Inlet, after the businessman who had arranged the Stinsons for him in 1927. Cape Northrup, after the co-designer of the Lockheed Vega. The Lockheed Mountains. The Bowman Coast, after the president of the American Geographical Society. Cape Mayo, after the chairman of the Detroit Aviation Society. Mount

Ranck, after his supporter at the Hearst Organisation. And, in perhaps the most blatantly commercial geographical name, Mobiloil Bay.

As he looked across to the west he saw wide ice-locked bays, which he believed were channels separating Graham Land from Antarctica. He named them Casey Channel, after R. G. Casey in London, and Lurabee Channel, after his Californian girlfriend Lura B. Schreck. The wider strait he named Stefansson, for his arctic mentor. After passing Stefansson Strait, Wilkins continued south:

> Ahead of us, this land extended as far as we could see, beyond a shoreline running roughly east and west. By now we were 600 miles from Deception Island, we had used nearly half our supply of petrol, and a dark storm was developing behind us. To go much further would be inviting trouble. Besides, crossing the Graham Land Plateau and discovering the channels, which apparently transformed the great peninsula into a chain of islands, we had discovered altogether eight new islands, three channels and a strait as well as an unknown land, which seemed to be part of the Antarctic continent. We wanted to fly westward across the islands and follow their western coasts northward, but the violence of the storm and our barely sufficient supply of petrol impelled us to take the shortest course for the return to Deception Island.

Wilkins saved the biggest name for last. The land that extended 'as far as we could see, beyond a shoreline running roughly east and west' he named Hearst Land, after the newspaper publisher. But whether Antarctica consisted of two or more large islands was still unknown.

190

After eleven hours of flying, Eielson and Wilkins returned to Deception Island. They had left at 8.30 in the morning, explored almost 1300 miles of unseen land, then returned in time to sit down and have their evening meal with the whalers. The first major flight in the Antarctic had shown the advantages of the aeroplane for exploring the continent. Unfortunately, it would also, in time, show the disadvantages. A land expedition in 1934, drilling down through the ice, would prove that the 'channels' and 'strait' Wilkins claimed divided Graham Land into a series of islands did not, in fact, exist. The land beneath the ice was above sea level, not below it. Graham Land was indeed a peninsula.

The season for flying on Graham Land begins and ends earlier than the season for flying at the Ross Sea. Wilkins knew that little useful flying could be done after the beginning of the New Year, and without a better runway, or a flat area of ice from which to get a plane into the air with a full load of fuel, he knew he would not be able to achieve anything more that season. He secured the two Lockheed Vegas and left them at Deception Island, hoping to return some time in the future to explore further. Then he and the other members of the crew returned with the whalers to South America. They were all back in New York by March 1929.

* * *

On 30 December 1928 Byrd had given the order to unload the *City of New York* onto the Ross Ice Shelf near Amundsen's old base. At the edge of the ice barrier the men started putting the supplies onto the ice, from where they had to be dragged five miles to the site Byrd had chosen. Four to five tonnes could be sledged across the ice each day. At that rate it would take a month to unload the *City of New York*. Meanwhile, the *Eleanor Bolling* was due to return from New Zealand at the end of January with more supplies, as well as with the Fokker and the Ford Trimotor. Only the smaller Fairchild was on the *City of New York*.

Slowly the work progressed, as the men hauled the supplies across the ice and began to erect the prefabricated sheds that would house them over winter. It was later estimated that they shovelled 2.5 millions pounds (1134 tonnes) of snow while burrowing down to erect their winter headquarters. On 4 January 1929, perhaps playing to his radio audience at home, Byrd named the base *Little America*.

On 15 January the Fairchild was assembled, and pilot Alton Parker was given the honour of making the first flight. Up to four people could squeeze into the fuselage, but only one, or perhaps two, could be accommodated in comfort. The three mechanics cut cards to see which one of them would have the honour of making the flight with Parker. Benjamin Roth won, which displeased Byrd, who felt the other two mechanics, Epaminondas Demas and Kennard Bubier, were more deserving. Both had been with the expedition longer and done more to make it happen. Roth, on the other hand, had joined shortly before the expedition left America. The Fairchild took off with Parker and Roth and made a short flight over Little America. Byrd wanted history written not as it happened, but as he preferred to think it had happened, so when he later wrote about the flight he ignored Roth and credited Demas and Bubier as being onboard with Parker. After the first flight the other pilots took the Fairchild up to circle Little America.

The *Eleanor Bolling* had still not arrived with the larger planes but Byrd was keen to make exploratory flights, despite it being late in the season. He had already learnt by radio that

Wilkins had completed his work and was returning north. On 27 January 1929 Byrd's meteorologist predicted good weather for flying. Byrd went up in the Fairchild, with Dean Smith as pilot and Harold June as reserve pilot and radio operator. Byrd was navigator. They flew 200 miles east towards King Edward VII Land before turning south into an unexplored area. Here they saw a new mountain range that Byrd named Rockefeller, after one of his major sponsors. Although the flight had not left the quadrant claimed by the British, the Fairchild had reached the limit of its flying range and Byrd was forced to turn back without finding anything new to claim for America. Fortunately, as the Fairchild flew over Little America on its return, Byrd saw that the *Eleanor Bolling* had arrived with the two larger planes.

By 18 February the Fokker was assembled and ready to make a longer flight. Bernt Balchen, the Fokker expert, would be the pilot, Byrd would navigate and Lloyd Berkener would be radio operator. The plan was to fly over the newly discovered Rockefeller Mountains and explore them more thoroughly. The specialist aerial photographer, Ashley McKinley, was upset that he was not included in the flight, especially as he had come on the expedition specifically to take photographs when new land was to be mapped. The Fokker took off and when Byrd, Balchen and Berkener reached the Rockefellers, they found the range covered in cloud. No mapping could be done, so they turned around and flew back.

When Byrd landed he was approached by his second-in-command, Laurence (Larry) Gould, on behalf of pilot Dean Smith and McKinley. The pair wanted to make their own flight. Perhaps sensing tension among expedition members who felt they were being overlooked, Byrd agreed, but ordered them to only make a short flight. Two hours after it had landed the

Fokker was in the air again, this time with Smith at the controls and McKinley navigating and taking pictures. Lloyd Berkener, the radio operator on the previous flight, went again. Once in the air, McKinley suggested they fly over the Rockefellers and map them if the clouds had cleared. All three felt they had nothing to lose. Smith thought he was being overlooked as 'first pilot', McKinley wasn't being allowed to take his photographs, and Berkener was returning to New Zealand on the *Eleanor Bolling* and would not be wintering over. This flight might be their last chance to discover anything. They radioed Little America for permission to fly over the Rockefellers. When Byrd replied, instructing them not to, Berkener simply winked at the others on the plane and said the transmission was garbled.

The Fokker headed east to the newly discovered Rockefeller Mountains, which the rebellious trio found clear of cloud. Beyond the Rockefellers they saw another mountain range. This was a much larger range, with a tall Matterhorn-like peak in the centre, and it continued far into the distance, finally disappearing over the horizon. Furthermore, it was outside the quadrant claimed by the British. Here was a discovery that was not only new, but one that could be claimed for America. Elated, the three flew back to Little America, arriving at nine pm. When they told Byrd of their discovery, they were not prepared for his reaction. Dean Smith wrote of their greeting:

We pulled off our furs, spread our maps on the center table, and, excited as children, told of our flight and our discovery.
'This Matterhorn peak, how far would you say it was from the eastern end of the Rockefellers?' asked Byrd.
'We flew on for at least forty-five minutes and were still not more than halfway. I'd say it was at least a hundred and fifty miles.'

'How precisely can you spot it on your map?' Byrd now asked.

McKinley and I compared notes and conferred at some length.

'From our longitude here I'd say it lies pretty close to northeast by east, call it sixty degrees. I'd put it somewhere in here,' and I drew a circle about thirty miles in diameter on the map.

Byrd spoke very seriously. 'This is most important. I congratulate you gentlemen on confirming my discovery. You have located this new land in almost exactly the place where I saw it this morning.'

'You saw it this morning!' exclaimed McKinley. 'But you didn't say anything about it after the flight.'

'No. I wanted to be sure before I announced it. But I did mark it on my map. Wait, I will show you.'

Byrd went into his room, closing the door behind him. We all sat mute. I caught Balchen's eye. He shrugged and rolled his eyes to the ceiling. Gould looked amused.

After about five minutes Commander Byrd returned, spreading his map on the table.

'Here is the course of our flight this morning,' he said, pointing to a penciled line. 'And over here is where I marked the new peak.' He showed us a heavy cross, drawn with a softer pencil than the course of the flight itself. Sure enough, if transposed to my map his cross would fall close to the center of my circle.

'Now that you too have seen this mountain, I feel justified in announcing the discovery. I have decided to call the area Marie A. Byrd Land in honor of my wife.'

Did Byrd really see Marie A. Byrd Land first, or did he lie and steal the kudos from the three men who kept on flying in that direction against his orders? The latter seems more likely. Balchen, who was the pilot on the earlier flight, makes no mention of discovering the new range. Only that they saw the mountains Byrd named Rockefeller, in the distance, then headed back to Little America. Later, Byrd told differing versions of when he first saw the 'Matterhorn peak'.

Nevertheless, Byrd went into print claiming to have seen the land first and today maps usually shorten the name of the immense area east of the Ross Sea simply to 'Byrd Land'.

After this, Byrd could at least be satisfied that the expedition had discovered, claimed and named new land in Antarctica. He had done enough to satisfy his backers for the summer and he could settle down to prepare his men for the long winter ahead. The *Eleanor Bolling* and the *City of New York* returned to New Zealand.

Only Larry Gould, the second-in-command, and a geologist, continually asked Byrd to make a further flight. The Rockefellers had been discovered. Gould wanted to fly there, land and take rock samples. All known wisdom about the weather told Byrd it was too late in the season for any more flying, but Gould persisted in asking, and Byrd finally gave in. The meteorologist gave them the okay on 7 March. Byrd gave Gould the choice of plane and crew. He chose the Fokker, with Balchen as pilot and Harold June as radio operator/backup pilot. The trio took off at three pm and headed for the Rockefeller Mountains, some 135 miles away. It would be the expedition's first landing on unknown ice.

Two hours later, the dots and dashes heard on the radio at Little America told Byrd that Balchen had successfully landed the Fokker. The signals continued to come through, saying that the trio were unable to take off again because of deteriorating weather. A day later they radioed that their plane had been destroyed.

A week went by. Then the signal from the trio camped at the foot of the Rockefellers stopped. Byrd was in a difficult situation. The exact location of the men was unknown. The Ford Trimotor was not yet assembled, so the only plane available was the small Fairchild, which could hold a maximum of five men. Two were required to make the rescue flight: the pilot and the radio operator/navigator. That meant the three men could be brought back in one flight. Inexplicably, Byrd felt he should go himself, either out of a sense of duty to his stranded men or, as some of his critics point out, to ensure his name was at the head of every newspaper story: the hero having to go and save the men. But Byrd was not a competent radio operator, nor was he a competent pilot in his own right. So his going along meant there would be six men to return to Little America, and that meant two flights.

The weather cleared on Sunday 17 March, ten days after the original trio had taken off, but Dean Smith was unable to get the engine of the Fairchild started. The weather stayed clear and the flight was planned for first thing next morning. Smith and his radio operator, Hanson, had the plane ready, but there was no sign of Byrd. According to Smith, he went to the Commander's room and knocked. Byrd called out to Smith, asking him to send the doctor in. The doctor went in, came back out, and then went in shortly after carrying three bottles of brandy. The men heard nothing until four in the afternoon when, still according to Smith, Byrd walked stiffly to the plane, his face set and white. With Byrd and Hanson crouched in the back, Smith got the Fairchild airborne and headed for the area at the southern end of the mountain chain where it was believed the marooned men were waiting. Seeing flags on the ground, Smith circled and landed.

On the ground the stranded trio told their story. They explained how poor weather had prevented them from taking off, and how, a day later, the storm had blown the wood and canvas Fokker away like a kite in a gale. After the explanation, Smith flew Balchen and June back to Little America, waited for another break in the ever-deteriorating weather, then returned five days later to collect Byrd, Gould and Hanson.

The season for flying was well and truly over. Byrd had lost his main support plane, but he had established his base and got his men safely ashore. He had discovered and named new land in Antarctica, and he could console himself with the knowledge that Wilkins was back in America without having made a long-distance flight across the continent or having reached the South Pole. Byrd now had to wait out the winter, so that when the sun reappeared in the spring he would be ready to fly to the South Pole.

14

Winter in America

Wintering at Little America meant that Byrd, along with forty-one companions, had to settle down to seven months of hibernation, boredom and oppressive overcrowding. Their 'city at the bottom of the world' consisted of a large administration building joined by a series of tunnels to a cluster of huts. All were under the snow; they referred to it as 'the warren'. Ventilation tubes supplying air from the surface had to be continually cleaned to prevent blocking. Throughout winter cliques formed, rivalries erupted, unpopular men were ostracised and Byrd brooded and waited for the coming sun so that he could fly to the South Pole.

On 9 May 1929, just three weeks after the sun had disappeared below the horizon, Byrd broke out the alcohol because the men wanted to celebrate the anniversary of the North Pole flight. Many of the men, Byrd included, got roaring drunk. Once the drinking started, however, it was difficult to stop. Some men were drunk every night for weeks. More than once Byrd was carried back to his bunk.

With Wilkins having returned north, Byrd believed the way to the South Pole was clear. With no competitor, he now believed that the biggest threat to his success, and thus to the further enhancement of his public image, could only come from within. He began to worry about members of his expedition publicising what was really going on at Little America.

As Byrd brooded he became increasingly paranoid about the loyalty of his men. He made up lists of those he considered most loyal and least loyal. Byrd wanted the level of loyalty and secrecy that was promoted within the Masonic Lodge, but there were Masons at Little America, such as Bernt Balchen, whom he didn't trust. Byrd formed his own secret club, which he called his Loyal Legion, and would single out a potential inductee and talk to him privately. He would broach the subject of loyalty and ask the word of the potential inductee not to mention the conversation to anyone. When he was satisfied with the response, Byrd would invite the man to join the fraternity. If he agreed, Byrd would then have him recite an oath:

> I solemnly swear on my word of honour and by all that I reverence and hold sacred, and without hesitation or mental reservation, that I will divulge to no one in any way and in no manner anything in connection with the Loyal Legion . . .

The oath then went on to have the inductee swear not to learn the names of the other members, to follow Byrd's orders, and:

> . . . that in the case of disloyalty displayed in a crowd when you [Byrd] are present I will act in response to a predetermined signal and predetermined course of action . . . I will protect the expedition from [traitors] within.

For Byrd, reaching the South Pole was important, but returning to enhance his public image was more important. As pilot Dean Smith would later write:

A trained cinematographer, George Hubert Wilkins went on his first polar expedition in 1913. The expedition was a shambles, and created animosity that would later cause Wilkins to leave Australia permanently. (Byrd Polar Research Center)

Richard Evelyn Byrd as a young officer in the United States Navy. Repeatedly passed over for promotion, partly because of a foot injury, Byrd took to flying and saw aviation 'firsts' as a way of advancing his career. (BPRC)

Wilkins (right) at the Western Front in October 1918. He became the only official Australian photographer, in any war, to receive a combat decoration. The war made him determined to help raise humanity to a higher state of civilisation. (Australian War Memorial EO3915)

Byrd with one of the flying boats he took to Greenland in 1925, where his flights over the ice convinced him that planes were suitable for exploring the Arctic. Frustrated on this expedition, he resolved to be the first to fly to the North Pole. (BPRC)

The Italian-built airship *N1*, which Roald Amundsen renamed *Norge* (Norway). Repeated plane crashes had convinced the veteran polar explorer that an airship was the better way to reach the North Pole. (Topfoto/Austral)

Frustrated when Amundsen would not allow him to dock at the Kings Bay jetty, Byrd had the unassembled *Josephine Ford* loaded onto a makeshift raft and floated ashore. The watching Norwegians marvelled at the 'can-do' spirit of the Americans. (BPRC)

Once ashore, the *Josephine Ford* was quickly assembled and a runway stamped out on the ice. Unfortunately, the fully laden plane was too heavy for its skis and, as Amundsen's airship prepared to depart, Byrd was forced to seek help from the Norwegians. (BPRC)

The Fokker Trimotor that Wilkins named *Detroiter*. The first time the engines were started a reporter walked into one of the propellers. It is seen here after crashing on its maiden flight. The crew considered the plane jinxed, yet it would become one of the most successful planes in aviation history. (BPRC)

Wilkins' single-engine Fokker, *Alaskan*, at Barrow in 1926. Before it could be flown the engine had to be warmed under a canvas covering and the ice scraped from the wings. (BPRC)

Roald Amundsen (left) and Lincoln Ellsworth. Although he had been the first man to reach the South Pole, Amundsen was broke and needed Ellsworth's money to make what he called 'the big trip'. (Topfoto/Austral)

General Umberto Nobile. A bitter public dispute with Amundsen forced him to save face for Fascist Italy, but after another flight to the North Pole it all went horribly wrong for the proud Italian. (Granger Collection/Austral)

Bernt Balchen (left) and Byrd's North Pole pilot Floyd Bennett. The two became friends and Bennett encouraged Balchen to come to America. On his deathbed Bennett spoke to Balchen about the North Pole flight. (BPRC)

Famous aviators gather for a publicity photograph in 1928. Standing (left to right) are Carl 'Ben' Eielson, the newly-knighted Wilkins, Byrd, Clarence Chamberlain, who followed Lindbergh across the Atlantic Ocean, and Bernt Balchen. Sitting between Wilmer Stultz and Louis Gordon, the men who flew her across the Atlantic, is Amelia Earhart. (Hatton Eielson Museum)

Wilkins sits atop his Lockheed Vega. The streamlined design and light weight were revolutionary in 1928, allowing the plane to fly faster and further than the heavier, bulkier Fokkers and metal-bodied Ford Trimotors. (BPRC)

Eielson (left) and Wilkins pose in front of the Lockheed Vega they flew across the Arctic Ocean. Although comfortable using a camera, Wilkins was rarely comfortable in front of one. Here he stands stiffly, looking off into the distance. (BPRC)

When Wilkins announced a submarine would be more suitable for reaching the North Pole, his planned expedition became a celebrity event. Walt Disney drew a cartoon showing Mickey Mouse setting off for the Pole in a submarine. (BPRC)

Byrd's massive metal-bodied Ford Trimotor is unloaded at his Antarctic base, Little America. (BPRC)

Aged nearly 70, on his last trip to Antarctica, Wilkins flies a small Australian flag while drinking a Ballarat Bitter with a penguin. Shortly after, he was told he had to leave Antarctica. (Davies Family)

Suzanne and Wilkins, taken some time in the early 1930s. The marriage lasted almost thirty years. Suzanne was content to pursue her singing career while Wilkins travelled the world. The pair never lived together for more than a few weeks at a time. (BPRC)

Byrd (left) and Bernt Balchen, when they last met in 1953. At the meeting the two men got into a noisy argument, which was reported in the press. Byrd's supporters would later claim that Balchen was prejudiced against Byrd and fabricated details of the *Josephine Ford*'s flying capabilities. (BPRC)

The Byrd expedition was not a scientific knowledge-seeking effort such as we have come to expect of a government agency or one of our non-profit foundations. It was a business enterprise, a private venture promoted, organised, and operated by Commander Byrd for his own objectives. To be sure, some of these objectives were scientific ... but such purposes were subordinate to the factors of dramatic publicity and commercial success.

The expedition was Byrd's own show: he was producer, director and star. For him to realise the maximum profit from this show, and for him to have the following that would enable him to stage subsequent productions and star in them too, it was important that he be constantly brought before the public's eye in a manner befitting his role and with care that no one steal his scenes.

Byrd's Loyal Legion was a way of ensuring that the enormous commercial investment he was making in his public image and celebrity would be protected. Bernt Balchen, despite being a Mason himself, was never invited to join.

Even though he was wintering at the bottom of the world, Byrd could continue to build his celebrity through the pioneering use of radio. Morse code was sent and received daily, and once a week Little America enjoyed the luxury of receiving voice transmissions. Every Saturday at four pm the men would assemble in the mess room and listen to the crackling sound coming out of the loudspeakers. The programs were beamed to them by General Electric's station WGY in Schenectady and Westinghouse's KDKA in Pittsburgh. The stations produced the programs for Little America on alternate weeks, and the programs were also broadcast to the general public in 'big America'.

Sometimes the transmissions were hard to hear at Little America, and music never came through very well, but each week the men would gather together and listen to guests and news from home. Celebrities regularly came on the programs and sent greetings to the isolated crew. Harpo Marx, the mime who never spoke in his regular appearances in the Marx Brothers' movies, broke his silence to speak to the men. And relatives would also send personal greetings. More than any other single factor, the radio broadcasts kept up spirits and morale throughout the winter.

But all that changed in early September when an unexpected voice crackled through the loudspeakers: 'Hello, Little America, this is Sir Hubert Wilkins.'

Byrd listened in stunned silence as his rival explained that he had decided to return to Antarctica this season and was planning to fly across the continent. What's more, the Australian cheekily invited himself to Christmas dinner at Little America. Byrd's paranoia now turned to rage. Wilkins was returning south and Byrd was in a race once again.

* * *

After his pioneering flights in the Antarctic, Wilkins and his small crew had returned to the United States. Wilkins said goodbye to Ben Eielson, who wanted to go to Alaska and establish Alaskan Airways. Wilkins also wanted to return to the Arctic, but now had his sights firmly set on submarine travel. In New York he approached the pioneer submarine builder Simon Lake.

Lake had built his first crude wooden submarine in 1894, before following it up with a larger one in 1897. He then began designing his Protector class. These impressed people of the period, with features such as large wooden wheels for rolling along the seabed and 'keel drop weights', whereby heavy weights were lowered to the seabed and the submarine's depth altered by hauling in or letting out the cables attached to them. Lake sold five Protector-class submarines to Russia in 1904 but the design was quickly superseded. As with the aeroplane, submarine design advanced greatly during World War One. But that didn't stop Lake trotting out the Protector design when Wilkins came calling. Lake still owned a twenty-three-year-old Protector, which he promptly named *Defender* and offered to Wilkins. What's more, the publicity-seeking Lake immediately went into print with the plan for the voyage:

> This little submarine with the incurably Jules Vernean air, immersed in the Stygian gloom beneath the icy crust of the Arctic Sea, is the 93 ft *Defender* designed by Simon Lake, actually rebuilt from a boat of 1906 ... This is the boat in which Sir Hubert Wilkins ... and a 'private and competent crew of ten volunteers' provided by the Lake Torpedo Boat Company, proposes to voyage 2,000 miles beneath the ice of the Arctic Sea in crossing the Pole from Spitsbergen to Alaska.

Wilkins seemed unimpressed with the boat but was content to let Lake, the submarine expert, look after it while he drummed up sponsorship for the expedition. His first stop was the Hearst Organisation.

In New York, Hearst had a proposition for his polar explorer. Hearst was sponsoring the German airship, the *Graf Zeppelin*, on a round-the-world flight. Would Wilkins care to go along and report on the flight for the Hearst papers?

It was a project, and an opportunity, that appealed to Wilkins. A cosmopolitan group of international celebrities and specialists, floating peacefully across boundaries as it linked the world and demonstrated mankind's inventive spirit and ability to master the elements – all taking place in a German airship barely a decade after mankind had come close to destroying itself on the battlefield. The *Graf Zeppelin* flight sat neatly with Wilkins' emerging ideas on the future of humanity.

Wilkins travelled to Germany, where he joined the other passengers for the flight. It did not get off to a good start. The airship lifted off from its base in Friedrichschafen, Germany, and headed west to cross the Atlantic. Engine problems set in almost immediately and the *Graf Zeppelin* was forced to land in France. The French, still with memories of the Great War, and always wary of the Germans, surrounded the airship and placed everyone under guard. Wilkins managed to slip away and write some copy for the Hearst newspapers, before learning that the *Graf Zeppelin* would return to Germany to have its engines completely overhauled. With time on his hands, Wilkins travelled to London to visit friends.

In London he received a telegram from Suzanne Bennett. She had been hospitalised in New York and Wilkins immediately travelled there to visit her. The reason for her hospitalisation is unknown, but when Wilkins returned to Europe to rejoin the *Graf Zeppelin* he left behind a promise that, at the completion of the flight, he would marry Suzanne.

On 31 July 1929, the *Graf Zeppelin* again left Friedrichschafen. This time it flew successfully to Lakehurst, New York, before continuing on its round-the-world flight. Its group of international celebrities were accommodated in style: not cramped in a small, flimsy aeroplane, but sitting and sleeping in comfort, drinking fine wine, eating fine food and listening to music.

On the journey Wilkins had time for lengthy discussions with the airship's builder, Dr Hugo Eckener, and the two became friends. They discussed Arctic travel and Wilkins' planned submarine voyage. Hearst had sponsored both men and the two hit upon the idea of a rendezvous between Wilkins' submarine and the *Graf Zeppelin* at the North Pole. The submarine could drill a hole in the ice and surface, the airship could descend and they could exchange passengers and mail. What headlines that would make! After the round-the-world flight concluded, the two men pitched the idea to Hearst and Hearst bought it.

But while the submarine was being made ready by Lake and the *Graf Zeppelin* was fulfilling other duties, Hearst proposed that Wilkins still had time to return to Antarctica and beat Byrd to the South Pole. A quick calculation showed Wilkins that he could go south, fly across Antarctica, then return in time to take his submarine to the North Pole. Further mapping of Antarctica to help locate sites for meteorological stations, plus proving that submarines were the ideal way to travel in the Arctic – all in the space of a couple of years. Humanity would be well served.

By the time Wilkins had returned to New York, Suzanne had made a full recovery from her ailment and, in keeping with his promise, Wilkins married her on 30 August 1929. By all accounts it was not an unhappy marriage in its early years. The two, even though they lived separately, were often together at social functions. By and large, Suzanne pursued her acting and singing career, while Wilkins continued to explore the polar regions.

However, it is clear that Suzanne began exerting her influence over Wilkins from the outset. Almost from the time of their first meeting, she was referring to him as 'Sir Hubert' rather than 'Sir George' because she felt it sounded more dignified. Wilkins, who had for over forty years been known as George, Captain George or, more recently, Sir George, now asked people to call him Sir Hubert. The name change, in a small way, contributed to confusing his place in history. Even today, newly published books, when referring to his photographic work in World War One, will mention Hubert Wilkins on one page and George Wilkins on another.

* * *

Byrd's plan to reach the South Pole was modelled on that of Amundsen eighteen years earlier. Like Byrd, Amundsen had used the first summer to establish his base, then wintered over so that he could start early in the spring. Byrd had made his base at the same place as Amundsen and planned to follow the same route to the Pole: first across the Ross Ice Shelf to the Queen Maud Mountains, up Axel Heiberg Glacier to the 10,000-foot (3000-metre) plateau, then straight to the South Pole. Like Amundsen, Byrd would have dog teams lay depots of supplies along the route before the final dash to the Pole. Only in the final climatic dash for the Pole would Byrd's plan differ from Amundsen's. Amundsen had used skis, sledges and dogs. Byrd would use the Ford Trimotor.

After arriving at the place he named Framheim on 14 January 1911, Amundsen had unloaded his ship and erected his hut within thirteen days. In three sledge journeys covering up to fifty miles per day, the Norwegians established depots with three tonnes of supplies along the route to the South Pole. The farthest depot was 280 miles away. Amundsen and his men then settled down to wait out the winter and, in the spring, get the jump on Robert Falcon Scott. Not knowing Scott's progress, Amundsen had been anxious to start as early as possible. Now, eighteen years later, with Wilkins returning to the Antarctic, so was Richard Evelyn Byrd.

In the first summer Byrd's sledge teams had not been as productive as Amundsen's. Two attempts had got a small amount of supplies just forty-four miles from Little America. It was over 400 miles across the ice to the foot of the mountains, and 400 miles more to the Pole. Worse, Byrd had already lost one of his backup planes. Now, after waiting out the winter and then hearing Wilkins' voice crackle through the loudspeakers in the mess room, Byrd was almost beside himself with anxiety. The Ford Trimotor could not fly all the way to the South Pole and back without landing to refuel, so a cache had to be laid at the foot of the Queen Maud Mountains. And the Ford had still not been flown in the Antarctic and would need at least two shakedown flights to test it and measure its fuel consumption.

Byrd knew he had to get his sledge parties out on the trail, and began urging them to be prepared to leave in early October. Malcolm Hanson had been making special radios for the sledge teams, but it was taking longer than expected and Byrd became increasingly terse with him. When the planned departure date of 7 October arrived and the radios were still not ready, Byrd was livid. On the same day, the canvas bags used to carry supplies on the sledges were found to be rotten and had to be remade. Poor weather set in and the temperature dropped. The sledge parties argued that it was too early to leave, but Byrd persistently forced the issue until they set off on 13 October. They returned the same day, saying the sledges wouldn't pull over such dry, sand-like ice in the cold weather. Byrd relented and told them to wait for warmer weather. But his mood became colder.

The sledge parties left again two days later, but they radioed on the first night that they had only travelled a few miles from

Little America before making camp. Another sledge party left on 20 October and eight days later reported that they had only travelled 110 miles. Meanwhile, the first sledging party had been slowed down by dangerous crevices. At this rate it would be weeks before either party could get the necessary fuel supplies to the base of the Queen Maud Mountains.

Byrd had no choice but to risk the Ford Trimotor to lay the fuel depot. The big plane was prepared and taken up for a test flight on 14 November. Four days later it set out on the depot-laying flight. Dean Smith was pilot and Harold June was co-pilot. McKinley was aerial photographer and Byrd navigator. The flight to the Queen Maud Mountains would also be used to check out the plane's cruising speed and fuel consumption. Shortly after take-off, Smith and June, sitting beside each other at the dual controls, noticed that the tachometer for the centre engine was not working. They would not be able to control the speed of the engine accurately, and therefore could not control its fuel consumption. They decided not to tell Byrd.

The plane flew out over the ice, following the trail set by the sledging parties. After four hours in the air they sighted the Queen Maud Mountains. Smith identified what he thought was the Axel Heiberg Glacier, which Amundsen had used to reach the plateau. He flew around, headed the Ford into the wind and masterfully landed the big plane on skis. The fuel was quickly stowed and the depot marked with flags while the engines were kept running. Byrd wrote that he confirmed his position with several sextant sights of the sun:

> Smith remained in the cockpit, carefully nursing the engines, while June, McKinley and I prepared the depot. I paused long enough to take several sights of the sun, which gave us a longitude line on the chart and indicated that we were

about where we thought we were. That done I pitched in and helped the others unload.

Byrd now made a strange decision, given the circumstances. He ordered the plane to fly east over Marie Byrd Land before returning. Perhaps he now wanted to see the land he had named after his wife, not for the second time but the first. In any event, he was denied the chance. Harold June reported that the long dipstick showed they were burning fuel faster than expected and barely had enough to get home. Neither pilot nor co-pilot had yet told Byrd about the broken tachometer. Reluctantly, Byrd conceded that they must head straight for Little America. On the flight back Smith and June realised they were not going to make it. Still neither man reported it to Byrd. Nor did June, who was also operating the radio, report anything wrong to Little America. Still 130 miles out, the central engine of the Ford began to splutter.

Back at Little America the radio operator listening to the transmission suddenly heard it go dead. The man in command of Little America – and now, with the loss of radio contact, of the entire expedition – was William C. Haines, a meteorologist. Haines was, in fact, the fourth-in-command of the expedition but the first and third, Byrd and McKinley, were on board the now silent Ford. The second, Larry Gould, was in one of the sledging parties. The decision about what to do was up to Haines. He waited three hours to ensure the Ford's radio simply hadn't stopped working, then ordered Bernt Balchen and Carl Petersen to load some spare fuel into the Fairchild and go to look for them. Balchen and Petersen took off in the Fairchild at ten pm and an hour later radioed that they could see the downed Ford and that they were going to land near it.

Once on the ground Balchen and Petersen found the four crew members of the Ford and learnt what had happened. When the central engine had begun to splutter, June, who was operating the radio, immediately stopped what he was doing and cut the two outboard engines. Then he quickly began to pump the outboard engine fuel to the tank of the spluttering central engine. As the backup pilot, and a man who had flown the Ford Trimotor, June knew instantly that Smith's only chance of landing the big plane was using the central engine, as the two outboard engines provided auxiliary power only. The Ford had dropped 400 feet before the central engine picked up and ran smoothly. Smith now headed on grimly, flying the Ford on the centre engine only, determined to get as close to Little America as possible. They travelled another thirty miles before the plane was completely out of fuel. Against the odds, Smith achieved a 'dead stick landing' on the unknown ice surface.

The four men had clambered out; Smith, June and McKinley immediately beginning the messy job of draining the engine oil before it froze. According to Smith, Byrd had set up his tent, crawled into his sleeping bag and gone to sleep. Four hours later, Balchen and Petersen arrived in the Fairchild. They unloaded 100 gallons of fuel and helped pour it into the Ford. Byrd was still not in good humour. Once the big plane was fuelled, Byrd ordered Balchen and Peterson to return to Little America in the Fairchild. It was a brash thing to do, given that the engines of the Ford had to be turned by hand to be started.

Smith, June and McKinley began the dirty job of putting the oil back in, then attempted to start the engines by swinging the propellers manually. Byrd excused himself from this duty, citing a bad back. After repeated tries, Smith, June and McKinley conceded they couldn't start the engines, drained the oil again and waited for help to return from Little America.

Smith later wrote that they would have started the engines had Byrd helped with the swinging of the propellers.

Now they had to wait for Balchen and Petersen to come and assist them a second time. The pair returned a few hours later and Balchen adjusted the engine settings. They got the engines going and this time waited for the Ford to climb safely into the air before they climbed into the Fairchild and followed it back to Little America.

The next day Byrd seemed in even worse humour. He took Balchen for a walk and asked him why the Ford had not been able to reach the Queen Maud Mountains and back, a total distance of only 800 miles. Balchen wrote:

Next morning I am the one that Byrd takes for one of his little walks. He is still brooding about last night, I can see, and he curtly demands to know why their fuel consumption was higher than expected. I reply that I cannot give the answer right now but I suspect the pilot did not lean his mixture properly. 'I'll go over the whole engine installation thoroughly,' I promise him, 'to make sure my figures are right.' I take out of my pocket my little slide rule, the same one I used in crossing the Atlantic. 'I've been keeping very careful figures on mileage and fuel consumption, just as I did on the *Josephine Ford* and *America* ...'

He interrupts, his eyes full of cold fire. 'Forget about that slide rule. From now on, you stick to flying. I'll do the figuring.'

I do not know what I have said to make him so angry, so I do not say anything more. He keeps on walking ... He whirls on me: 'How is it you always manage to do the right thing?' he accuses. 'Why do I always have to come back to you?'

I have no answer, because it is hard to understand why it is wrong to do something right. What he says next is even harder to understand.

'I made up my mind a long time ago you'd never be my pilot,' he says in irritation. 'But now I have no choice. You will fly to the South Pole with me.'

Of course, Byrd did have a choice. Dean Smith had long been considered the leading pilot of the group and the man expected to make the flight to the South Pole. His handling of the big Ford at the foot of the Queen Maud Mountains and the later dead stick landing had been impeccable. But now, somehow a reminder of the North Pole flight and Balchen waving his slide rule in front of Byrd's face had left Byrd with 'no choice'. Bernt Balchen would be the pilot for the South Pole flight.

Byrd began preparation for another base-laying flight. A few days later, news came by radio that made him change his plans yet again. Sir Hubert Wilkins had just made his first flights of the season in the Antarctic.

15

Where Amundsen Stood

Wilkins had headed for Antarctica in the southern summer of 1929 without Ben Eielson. His friend, with whom he had shared so many adventures, had finally been persuaded by his family to stop the dangerous work of piloting planes over the unexplored regions of the world. Instead, Eielson had chosen to turn his attention to his dream of establishing Alaskan Airways. In early October Eielson had received an offer that would help fund his new venture. A ship belonging to the Swenson Fur Trading Company was frozen in at North Cape, Siberia, with fifteen people and a valuable cargo of furs on board. Eielson had been offered $50,000 to bring the people and the cargo back to Alaska. So, on 9 November, while Wilkins was establishing himself at Deception Island in Antarctica, Eielson took off from Nome, Alaska, with mechanic Earl Borland, to fly across the Bering Strait. They crashed, and the wreckage of their plane, along with their bodies, was not found until two months later.

In Antarctica, radio messages informed Wilkins of Eielson's disappearance and the subsequent search, but there was nothing he could do as he prepared for his flights at the other end of the globe. He later wrote:

Eielson and I together had seen, in the North and in the South, more than half a million square miles of the earth's surface that no other human eyes had ever seen. We had flown five thousand miles on a straight line over unknown coastlines and seas and had added literally hundreds of terrain features to the charts and maps of the known world.

None of these would have been known so soon but for Ben Eielson's superb mastery of his job, his cool head, and his gallant spirit. He was a splendid companion, as well as an expert pilot, whose personality had helped me as much as his professional skill. Eielson will live in exploring history as long as men fly over the earth. Typically, he died while trying to effect the rescue of a fur-trading ship caught in the ice. His death was a great loss to aviation and to everyone who knew him. It was a great loss to me.

Wilkins continued with his preparations. He had brought a small tractor so that, if necessary, he could bulldoze a runway on Deception Island. He also had support from the British government, which had provided £10,000 and arranged the loan of the Discovery Committee ship, the *William Scoresby*. If he was unable to take off from Deception Island, then the ship would meet him there and take him, with his planes and crew, west along the unexplored coast so that he could locate suitable take off points. With two new pilots, Al Cheesman and Parker Kramer, along with a small support crew, Wilkins arrived at Deception Island on 1 November. He wrote:

When I left Montevideo with the whalers, aboard the *Hectoria* again, I was hoping to find normal weather in the Antarctic, with ice solid enough to serve as a landing field for the planes, but as we approached Deception Island we saw no sign of ice at all. The previous year had been unaccountably warm, yet we had encountered pack ice three hundred miles north of Deception. Now the sea was open and the ice in the harbour even thinner than in 1928.

We were amazed to find the edge of the pack lay as much as three hundred miles south of the island. The continuing warmth had now melted the floating bits and the great mass of ice at the South Pole was still diminishing in size.

For Wilkins, with his focus on the possibility of long-range weather forecasting, the phenomenon took on more importance than his ability to get airborne.

Thinking back on it later, I believed that this unusual phenomenon may have had a long-range effect on climatic conditions throughout the world, or may have been somehow related to them. This six hundred mile retreat of the ice in the Antarctic summer of 1929–30 was followed by the memorable drought in the [northern] summer of 1930, during which many parts of the United States, for example, saw the ground turn as dry and hard as any season in memory.

At Deception Island the two Lockheed Vegas, which had been left there the year before, were not even covered with snow. The mechanics soon had them ready for flying. The small tractor/bulldozer, which had been brought along to help make a runway on Deception Island, made little impact on the exposed basalt rock. Wilkins' only chance to make a long-distance flight was to wait for the *William Scoresby* to arrive and take him and the planes further west, in the hope of finding suitable flat snow on which to take off. While he waited he made short exploratory flights from the rough airfield he had built the previous year. The news was radioed to the Hearst Organisation and relayed to Little America on 19 November 1929. The main result was to spur Byrd on to reach the South Pole as quickly as he could.

* * *

On hearing the news Byrd announced that there would be no more shakedown flights. 'Don't forget that Wilkins is out to beat us,' he told his men.

Although the ground support party had still not reached the base of the Queen Maud Mountains, Byrd decided that as soon as the weather was favourable he would fly direct to the South Pole. The change of plans was not radioed to the ground party for fear that Wilkins would eavesdrop on the transmission and take off for the Pole immediately. Byrd would write in his log:

In its 10 o'clock report the Geological Party says the weather continues unchanged – 'excellent'.

Haines is making the charts. He believes that within another ten or fifteen hours we shall have the weather we want.

It would be asking too much to demand perfect weather throughout the flight. A south wind, for example, which generally brings clear skies, must of necessity be a head wind on the outward trip, when the Ford would be carrying its heaviest loads. But a north wind, which might provide a very helpful boost, unfortunately brings as a rule clouds formed by the condensation of the warmer air from the water as it strikes the Barrier.

Byrd knew that the flight to the South Pole would be particularly hazardous. The return trip was 1600 miles. The distance was not a great deal longer than the North Pole flight, but was complicated by the fact that after flying 400 miles from Little America, across the Ice Barrier, the plane then had to climb over 10,000 feet (3000 metres) to clear the Queen Maud Mountains. At the North Pole is a deep ocean covered with a thin crust of ice. The South Pole, on the other hand, sits in the middle of a land mass and 10,000 feet above sea level. Climbing to that height, with the plane almost fully laden, would be no easy matter.

At noon on 28 November, Larry Gould, now near the foot of the mountains, radioed that the clouds were beginning to clear. It was as good as Byrd could expect, so it was time to go. Balchen would be pilot, Harold June would be co-pilot and radio operator, McKinley would come along as aerial photographer and Byrd would be navigator. At 3.29 pm the Ford Trimotor, which Byrd had named the *Floyd Bennett*, lifted smoothly into the air to the cheers of every man on the ground at Little America. The plane circled once and headed south, following the ground trail and overflying Gould's party waiting faithfully at the 7th Depot. Then in front of them appeared the Queen Maud Mountains. A decision now had to be made as to which route to take to reach the plateau beyond. Byrd would write:

> At 9:15 o'clock we had the eastern portal on our left, and were ready to tackle the Hump. We had discussed the Hump so often, had anticipated and maligned it so much, that now that it was in front of us and waiting in the flesh – in rock ribbed glaciated reality – we felt that we were meeting an

old acquaintance. But we approached it warily, respectfully, climbing steadily all the while ...

I stood beside Balchen, carefully studying the looming fortress, still wondering by what means we should attempt to carry it. In the end we decided to choose Liv's Glacier, the unknown pass to the right, which Amundsen had seen far in the distance and named after Dr Nansen's daughter. It seemed to be wider than Axel Heiberg, and the pass not quite as high.

The flight south was, according to Byrd, carefully managed and calmly carried out. In his account, Byrd, as always, orchestrated the affairs, made the decisions and issued the orders to men who were grateful to receive his guidance and instruction. Bernt Balchen left a different version. When Balchen was interviewed by author Richard Montague in 1970, he claimed that Byrd didn't know where he was and was drunk for a great deal of the flight. In fairness to Byrd, Balchen's claims were made after Byrd was dead and Balchen had become bitter towards him. However, Balchen also told Montague that the preparation and early stages of the flight were confused and disorganised. Apparently, at the last moment before taking off, Byrd had suddenly ordered an extra 250 pounds of supplies to be loaded aboard. Now, as Balchen struggled to hold the plane and get it to fly up the Liv Glacier, he was constantly shouting at Byrd to throw unnecessary weight overboard. Byrd finally complied.

The flight up the Liv Glacier was fraught with danger and perhaps the most difficult flying episode that Byrd had ever undertaken. Balchen wrestled the controls to continually gain altitude while the swirling winds buffeted the plane. After some of the supplies were thrown out the big Ford crept up a few hundred feet in altitude, but still the glacier rose in front of them. Balchen wrote:

> The Liv Glacier is like a great frozen waterfall, halted
> in the midst of its tumbling cascade and immobilized
> for all eternity. Sheer cliffs rise above us on either side,
> and the canyon narrows as we wind our way upward. A
> cataract of ice looms ahead, and there is no room to turn
> around now.
>
> A final icy wall blocks our way, steeper than all the
> others. A torrent of air is pouring over its top, the plane
> bucking violently in the downdraft, and our rate of climb is
> zero. June jettisons the second sack, and the Ford staggers
> a little higher, but still not enough. There is only one thing
> left to try. Perhaps at the very edge of the downdraft is a
> reverse current of air, like a back-eddy along the bank of a
> rushing river, that will carry us upstream and over. I inch
> my way to the side of the canyon, our right wing almost
> scraping the cliff, and all at once we are wrenched upward,
> shooting out of the maelstrom of wind, and soar over the
> summit with a couple of hundred feet to spare.

Byrd would write that his navigation was calm, constant and competent. He continually knelt and checked the ground speed and drift indicator, took his sextant readings and compared them with his dead reckoning. Although Balchen would write that after they had cleared the Liv Glacier and reached the plateau he received no instructions from his navigator, Byrd has told a different story. According to Byrd:

> Whenever I noted any change in the direction or strength
> of the wind, I would steady Balchen on his course with the

sun compass, first shaking the trolley line to attract his
attention, then waving him on the new course.

So the Pole, the mysterious objective, was actually
in sight. But I could not spare it so much as a glance.
Chronometers, drift indicators and compasses are hard
taskmasters.

At six minutes after one o'clock, a sight of the sun
put us a few miles ahead of our dead reckoning position.
We were very close now. The sight was a check, but I
depended more on the previous sight. At 1:14 o'clock,
Greenwich Civil Time, our calculations showed that we
were at the Pole.

Balchen explains it with less emphasis on Byrd's navigation
and instead implies that it was his dead reckoning that found
the Pole:

The right engine backfires, and misses a couple of beats,
and June reaches for the dump valve again. At our altitude
of 11,000 feet, two engines could never keep the Ford
airborne. I figure that I may have leaned the mixture a little
too thin, and adjust it just a fraction. The right outboard
picks up and runs smoothly once more.

According to my dead reckoning, we should be at the
Pole in another fourteen minutes. Our position is Lat.
89 degrees 40' S., about twenty miles away, so our goal
must actually be in sight at this moment. I send a message
back to Byrd on the trolley cable that connects the cockpit
with the navigator's compartment. Fourteen minutes later,
at 1:14 in the morning, Byrd sends a message forward on
the trolley for June to broadcast to the base:
'We have reached the South Pole.'

The Ford Trimotor circled the South Pole and headed north. Byrd wrote:

> For a few seconds we stood over the spot where Amundsen had stood, December 14, 1911; and where Scott had also stood, 34 days later, reading the note which Amundsen had left for him. In their honor, the flags of their countries were again carried over the Pole.

The *Floyd Bennett* now headed north to descend the Axel Heiberg Glacier and find the depot of fuel laid at its foot. According to Balchen, as soon as they had turned their backs to the Pole, Byrd started hitting the cognac. When the Ford descended the glacier the pilots could find no sign of the vital fuel depot that had been flown there just two weeks earlier. Smith and June had been pilots on that flight and Smith later claimed that he had received no navigational instructions from Byrd, and that he had picked out what he thought was the Axel Heiberg Glacier, based on Amundsen's descriptions. When they had landed at the foot of the glacier Byrd had got out and, standing on firm ground, taken his sextant readings of the location of the depot and had agreed that they were where they ought to be.

Now, a fortnight later, Balchen and June were unable to locate the depot. As June had been on the previous flight, Balchen handed him the controls so that he could fly around and attempt to recognise the terrain. It was a critical period: without the depot the men would be stranded some 400 miles from Little America without fuel. Fortunately, as they flew west June saw the depot. It had been mistakenly laid at the foot of the Liv Glacier, approximately fifty miles from where it was supposed to be. Byrd's navigation had proven inaccurate again.

According to Byrd:

> The skis touched the surface at 4:47 o'clock. Taking the
> fuel aboard was quite a problem. Each can had to be broken
> open and poured, one by one, into the wing tanks, and
> we soon tired of lifting them to June, who was doing the
> pouring. It was six o'clock before we rose from the Barrier,
> and headed north on the last leg of the flight.

According to Balchen, when they landed at the depot
Byrd whooped and hollered, 'We made it. We made it,' and
continued drinking, leaving the others to do the heavy lifting
of the fuel drums. He finished his supply of cognac and began
to sober up on the four-hour flight to Little America. But his
navigation remained in question, especially after his inability to
know the location of the fuel depot at the base of the Queen
Maud Mountains.

After the South Pole flight Byrd made only one more
long-range flight from Little America. On 5 December he told
pilots Parker and June to ready the Ford Trimotor, and at eleven
am the plane took off with the pilots, Byrd and photographer
McKinley on board. Without explanation, Byrd ordered June,
who was at the controls, to fly to Marie Byrd Land, perhaps
seeking again to view it for the first time. After successfully
sighting the land named for his wife, Byrd started to drink
brandy; by the time the plane returned to Little America he was
roaring drunk. This time various crew members noted in their
diaries how drunk their commander was. Byrd was carried to
his bunk and, despite there being some two to three months of
fine weather still ahead, the season's flying was over.

Back in big America a special bill was rushed through
Congress, promoting Byrd to Rear Admiral. In six years the

polar aviator had risen from Lieutenant to Admiral purely on political promotion.

* * *

After the arrival of the *William Scoresby*, Wilkins loaded his planes on board and, with his crew, sailed south along the west coast of Graham Land to Port Lockroy. From here, on 19 December, he made his first major flight of the season, taking off from the harbour with floats fitted to the plane. He crossed Graham Land and explored the east side for landing fields. A week later the *William Scoresby* sailed further south and Wilkins explored Charcot Land.

With the weather deteriorating, the *William Scoresby* sailed farther west and further flights were made of previously unexplored areas of the coast. But poor weather and the inability to find suitable areas to take off on skis again prevented the trans-Antarctic flight. Frustrated, Wilkins called an end to the season's flying. Nevertheless, he had learnt a great deal about the previously unknown areas east and west of Graham Land, and headed north with knowledge that would soon lead to the first crossing of Antarctica.

* * *

Having reached the South Pole, Byrd's main objective was to get back to America and reap the benefits of his enhanced status. Most of December was spent packing up and getting ready to leave when the ships arrived. The *City of New York* left Dunedin on 5 January and tied up against the ice on 18 February. Within twenty-four hours the men had loaded everything they were taking home and were ready to go.

The *City of New York* rendezvoused with the *Eleanor Bolling* and headed for New Zealand. On the way Byrd had all members of the expedition sign a new statement promising not to release photographs or be interviewed by reporters. He was determined to maintain control of his men and his public image back in civilisation.

Byrd was fairly sure that he had most of the crew under control, but he still had suspicions about pilot Dean Smith. It was well known that Smith had kept a detailed diary of the whole adventure. He had recorded the bad times as well as the good, including the drinking, squabbles and what he saw as Byrd's shortcomings. It was also known that Smith had been offered money for his story by the Hearst newspapers. Towards the end of their journey home, Smith discovered that his locker had been broken into and his diary stolen. He never saw it again. Fellow pilot Harold June later confessed that he had been ordered to take it and give it to Byrd.

After passing through the Panama Canal, the *City of New York* and the *Eleanor Bolling* reached New York on 19 June 1930. When Byrd stepped ashore he was treated to a ticker-tape parade – his second. A day later he and all the members of the expedition travelled by specially chartered train to Washington, where they were received at the White House by President Herbert Hoover. Banquets, honours and awards followed at an almost exhausting pace.

16

The Last Place Left to Explore

Wilkins and Byrd returned to a different world to the one they had left. It was a world firmly in the grip of the Great Depression, the worst and longest period of high unemployment and low business activity in the twentieth century. A time when millions of people in many countries were unemployed, and when industries and banks were closing.

Despite this, Wilkins was determined to realise his ambition of a submarine expedition to cross the Arctic Ocean. He was offered an O-class submarine by the US Navy which, despite being underpowered and outdated, was far superior to the wooden-wheeled Protector that Simon Lake had first proposed. William Randolph Hearst had promised additional funding if the submarine reached the North Pole and exchanged passengers and mail with the *Graf Zeppelin*, but Wilkins still needed money to get his expedition underway. He turned to Amundsen's former partner, Lincoln Ellsworth, whose enormous fortune had not been affected by the stock market crash. Ellsworth added his name and $70,000 to the expedition.

The Wilkins–Ellsworth Trans-Arctic Submarine Expedition was officially launched in New York on 24 March 1931. It was a celebrity event with film stars, politicians and dignitaries attending. Walt Disney even drew a cartoon of Mickey Mouse navigating his way through ice floes in a submarine and presented it to Wilkins. Aware of the importance of publicity to the Hearst organisation, Wilkins christened his submarine *Nautilus* after the boat in Jules Verne's novel *Twenty Thousand Leagues Under the Sea*. And he installed a small musical organ to play while travelling under the Arctic ice, just as the fictitious Captain Nemo had done.

The submarine left New York on 2 May. Constant problems had meant that Wilkins was getting away late, so the plan to cross the Arctic Ocean was reduced to reaching the North Pole and returning to Spitsbergen. On its voyage from New York to Europe the *Nautilus* continually broke down. Eventually, it sent out a distress signal and the battleship USS *Wyoming* met it mid-Atlantic and towed it to Ireland. It underwent repairs before limping its way north to Norway. By now, plans to rendezvous with the *Graf Zeppelin* had been abandoned, so Hugo Eckener took the big airship on a tour of the islands north of Russia instead.

Wilkins finally coaxed the submarine north to reach the ice pack on 22 August, where he discovered the bow planes used for diving had sheared off while pushing through the ice floes. The unwavering Wilkins urged his disgruntled crew onward and managed to make short excursions under the ice to prove it could be done. After fifteen days of edging around the ice pack and collecting scientific data, Wilkins returned to Norway. By this time the *Nautilus* was in such poor condition that it was not considered safe enough to sail back across the Atlantic. Instead it was scuttled in deep water off Bergen.

In recent times it has become popular to say the *Nautilus* was sabotaged – that the submarine expedition was to be Wilkins' crowning glory and the highlight of his career, but he was undone when the cowardly crew purposely destroyed the submarine's ability to dive. This is not true for three reasons. To cut the bow planes off underwater, the diver on the submarine – a man named Frank Crilley, who was a winner of the Congressional Medal of Honour – would have had to get into his deep-sea diving dress and go over the side. This is a three-person operation (the diver and two tenders). It would have been impossible to do this in secret on the small submarine, particularly because the diver would have needed to be in the water for a couple of hours to cut the bow planes with a hacksaw. Secondly, Wilkins, in the report he wrote at the time (as opposed to his semi-fictitious writing many years later), doesn't mention it. He writes at length about the attitude of the crew and details all the problems he had, but does not mention sabotage or the crew damaging the submarine on purpose in any way. If there had been sabotage he would certainly have brought it up in that detailed report. Thirdly, the last surviving crew member, Ray Drakea, laughed at the idea the submarine had been sabotaged. 'Weren't no sabotage,' he said in 1999. 'That submarine was just old and falling apart.'

Still, for many authors the story of sabotage makes better reading than admitting that Wilkins made poor choices, both in the submarine and the people entrusted to modify it for Arctic travel.

Wilkins' failure to reach the North Pole or rendezvous with the *Graf Zeppelin* meant the additional funding from the Hearst organisation was not forthcoming. This left the Wilkins–Ellsworth Trans-Arctic Submarine Expedition severely short of funds and unable to pay off the crew. Lincoln Ellsworth, who had never actually seen the submarine, loaned Wilkins $20,000 to clear the debt. The first attempt to reach the North Pole by submarine was over and Wilkins had lost all his money. What's more, he was now indebted to Lincoln Ellsworth.

Ellsworth still harboured the dream of seeing his name writ large in polar history books, but the opportunities for polar firsts were diminishing fast. Only one of any consequence seemed to be left. No one had yet crossed Antarctica, either on land or in the air. Shackleton had attempted it. Others, including Wilkins, had planned it. Plenty had talked about it. Now, in 1931, Lincoln Ellsworth dreamt it and backed his dream with his wealth. To repay his debt, Wilkins agreed to organise the first crossing of Antarctica, this time with Ellsworth sitting in the hero's seat. Wilkins organised the expedition ship, a former Norwegian whaler, and hired the best available polar pilot, Bernt Balchen. Balchen was sent off to see Jack Northrup, the designer of the Lockheed Vega, to get him to design a plane specifically for polar conditions. Ellsworth, for his part, went holidaying in Europe with his new bride. He also used the time to collect memorabilia associated with his hero, Wyatt Earp.

The expedition was ready by 1933 and travelled to Dunedin, in preparation for sailing south. Here Ellsworth joined the expedition, met most of the crew and saw his plane and expedition ship, which he named the *Wyatt Earp*, for the first time. Ellsworth, Wilkins, Balchen and the mostly Norwegian crew sailed to the Ross Sea, where they planned to set up a base near Byrd's Little America. Byrd had had more success taking off from this side of the continent than Wilkins had on the other, so basing themselves at the Ross Ice Shelf seemed the smart thing to do.

But there were no plans to winter over. They would get the *Wyatt Earp* next to the ice shelf, get the plane off and fly to Graham Land, then wait for the *Wyatt Earp* to sail around and pick them up. They could then leave with the job done. Balchen would be pilot and Ellsworth would navigate in the two-seater plane. Wilkins would be in command of the *Wyatt*

Earp and in no time he could be back up north, his debt to Ellsworth repaid, and able to get on with the job of finding a more reliable submarine. That, at least, was the plan.

The *Wyatt Earp* reached the Bay of Whales in the Ross Sea on 7 January 1934 and the plane, the *Polar Star*, was unloaded onto the ice. During the night of 12 January heavy seas pounded the ice, which started to crack. The *Polar Star* sank up to its wings and had to be taken back on board the *Wyatt Earp* with the undercarriage damaged. The Ellsworth Trans-Antarctic Expedition for 1933–1934 was over before it got off the ground. The expedition returned to New Zealand and Wilkins went to England to attempt to get the British Navy to loan him a submarine.

But Ellsworth still wanted to fly across Antarctica, so Wilkins agreed to come on a second expedition with him. Nine months later the *Wyatt Earp* headed south again. This time, however, Byrd was back at Little America, so Wilkins reversed the direction of the planned crossing, making the start from Graham Land.

On 14 October 1934 the *Wyatt Earp* arrived at the now abandoned whaling station on Deception Island. This early in the season, the snow was thick, as was the ice in the harbour. Ellsworth would not have the same difficulties getting his plane airborne. Two weeks after arriving, the *Polar Star* was unloaded, assembled and ready for Bernt Balchen to take it up for a test flight. When he tried to start the engine there was a loud crack, like a pistol shot, and the propeller stopped turning. Lubricating oil, placed in the cylinder to prevent corrosion during the sea voyage, had not been removed and when the engine was turned over a connecting rod had broken. Worse, it was discovered that no spare had been brought. A radio message was sent requesting a rod be flown to Chile's southernmost port, 900 miles from

Deception Island. On 31 October the *Wyatt Earp* set off to fetch it, returning three weeks later. But by now the snow had melted and the ice in the harbour was thinner.

Based on his previous experience, Wilkins wasn't about to go searching to the west. Instead he recommended that the *Polar Star* be loaded aboard the *Wyatt Earp* and the expedition sail east into the Weddell Sea. They reached Snow Hill Island, which they found suitable for a landing field, and waited for the weather to clear. They waited some four weeks, during which time Ellsworth sank into depression and considered abandoning the flight altogether. Wilkins radioed America seeking the funds to purchase the plane from Ellsworth and make the flight himself, but before he could get an answer the weather cleared. Ellsworth's spirits lifted and, on 3 January 1935, he and Balchen took off. They were in the air an hour when Balchen saw a towering white cloud bank that he judged to be too high to fly over. Not consulting Ellsworth he turned the plane around and flew back to Snow Hill Island. Ellsworth was extremely upset and stormed from the plane without speaking to anyone. His second expedition to the Antarctic was another non-event. The *Wyatt Earp* headed north again.

Ellsworth was keen for a third attempt, while Wilkins was keen to get on with his next submarine expedition but, as he wrote to a friend: 'I gave Ellsworth my word that I would help him do the job and a promise is a promise after all.'

Wilkins kept his word and sailed south with Ellsworth a third time, to land at Dundee Island, near the tip of Graham Land, on 18 November 1935. Bernt Balchen had been replaced as pilot by a quiet English-born Canadian, Herbert Hollick-Kenyon. Armed with Wyatt Earp's gun belt, which he intended to carry across the continent, Ellsworth climbed aboard the *Polar Star*. Hollick-Kenyon got the plane airborne and the pair flew for two hours before Hollick-Kenyon turned around due to a fuel leak. A day later they tried again and Hollick-Kenyon turned back because of bad weather. Ellsworth stormed from the plane without speaking and sulked in his quarters until Wilkins persuaded him to have another attempt.

This he did on 23 November. This time Hollick-Kenyon not only got the plane in the air successfully, but managed to keep it flying south along Graham Land and passing what Wilkins, in 1928, had named Hearst Land. The pair continued their flight across the continent, with Ellsworth alternating between writing poetry and naming the land and mountains he saw. After almost 14 hours in the air they should have been nearing Byrd's old base of Little America II (which had been established on Byrd's second expedition south) but nothing resembling Marie Byrd Land was coming into sight. Hollick-Kenyon and Ellsworth exchanged notes, with Ellsworth admitting that he had no idea where they were. Hollick-Kenyon landed the plane so they could take accurate sextant readings. On the ground Ellsworth took repeated readings and came up with wildly different positions. Having named the area James W. Ellsworth Land after his father, he and Hollick-Kenyon got back in the plane and headed in the direction they hoped would lead to Little America II. The *Polar Star* landed four more times and each time Ellsworth tried unsuccessfully to take sextant readings. Finally, Hollick-Kenyon discovered that the index mirror screw was not set properly and, after making adjustments, he roughly calculated their position.

By this time the *Polar Star* did not have sufficient fuel for another flight so Ellsworth and Hollick-Kenyon equipped themselves with provisions and walked out on sorties to find Byrd's old base. Ten days later they found an air vent protruding through the snow and dug down to Little America II. Inside they found food, fuel and books to read. They settled down to wait for the *Wyatt Earp*. The first crossing of the continent of Antarctica was successfully completed. Wilkins sailed the *Wyatt Earp* around to pick the pair up, then the whole expedition returned to the United States.

His promise kept, Wilkins again turned his attention to taking a submarine to the North Pole. While he was trying to raise money and support, he volunteered to search for some Russian aviators who had disappeared while flying across the Arctic.

Before he left to begin the search, Wilkins was approached by Harold Sherman, a writer specialising in exploring the metaphysical. Sherman believed the dead could communicate with the living and that mental telepathy was a fact waiting to be proven by science. Sherman proposed a scientific experiment to Wilkins. While Wilkins was in the Arctic, once a day, at a prearranged time, he was to stop what he was doing and focus his thoughts on what he saw in front of him or what situation faced him. At the same time, in his studio in New York, Sherman would concentrate and write down what mental impressions he received.

At first Wilkins didn't take the idea seriously. He kept a diary of his impressions but admitted he often forgot to concentrate his thoughts at the agreed time. Nevertheless, after the unsuccessful search for the Russian aviators, Wilkins returned and he and Sherman presented their notes and diaries to an independent third party. The results were astounding. Sherman often described, in minute detail, things that Wilkins had witnessed. The two men co-wrote a book detailing their experiment called *Thoughts Through Space*.

For Wilkins, the experiment opened up a whole new area of interest for his restless enquiring mind. If mankind could not live peaceably by sharing the food, land and resources of the planet, he reasoned, then perhaps humanity could raise itself to a higher state of civilisation by exploring the previously unexplored powers of the human mind.

Sherman now told Wilkins about another metaphysical project with which he was associated. A Dr William Sadler was channelling information from an unknown spiritual source. The information concerned everything anyone would wish to know about the origins of the universe and the evolutionary development of man. Importantly, the information being received (and carefully recorded) married known scientific fact with Christian belief. Certain life forms were allowed to evolve on the planet Earth (called Urantia) before Adam and Eve were despatched to begin a colony here. Wilkins became absorbed in the work of Dr William Sadler and regularly studied transcripts. Later, after many years of channelling, Wilkins contributed money to the publication of the Urantia Book. From the time of its publication until his death, he carried a copy of the 2000-page book wherever he went.

After the failed search for the Russian aviators, Wilkins realised his chances of getting a submarine for another Arctic expedition were remote. The storm clouds of war were gathering over Europe and governments were not selling or loaning their submarines. Nor was anyone interested in sponsoring him.

Wilkins was approaching his fiftieth birthday and, since leaving Australia almost thirty years earlier, he had never owned a home or lived in one place for more than a few weeks. Suzanne and he had been married for nine years, and the singer and actress, twenty years his junior, was now regularly seeing other men. Wilkins decided it was time they should both go home to Australia. He just needed something to occupy his restless mind.

The Australian government was showing interest in setting up Antarctic bases, so Wilkins hit upon the idea of having himself put in charge of the program. He knew he would be up against his old adversary, Sir Douglas Mawson, so he devised a cunning plan to get the government to back him. First he had to convince the Australian government that the Americans were intent on claiming Australian Antarctic territory. To do this, he had the *Wyatt Earp* refitted to make it more comfortable. Then, appealing to Lincoln Ellsworth's vanity – never a difficult thing to do – he convinced the American to sail south one more time in order to explore more of the frozen continent. Wilkins and Suzanne travelled by passenger liner to Australia, where they met up with Ellsworth. A crew sailed the *Wyatt Earp* there. Then, taking a small plane on board, Wilkins and Ellsworth sailed to the Antarctic coast, smack in the middle of the Australian territorial claim. Ellsworth and a pilot made a flight directly inland, with Ellsworth busily dropping steel canisters claiming the land for the United States. Wilkins radioed the Australian government, saying it needed to set up manned stations in the area to counter the claim. Even better, Wilkins went on, he had negotiated to buy the *Wyatt Earp* and all its equipment from Ellsworth. Here was the complete package; the ship, the equipment and the man to head it all. The plan certainly got the attention of the government. Wilkins and Ellsworth returned to Australia and the pair met with Mawson.

Mawson, who had the ear of the government, and who never missed an opportunity to call Wilkins a showman and his expeditions 'stunts', delivered the verdict. Yes, the government would buy the *Wyatt Earp* and the equipment to set up the bases along the coast. But it would be Mawson, not Wilkins, who would head the whole operation. Wilkins was devastated. Ever since he had stepped off the *Karluk* with Stefansson in

1913, a decision that led to the death of one of Mawson's friends, Australia's two greatest polar explorers had been bitter rivals. Now, with Australia about to undertake a long-term program of Antarctic research, Mawson had shut the door in Wilkins' face permanently.

Wilkins left Australia in 1939 and vowed never to return. Except for a brief stopover when he was travelling on a US Navy ship – when he had no say in the matter – he never did.

Wilkins had only been back in America a short time when Germany invaded Poland and World War Two began. He offered his services to the Australian government, but Australia, which had automatically followed Britain into the war, had little need for a fifty-something polar explorer. Wilkins then began working for America as a consultant on survival in polar conditions. In 1942 he became attached to the Quartermaster Corps of the US Army and when, after the war, the research functions of the corps were moved to Natick, Massachusetts, Wilkins followed. Having never owned property in his life, the continuously wandering Wilkins simply rented a hotel room at the nearby Park Central Hotel, Framingham.

Knowing that she would now live permanently in America, Suzanne bought a farmhouse near Montrose, Pennsylvania, in 1940 and divided her time between there and her apartment in New York. The large house became the repository for Wilkins' lifetime collection of films, photographs, correspondence, artefacts and journals. He bought a 1939 Chevrolet station wagon and would regularly drive out to visit Suzanne and leave more of his material at the farmhouse. In the meantime, Suzanne became the companion of Winston Ross, a singer that she and Wilkins had heard at a New York nightclub. Ross eventually moved to the farmhouse to live permanently with her.

During the International Geophysical Year (IGY) of 1957–1958, twelve countries, including the United States and the Soviet Union, collaborated in an effort to study the polar regions and their impact on the world's weather. Several countries established permanent bases on Antarctica and floating weather stations in the Arctic.

In November 1957 Wilkins travelled to Antarctica at the invitation of the US Army. Jim Waldron, a pilot with the US Air Force, was at the base at McMurdo Sound, at the edge of the Ross Ice Shelf:

> I returned from a flight one day and found my things had been moved and an extra bunk put in my room. I soon discovered my new room mate was the polar explorer, Sir Hubert Wilkins. I had heard of Sir Hubert of course, because we had studied Arctic and Antarctic lore.
>
> He always carried this big blue book with him and I asked him about it. He told me that the book was like the bible of a religion he belonged to. He told me there were planets throughout the universe and on each planet certain selected individuals, usually only two or three, would be invited to join this religion, and that he was one of the people chosen on Earth. He was very convinced about it all.

While he was in Antarctica, Wilkins hoped to be invited on a flight over the South Pole so that he could complete what he had started thirty years earlier. But he made the mistake of publicly criticising the American base at McMurdo Sound. Paul Dalrymple, who was at the base with Wilkins, recalled:

> Sir Hubert said he was going to the South Pole and he was excited about the prospect. But he criticised the conditions and Admiral Dufek, who was in charge of establishing the

US base at the South Pole [and who was with Byrd at Little America II in 1933-1934] told Wilkins he was no longer welcome at the American base.

Sir Hubert came to me because I was flying to the South Pole the next day. He asked me to take his parka with me. It was an Eskimo parka and he'd worn it on his flights in the 1920s. I told him I couldn't take it. When I woke up the next morning Sir Hubert had left the base, but his parka was hanging on the end of my bed.

Later, after Sir Hubert died, I went to his memorial service, intending to give the parka to Lady Wilkins. But she turned up drunk with her lover. It's no secret there was no love lost between Sir Hubert and Suzanne. Anyway, I decided not to give her the parka and donated it to the Christchurch Museum [New Zealand].

Wilkins returned to America in April 1958. He had witnessed one of his dreams, the thorough mapping of the polar regions with a view to establishing permanent meteorological stations, come true. He was about to witness another.

In 1946 the heads of the Manhattan Project, which had developed the atomic bombs in World War Two, turned their attention to harnessing nuclear energy to propel ships. In December 1951 the US Navy began constructing what would become the world's first nuclear submarine. As Wilkins had, the Navy named their new submarine the *Nautilus*. It was launched in January 1954 and immediately showed its superiority over conventional submarines, which had to surface every few days to recharge their batteries. Two more nuclear submarines, the *Skate* and the *Swordfish*, followed soon after.

With submarines capable of staying submerged for weeks at a time, the US Navy began to consider extended cruises under the Arctic ice. The *Nautilus* and the *Skate* were assigned to explore the possibilities. In August 1958, the *Nautilus* entered the Arctic Ocean via the Bering Strait, while the *Skate* waited at the edge of the ice pack, north of Spitsbergen. The *Nautilus* reached the North Pole on 3 August. It remained underwater and continued across the Arctic Ocean, before surfacing at Spitsbergen. Then the *Skate* commenced its voyage, reaching the North Pole on 12 August. It continued across the Arctic Ocean, surfaced in an open lead to rendezvous with a floating weather station off the coast of Alaska, then submerged and crossed the Arctic Ocean again, eventually arriving at Bergen, Norway.

The commander of the *Skate*, James Calvert, immediately sent a message to Wilkins:

> The majority of your aims and predictions of nearly thirty years ago were realized this summer. The men of the *Skate* send a sincere salute to a man who has many times shown the way.

On his return to America, Calvert invited Wilkins to come aboard and inspect the *Skate*. On 18 October, Wilkins accepted the offer. Calvert wrote:

> Sir Hubert remained aboard the *Skate* for lunch, and afterward we briefly discussed her voyage north. I felt a little ashamed telling him about the wealth of mechanical devices we possessed – the finest money could buy. Everything, which for him had proved bulky or useless, had, after twenty-seven years of intensive submarine development, either been replaced by something far better or improved beyond recognition.

But Sir Hubert took all this progress in stride – he had the wisdom to know that it is courage and imagination which matter most . . .

'Now that you have everything you need to do the job,' said the old explorer suddenly, 'you must go in the wintertime.'

I was startled, but I knew what he meant. Every bit of submarine exploration in the Arctic had been done in summer, when polynas [open leads of clear water] are abundant. In winter they would be frozen over and open water nonexistent or very difficult to locate.

'You haven't really opened the Arctic Ocean for scientific investigation,' Sir Hubert went on, 'or military or commercial use, for that matter, if you merely demonstrate what you can do in summertime.'

Then one long sigh escaped him, and he sat for some time with a faraway look and a half-smile. I'm sure he found it hard to face the fact that the years were past when he could take part in such an adventure.

Six weeks after his meeting with Calvert aboard the *Skate*, Wilkins died in his hotel room in Framingham, Massachusetts.

Calvert continued to be interested in the possibility of taking the *Skate* to the Arctic in wintertime. He was ordered to attempt it and the voyage was planned for March 1959. Shortly before departing Calvert was asked by Admiral Frederick Warder if he would take Wilkins' ashes with him and scatter them at the North Pole. He wrote:

'The *Skate* would be honoured, Admiral,' I said. 'But to surface right at the Pole is a pretty big order. We couldn't do it last August, and I don't hold much hope for the winter.'

The Admiral suggested that we might perform the
task while submerged, using a special ejector – possibly a
torpedo tube.

I shook my head vigorously. 'No there's no meaning to
that. He wouldn't have wanted it that way.'

The Admiral agreed. 'You're right – either do it on the
surface, or bring the ashes back and we'll have somebody
do it at a more favorable time.'

This ended the conversation, but not my thoughts
about it. Somehow, I felt, we would have to find a way.

On 17 March 1959, the nuclear submarine USS *Skate* broke
through the ice and became the first vessel to surface at the
North Pole. In the eerie dark, lit only by flares, crew members
climbed down to stand on the ice. The Australian and the
United States flags fluttered from the conning tower. Calvert
spoke:

On this day we pay humble tribute to one of the great men of
our century. His indomitable will, his adventurous spirit, his
simplicity, and his courage have all set high marks for those of
us who follow him. He spent his life in the noblest of callings,
the attempt to broaden the horizons of the mind of man.

Some of his personality is expressed in this prayer
he wrote himself: Our heavenly Father, would thou give
us liberty without license and the power to do good for
mankind with the self-restraint to avoid using that power
for self-aggrandizement . . .

Lieutenant David Boyd then upended an urn and the ashes were
instantly scattered to the wind. George Hubert Wilkins, the
farmer's son from South Australia, had reached the North Pole.

* * *

Harold Sherman, with whom Wilkins had collaborated on the book *Thoughts Through Space*, believed that a person's thoughts continued after death and that it was still possible for the living to communicate with them. For about a year after Wilkins' death, Sherman continued to 'receive messages' from him. The first came on 25 April 1959:

> Hello Sherman. It is not easy to get through. I have been trying for some time. I find that each mind is like a miniature universe, a collection of magnetized ideas or concepts, revolving around a nucleus or center which represents the entity itself.
>
> The universe is not at all like man has described it in his books and scientific treatises. It is difficult to get away from a planet on which you are born because of the hold its energy particles have upon you. That is why I am glad I had the body the world knows as Wilkins returned to the fires, so that the ashes might more speedily be freed from any identification with me.
>
> It was a source of profound satisfaction to have those ashes released at the North Pole, and to have it done by these new under-ice pioneers. They are going to realize my dreams. Dreams I find, which no single entity really completes in any life, but leaves for others to carry on.

Within a year 'Wilkins' was warning Sherman of Russian plots to manipulate the weather in an effort to ruin the American economy.

* * *

In his will Wilkins left everything to Suzanne – not just any money he had, but also his films, photographs, records and their copyright. Suzanne, assisted by Winston Ross, then set about ensuring that her husband would be remembered as she wanted him to be remembered. She began by censoring much of his material. Anything with references to other women in his life was destroyed. Diaries and manuscripts were re-typed, often sloppily, with sections edited out or rewritten, then the originals destroyed. Exactly how much of Wilkins' original material was destroyed we will never know. With what they decided to keep, Suzanne and Ross then attempted to establish a Wilkins Memorial Foundation in a shed on Suzanne's property. Not surprisingly, few people came to the remote farm and the material languished.

Suzanne died in 1975 and she bequeathed what was left to Winston Ross, who continued to be careless with it, giving many of the artefacts away. When Australian entrepreneur Dick Smith visited the farmhouse, Ross sold him Wilkins' 1939 Chevrolet station wagon, a polar sledge and other artefacts. Smith had the foresight to ship them back to Australia in the hope that a museum might one day be interested. Next, in an attempt to raise money, Ross and his new partner, Marley, decided to sell what they could. Of particular value was a collection of stamps. Paul Rodzianko, who became involved in the process of this sale, explained:

> It was clear from the outset that neither of the custodians
> of the materials had any idea of what anything was worth
> and in fact were keeping things in such a horrid state that
> all of it was gradually being destroyed by the conditions
> and their sloppiness. Another collector friend and I made an
> agreement to acquire the postal history of the Foundation,

or to sell it to third parties so that repairs could be made to the house and memorabilia and some sort of museum be organised. But it quickly became evident that they were not interested in a museum but rather a fund to support them. This was not possible according to the tax law so it degenerated quickly.

Ross and Rodzianko were soon threatening each other with legal action. To avoid a costly court case, an agreement was reached for the entire Wilkins' Collection to be sold to the Ohio State University for $125,000 in 1988. That should have been the end of the matter, but it wasn't. Before the university could arrive with their trucks to collect the material, Ross, who felt unfairly pressured into the sale, hid a portion of it. The university, not knowing what should have been included, never realised much had been withheld. Winston Ross died in 1996, and the 'secret material' was taken over by Marley Ross, who died two years later. Next it went to her two sons from previous relationships.

At the time of writing, the material languishes. Attempts to have it donated to a museum, deposited with the Byrd Polar Research Center or even inspected by the author, have so far failed. There are clues to the volume and content of the material, but a full inventory has not been taken. Hopefully, this may change in the future and Sir Hubert's legacy will be more fully understood.

17

We Should Be at the Pole

Byrd also returned to Antarctica in the southern summer of 1933–1934, leading an expedition he had privately mounted and financed. He established Little America II on the Ross Ice Shelf, then Advance Base, 123 miles away at 80° 08' south. Here he planned to spend the winter alone. Why would someone want to spend an Antarctic winter alone in a small prefabricated hut? Byrd's justification was scientific: to take weather observations. But he wrote:

> This much should be understood from the beginning:
> that above everything else, and beyond the solid worth
> of weather and auroral observations in the hitherto
> unoccupied interior of Antarctica and my interest in
> these studies, I really wanted to go for the experience's
> sake. So the motive was in part personal. Aside from the
> meteorological and auroral work, I had no important
> purposes. There was nothing of that sort. Nothing whatever,
> except one man's desire to know that kind of experience to
> the full, to be by himself for a while and to taste the peace
> and quiet and solitude long enough to find out how good
> they really are.

Soon after Byrd was left alone at Advance Base, the men at Little America II, in contact by radio, became concerned about his mental state. His messages became increasingly despondent and they finally decided to risk a polar sledge journey in the middle of winter to rescue their leader. They arrived at Advance Base on 11 August 1934 and waited until Byrd had recovered before they transported him back to Little America II. His deteriorating mental state was blamed on carbon monoxide poisoning from a leaking stove pipe.

Byrd returned to Antarctica in 1939, as commander of an expedition that established Little America III and sent out five exploring parties. The expedition was cut short when America entered World War Two, and the base was abandoned in 1941.

After the war, Byrd commanded the US Navy's Operation Highjump, which was, at the time, the largest Antarctic expedition ever mounted. Operation Highjump sent 4700 men, thirteen ships and twenty-three aeroplanes to Antarctica. The expedition members mapped extensive areas and discovered new land, including twenty-six islands. During Operation Highjump, on 16 February 1947, Byrd made his second flight over the South Pole.

In 1955 Byrd was placed in command of a US Navy task force that would supply and maintain the permanent bases being established for the International Geophysical Year. Six bases, including one at the South Pole, were set up, and a runway was built at McMurdo Sound. Byrd visited Antarctica in the southern summer of 1955–1956 and flew over the South Pole for a third time on 8 January 1956. He was planning to return to Antarctica in the 1956–1957 season but was prevented by failing health. He died at his home in Virginia on 11 March 1957, and was survived by his wife and four children. Immediately after his death, *The New York Times* wrote:

The Antarctic has ceased to be an unknown 'sea' largely because of his work. The loneliest of all continents is now peopled with men from the far corners of the world.

It was Admiral Byrd more than any other one person, who made it known to the man in every street. As author and lecturer he literally popularized the Antarctic.

The United States is down there strongly because Richard Byrd drove the opening wedge and planted the American flag. The concept of Polar defense – North and South – was based on his explorations, at least in the beginning.

Such men are not easy characters, they burn with a bright flame. They go their way alone, partly because they stand on a narrow summit. They do not belong to friends or even, in a certain sense, to their families. They are men of the world, the sort of men who carry the world forward, who open horizons, who make a mark on history's pages that can never be erased. Richard Evelyn Byrd was such a man.

* * *

Byrd and Bernt Balchen were never friends, but after the Second World War what was once a coolness between the two grew to become open hostility. Byrd felt that Balchen was getting too much credit for what he considered were Byrd's own achievements. And Balchen felt that his promotion in the newly formed US Air Force was being blocked by Byrd's political influence. Byrd's brother, Harry, was a US senator during the period, and a member of the Armed Services Committee.

Balchen's biographer, Carroll V. Glines, in *Bernt Balchen: Polar Aviator* has carefully and systematically set out evidence to show how Byrd worked diligently to stifle Balchen's career and decrease his standing in the public eye. In 1953, for example, when a *Reader's Digest* article suggested that Byrd was assisted in his North Pole flight because Amundsen 'loaned him the services of 26 year-old Bernt Balchen', Byrd countered by having expedition members write statements saying it wasn't so.

The dispute simmered for years, often making the press. When a reporter asked Balchen why Byrd was blocking his career, Balchen replied, 'Because he didn't fly over the North Pole, and he knows I know it.'

The two men last met face to face on 13 October 1953 at a ceremony commemorating fifty years of powered flight. The meeting erupted into a noisy argument that was reported in *Newsweek*.

Eventually, Balchen decided to commit his doubts about the North Pole flight to paper. For his autobiography he would write:

> Take the strange contradictions in Commander Byrd's record of his North Pole flight. According to his own figures, the *Josephine Ford* was in flight 15 hours and 30 minutes and spent 13 minutes, sometimes Byrd put the time a minute longer, circling the Pole – which leaves a total of 15 hours and 17 minutes to fly 1,340 nautical miles (1,542 statute miles. The distance sometimes varies a few miles in different estimates). This means the average cruising speed would have been 87.2 knots (100.3 mph). From actual test data – plus my little pocket slide rule that Byrd despised – I compute that with ski installation the best cruising speed that could be squeezed out of the plane would have been no more than 74 knots (85.1 mph).
>
> In Byrd's stated time of 15 hours and 17 minutes, he

could therefore have travelled a maximum distance of only
1,131 nautical miles (1,300 statute miles), and the furthest
north latitude he could have reached was 88 degrees
15.5 minutes, or 104 nautical miles (120.2 statute miles)
short of the Pole. All his life I waited for Admiral Byrd to give
some explanation of the discrepancies in his log. To the best
of my knowledge he never did, at least not publicly.

But Balchen's publisher was forced to remove the offending paragraphs after legal threats from Byrd's family and supporters. A disgruntled Balchen kept a copy of the full manuscript and, ten years later, showed it to Richard Montague, who was researching his book *Oceans, Poles and Airmen*.

Balchen died on 17 October 1973, two years after the publication of *Oceans, Poles and Airmen*. He had been the only man to have flown the *Josephine Ford*, other than Floyd Bennett, and so was perhaps the only person qualified to accurately estimate its flying speeds. Byrd's supporters claimed that it was Balchen's animosity towards Byrd that caused him to fabricate figures about the flying speed of the plane. Nothing, they maintained, could ever be proven.

* * *

During the International Geophysical Year of 1957–1958, the Ohio State University served as a data collecting centre. In 1960 the University established the Institute of Polar Studies in order to bring together scientists from a variety of subject disciplines who were engaged in polar research. An archival program was commenced within the institute to collect the papers and records of explorers, or those otherwise engaged in polar research. The family of Richard E. Byrd began submitting his records to the Institute in 1985. Two years later, the name of the institute was changed to the Byrd Polar Research Center (BPRC). Three years later again, the BPRC obtained some of the papers and records of Sir Hubert Wilkins from Winston Ross. Byrd and Wilkins, in a sense, would come together in death, as they had done in life.

In 1996, seventy years after Byrd's North Pole flight, Dr Raimund Goerler of the BPRC Archival Program was going through a box of papers that had recently arrived from Byrd's family. Goerler discovered a small diary that had slipped down the side of the box. He examined it carefully and found it to be the diary/notebook that Byrd had carried on the North Pole flight. Goerler described it:

> In contrast to his lustrous public career, Byrd's private diary is ordinary – even shabby – in appearance. Its cover is faded black, and bears the printed title 'Diary, 1925' although the document contains passages written in 1926 and 1927. Byrd wrote most entries in pencil and with a hasty hand. Many pages are blank; some pages have notes and mathematical calculations that are randomly placed. Clearly the diary served Byrd as both a daily journal and a convenient message pad.
>
> Nevertheless this unappealing book is an extraordinary document. Byrd wrote the entries for himself, not for public inspection, although in 1928 he quoted from parts of the diary for his book, *Skyward*. At the time of its writing, the diary was a private notebook for recording Byrd's thoughts and observations about himself, about his colleagues and his rivals and about his family and the state of his career.

Importantly, too, the entries are in no particular order. Goerler explains:

> The diary's organisation is confusing and misleading. For example, it begins with Byrd's speculation about what the new year (1925) will bring. A few pages after this come the communications from Byrd to Floyd Bennett during the flight to the North Pole on May 9, 1926. Pages concerning the 1927 transatlantic flight follow. Next come daily notes about the USS *Chantier*'s cruise from New York to Spitsbergen and preparations for Byrd's 1926 flight to the North Pole. The diary ends with daily entries about Byrd's expedition with Donald Macmillan to Greenland in 1925, and mixed with these are still more notes about the North Pole flight.
>
> The disorder can be explained. Byrd began the diary in January 1925 and turned to it again on June 20, 1925, at the beginning of the expedition with Macmillan. In April 1926 the frugal Byrd used the blank pages of his 1925 journal to record his North Pole flight of that year, which ended on May 9; in June 1927 he used more blank pages to make notes about his transatlantic flight. Sometimes Byrd crossed out the printed dates for 1925; sometimes he did not.

The diary was a remarkable find. Byrd himself had made reference to it in his book *Skyward*, when he was describing the take-off for the flight across the Atlantic: 'I made notes in my log and remarks in my diary, the same diary carried over the North Pole with me.' Here then was the very diary Byrd had described. But would it reveal what had happened on the North Pole flight?

Goerler carefully and thoroughly transcribed all the notes made by Byrd in the diary/notebook. He also noted that some comments and navigational calculations had been erased. No one can say who erased these passages or when. It may have been Byrd, his son, or someone else. Goerler had the diary/notebook photographed, using ultraviolet light to ensure the erased passages could be detected and clearly read. It was hoped that in these navigational calculations the true course and extent of the 1926 flight could be determined.

In his report to the National Geographic Society, Byrd had claimed to have taken the necessary sextant readings to prove he had reached the North Pole. Would these readings be in his diary/notebook? With the calculations transcribed, Goerler offered them to three experts for interpretation. In his book, *To the Pole*, Goerler explains the results:

> Dennis Rawlins, an astronomer and the publisher of the scientific-historical journal *DIO & the Journal for Hysterical Astronomy* who has specialised in examining polar explorers' navigational records, inspected the diary and the navigational calculations and notes. He found erased sextant readings that differ from those in the official report submitted to the National Geographic Society. According to Rawlins, the erased readings prove that Byrd came no closer to the North Pole than 150 miles. Rawlins' report is contained in a fifteen-page letter of May 1996, to Raimund Goerler, now in The Ohio State University Archives.
>
> Colonel William Molett, an experienced polar navigator who taught navigation and has published on the subject, reviewed both the diary and Rawlins' report. He concluded that the erasures were miscalculations that Byrd realised were erroneous. He believes that Byrd

did not use the erased calculations and that there is no discrepancy between the official report and the diary. Colonel Molett's report is also in a letter to Raimund Goerler in The Ohio State University Archives.

Dr Gerald Newsom, professor of astronomy at Ohio State, also studied the diary. His evaluation is that the erasures are inconclusive. In his view, the erasures were the work of a navigator who, although tired, was still alert enough to realise he had made an error in his calculations. According to Professor Newsom, Byrd at a minimum got within 'tens of miles' of the North Pole and may have reached it.

With three different opinions from three experts, it is difficult for the layman to draw many conclusions. Rawlins said the calculations in the diary showed that Byrd got no closer than 150 miles from the Pole. Molett says they are probably miscalculations that Byrd knew were erroneous and therefore didn't use them. Newsom says similar; that Byrd knew the calculations were wrong, but still may have reached or got close to the Pole.

But there are no calculations taken at the North Pole. Of the calculations in the diary, the ones made closest to the Pole show a position some 150 miles away. If Byrd made calculations at the North Pole, as he claimed he did when he spent thirteen minutes circling it, he certainly did not make them in the diary/ notebook he carried and in which he made all his other notes and calculations.

In addition to the navigational calculations, there are five pages on which Byrd has written notes, either to himself or the pilot, Floyd Bennett. The notes are quoted here in their entirety and in the order they are written on the page, from top to bottom.

On the page headed 'Monday January 5, 1925':

We are making good speed. It looks like fog over the polar
sea. Send a radio back that we are making fast speed and
are about to pass Amsterdam Island. We have a little drift
to the left. Direction of wind from the east. Now we can't see
the edge of ice pack.

   I want to line up the mountain and Amsterdam Island.
I will do it from top side. Watch me. We have drifted way
over to the west. I am trying to get back on line. Please
head on, I tell you.

Page headed 'Tuesday January 6, 1925':

You are steering too much to the right. Set compass a few
degrees to left.
   Send a radio back that we are 85 miles due north
Amsterdam Island. Got over ice pack just north of land.
   I want to use a smoke bomb. Where is match to strike
with.
   Send radio that we are 240 miles due north
Spitzbergen. Then pull in your wire.
   You are keeping to the right 5 degrees too much.
   You must not persist in keeping too far right. ['Must' is
underlined three times.]
   Radio that we are 230 miles from the Pole.
   Radio
   Nothing but ice everywhere. No sign of life. Motors
going fine.

These entries, apparently made on the way to the Pole, show a
confident Byrd who knows exactly where he is. He knows he

is a few degrees off course, first drifting to the left because of the wind from the east, then too far right. Three times he gives his position exactly: '85 miles due north of Amsterdam Island', '240 miles due north of Spitzbergen' and '230 miles from the Pole'. These are exact positions, not approximations, and each time Byrd writes 'we are' not 'we should be'.

There are three other pages on which Byrd wrote instructions or notes to Bennett. One page, headed 'Cash Account November' has only one note:

There is a very strong wind please steer very carefully.

On the page headed 'Wednesday, January 14, 1925' there are the notes:

We should be at the Pole now. Make a circle. I will take a picture. Then I want the sun.
Radio that we have reached the Pole and are now returning with one motor with a bad oil leak. But I expect to be able to make Spitzbergen.

Then on the page headed 'Cash Account December' are the notes:

The stb [starboard] motor has an oil leak.
Can you get all the way back on two motors
What has been our average air speed
20 miles to go to Pole
How long were we gone before we turned around [erased]
Head the plane right at the sun

Under the question 'How long were we gone before we turned around?' Bennett has written, in large letters, '8½'. Twice on this page Byrd has made the mathematical calculation for multiplying 85 by 8.5.

Ever since Byrd returned from his North Pole flight people have questioned whether he had the time to fly all the way there and back. Many people have claimed Byrd couldn't possibly have made it. But no one has explained why he might not have flown all the way. Even his diary reveals that 'we are 230 miles from the Pole . . . motors going fine'. Why would this expert navigator turn around early? Why turn back when the goal of his life, plus the fame and fortune that Byrd knew would accompany it, was so close?

Byrd also wrote: 'We should be at the Pole now,' then: 'Radio we have reached the Pole.' This indicates that he believed he was there. So did he actually make it? Did a combination of favourable winds and exceptional performance from the plane actually get him to the North Pole? Did Bernt Balchen, the only man to fly the plane besides Floyd Bennett, later fabricate a lie about its performance because of his personal dislike for Byrd? Have the critics got it wrong all these years? Or did Byrd turn back early, mistakenly believing he had reached the North Pole?

The answer lies in Byrd's diary/notebook. And when we examine his words, in association with the known facts, a highly probably answer presents itself. The first clue lies in the National Geographic Society's article, which declared Byrd had reached the North Pole. A paragraph in the article reads:

Soon after leaving the Pole the sextant which Commander Byrd was using slid off the chart table, breaking the horizon glass. This made it necessary to navigate the return trip wholly by dead reckoning.

Byrd broke his sextant. According to what he told the National Geographic Society's committee he broke it shortly after leaving the Pole. This is a remarkable admission. Not only that he broke his sextant – an instrument vital to his ability to fly accurately to the North Pole – but also that he was only carrying one. He had no backup. It was common practice for all navigators to carry at least two sextants and treat them with the utmost care. Quite literally, their lives depended on them. Wilkins, in navigating the flight from Point Barrow to Spitsbergen, speaks of his *sextants*. In Byrd's own book *Skyward*, he quotes a description of himself given by Commander Towers:

> Byrd spent the afternoon vibrating between the forward and after cockpits, trying smoke bombs, sextants, etc. My cockpit was not very large, and with all the charts, chart desk, sextants, drift indicator, binoculars, chronometers, etc., stacked in there, very little room was left.

Twice in as many sentences Towers refers to *sextants*. Byrd carried more than one that time, but not, apparently, on the North Pole flight. Why is unknown, but it appears, by his own admission, that he was carrying only one and he broke it.

But when did he break it? On the return journey, as he claimed? In fact, Byrd would not have been using his sextant on the return journey. He needed it only to determine how far north he had travelled. To get back to base, he simply had to stay in a straight line until he reached Spitsbergen, and then follow the coast to Kings Bay.

Let's re-examine the flight, using the notes in Byrd's diary/ notebook, while bearing the broken sextant in mind.

Firstly, Byrd was an expert navigator. It was his field. Navigation for aviators was his speciality. He even invented the bubble sextant to allow fliers to take a reading of the angle of the sun when no horizon could be seen. If he was going to navigate his way to the North Pole, then the sextant and the sun compass would be the instruments he would use. His only other means would be by dead reckoning; that is, by measuring his speed for a period of time to calculate that he had reached where he wanted to be. Dead reckoning was not the navigation method of choice for an expert like Byrd. And even the committee from the National Geographic Society pointed out that they would not be willing to accept dead reckoning as proof that Byrd had reached the Pole.

So, Byrd and Floyd Bennett take off in the Fokker Trimotor *Josephine Ford* at thirty-seven minutes past midnight on 9 May 1926, in a plane with enough fuel to fly to the North Pole and back. On the diary notebook page headed 'Monday January 5, 1925' Byrd writes his first notes to Bennett at a time when they are 'about to pass Amsterdam Island'. At this point they are drifting to the left and he instructs Bennett to steer to the right: 'We have drifted way over to the west. I am trying to get back on line.'

The next instructions to Bennett are written on the page headed 'Tuesday January 6, 1925', about an hour later, when they are '85 miles due north of Amsterdam Island'. Bennett has overcompensated for the wind and is now steering too far to the right. Byrd uses this page to write further notes over the next few hours. Three times he gives exact positions, the last being '230 miles from the pole'.

A page at the rear of the diary/notebook, headed 'Cash

Account November', has only one entry: 'There is a very strong wind please steer very carefully.' It's impossible to say when this was written in context with the other statements, but it may have been at this point. There is nothing else on the page, which indicates that Byrd may have put the book down for a period of time, or at least closed it before making his next note. Otherwise, he would likely have filled the page with notes, as he did on the others.

These written notes, and his calculations, which have already been discussed, are the only pages written on the way to the Pole. The next notes are written when Byrd believes he has reached the Pole: 'We should be at the Pole now. Make a circle. I will take a picture. Then I want the sun.' And on the same page, but most likely written a few minutes later, after Byrd has taken his picture and Bennett has circled the plane and is heading back, is the note: 'Radio that we have reached the Pole and are now returning with one motor with bad oil leak. But expect to be able to make Spitzbergen.'

Between 'we are 230 miles from the Pole' and 'we should be at the Pole' something dramatic has happened and Byrd is no longer confident of his position. Suddenly, he is no longer the confident navigator using his instruments to calculate exactly where he is to the mile. Instead, he's making an estimate like a navigator using dead reckoning.

Could Byrd have broken his sextant – his only sextant – on the way to the Pole and not, as he claimed, shortly after reaching it and turning for home? It would explain why he is suddenly no longer confident of his exact position. It would explain why, as Dennis Rawlins claims, there are calculations for sextant readings to within approximately 150 miles of the Pole, but none for any time after that. It would explain why none of the experts who examined the calculations in the diary/

notebook found figures that showed Byrd at the Pole. And most importantly, it would explain the curious entries written by Byrd on the page marked 'Cash Account December'.

Let's assume that Byrd broke his sextant somewhere before reaching the Pole and we will see why these entries make sense. Byrd sets off confidently with his sextant and sun compass. He doesn't need to record speed or the time he leaves Kings Bay because he is going to navigate his way to the Pole by taking sextant readings. But somewhere around 150 miles from the Pole his sextant slips off the chart table and breaks. What does he do? Abort the flight? Of course not. He's very close, about two hours flying time, and he believes he won't have the opportunity to get another shot at the prize before Amundsen or Wilkins. He's still got his sun compass, so he can keep on a straight course. And he can revert to dead reckoning to make an estimate of how long he has to fly to reach the North Pole.

We'll never know what Byrd's dead reckoning estimates were, but while he's trying to calculate when he will reach the Pole, something else happens. The starboard motor develops an oil leak. The motor is still running – but for how long? When will it run out of oil, overheat and stop? Byrd is cramped within a wood and canvas plane, more than 500 miles from help, flying over polar ice with a motor that could stop at any time. And he's got everything riding on getting to the North Pole and back. So when, by his dead reckoning, he believes he has reached his goal, he writes to Bennett: 'We should be at the Pole now. Make a circle. I will take a picture. Then I want the sun.'

This last instruction means head straight for the sun, because the sun, at the time, was lying in the direction of Spitsbergen. This is not a man circling the Pole for thirteen minutes to take observations, as he later claimed. The oil leak means there is no time to waste. And he has no sextant with which to take observations. But he turns around genuinely believing he has achieved his goal and writes the note to Bennett: 'Radio that we have reached the Pole and are now returning with one motor with bad oil leak. But expect to be able to make Spitzbergen.'

Now it's a race against time, and a failing motor, to get back. (The oil leak was temporary, as it turned out, and the motor kept running.) Next come the notes written on the page, 'Cash Account December':

> The stb motor has an oil leak
>> Can you get all the way back on two motors

Bennett may have nodded an affirmative, or perhaps he shrugged his shoulders in a gesture indicating 'I don't know'. What else could he do? Anthony Fokker had claimed his big planes could still fly with one wing motor disabled; now they would find out. Byrd settles back to wait. He begins to wonder about the accuracy of his dead reckoning. Byrd hadn't noted the time the plane left Kings Bay. He must now check his dead reckoning with Bennett. He asks:

> What has been our average air speed

Somehow Bennett communicates eighty-five, meaning eighty-five miles per hour, the estimated cruising speed of the Fokker. Perhaps he points at the air speed indicator. As they were heading back, with a lightened fuel load and a tail wind, the air speed indicator could be showing close to eighty-five miles per hour. As Balchen would later write, after having flown the plane: 'I compute that with ski installation the best cruising speed that could be squeezed out of the plane would have been no more than 74 knots (85.1 mph).'

To calculate his position by dead reckoning, Byrd now needs to know how long they took to fly to the Pole. Next he writes the question to Bennett:

How long were we gone before we turned around

This question confirms that Byrd didn't know what time he left Kings Bay. Bennett writes '8½', meaning eight and a half hours. Byrd does his calculations – twice. Eighty-five miles per hour, multiplied by eight and a half hours. The answer is 722 miles. Byrd knows Kings Bay to the North Pole is approximately 750 miles. Under his calculations he writes:

20 miles to go to Pole

Dr Raimund Goerler has suggested that this entry was made on the way north, indicating that Byrd had twenty miles to go to reach the North Pole. It wasn't. It could not have been. The answer of twenty miles was only arrived at after the multiplication of eighty-five miles per hour by eight and a half hours. And those figures were supplied by Bennett. And the phrasing of the question as to the time of the flight was 'before we turned around'. The questions were asked on the way back. The calculations were made on the way back. The answer was arrived at on the way back. Byrd was not indicating that 'we have 20 miles to go to the Pole', but rather that 'we had 20 miles to go to the Pole'.

Byrd was on the way back when, by his own calculations, he realised he was twenty miles short of his goal.

But he had already radioed that he had reached the Pole. And twenty miles short on a 750-mile flight was no great issue, surely. From the height at which they were flying they would have seen the Pole.

But had they? Had they really got within twenty miles? Had the dead reckoning been accurate? Was the plane's average air speed really eighty-five miles per hour on the outward flight? That was a measure of their air speed. Who could estimate their ground speed – especially as there had been 'a very strong wind'? A headwind would mean their air speed would be higher than their ground speed. Had they really been flying at eighty-five miles per hour ground speed?

Byrd made no more entries in his diary/notebook. But somewhere on the return journey the realisation must have set in. Perhaps when they sighted Amsterdam Island and Byrd realised just how quickly they were returning. The return flight would be an hour and a half quicker than the outward flight. Eight and a half hours out. Seven hours back. How could that be? The only answer was a wind from the north. And that meant that their ground speed would have been slower than their air speed on the outward journey. At first Byrd had estimated he had reached the Pole. Then, after the plane had been turned around, he estimated he had twenty miles to go. Now, as he neared Kings Bay, he must have realised that he was further from the Pole than he had thought. Even if his air speed was ten miles per hour slower than he estimated on the outward journey, it would have left him more than 100 miles from the Pole. And then, returning from a trip of only 650 miles, a ten miles per hour tailwind would have got him back in seven hours.

What was Byrd to do? He was about to land at Kings Bay. Should he land and tell the world that he was not sure of exactly how far he had gone? That he, the navigation expert, had broken his only sextant on the way to the North Pole and then become preoccupied with an engine leaking oil? That he'd made an estimate and turned around before he realised the plane had been flying slower than he thought on the outward journey, and that he'd only realised on the way back when the wind brought them home so much faster?

As the *Josephine Ford* circled Kings Bay, Byrd must have needed time to think. He had arrived back earlier than expected, so his own crew weren't ready to greet him. They had received the radio message 'We have reached the Pole' after Byrd had flown eight and a half hours. They did not expect him back for another hour and a half. Nor, when they met him, would they have to ask if he had reached the Pole. He had already told them.

Ellsworth and Amundsen were there to watch the *Josephine Ford* as it circled to land at Kings Bay. They would co-write:

> The landing was made in splendid style, and was so well calculated that the machine stopped exactly on the same spot that it had left in the morning. There were not many who had managed to arrive in time, but we were enough to seize and haul the two heroes out of the machine and to give them a rousing cheer. Then a strange thing occurred – we set upon the two men and actually gave them a kiss on each cheek! We were in a great state of excitement and allowed ourselves to be carried away by our emotions. Of all the compliments these two men have ever received, they have scarcely had greater than they got from us at that moment. Nobody enquired, 'have you been to the Pole?' That went without saying, judging from the time they had been away. We knew exactly what these two wanted more than anything else in the world – namely, to get on board and into their bunks. Sixteen nerve-racking hours are enough for the strongest. So we took them by the arm and led them down to the shore.

Byrd was taken aboard the *Chantier* and left in his cabin. A newspaper correspondent wrote: 'We await confirmation.'

What did Byrd do in his cabin? Did he sleep? Did he go over the flight in his mind again and again? Did he look at the jottings in his notebook to see if he could determine how close he may have been to the Pole? Did he consider coming out to say, 'Sorry – I made a mistake. Give me a couple of days and I'll do it again'? He knew that Wilkins and Amundsen were both standing ready to make the flight that he had just got wrong.

Alone in that cramped, damp cabin, Byrd faced the biggest decision of his life. What should he say to the world that was waiting outside? If he admitted he did not make the Pole he would face a career in decline. He would be in debt. He would have failed. If, on the other hand, he emerged to say he had reached the Pole, his future would be assured. The fame, fortune and respect he desperately craved would all be his. What should he say to the world that waited for his announcement? He would later write:

> In Bennett and me mothers saw their sons, wives their husbands, sisters and brothers. In us men saw what they too might have done had they had the chance. In us youth saw ambition realised. In us America for the moment dramatised that superb world-conquering fire which is American spirit. For the moment we seemed to have caught up the banner of American progress. For the moment we appeared to typify for them the spirit of America.

For a proud patriot like Byrd, who genuinely believed success was his birthright and greatness his destiny, there was really only one choice he could make. He had a duty to that world, that

America, that was depending on him. He had a duty to his crew and supporters. He had a duty to himself and his family.

He emerged from his cabin to declare that his calculations had shown him at the North Pole. He fabricated the story about circling the Pole for thirteen minutes and taking repeated sextant readings. And once he had lied, he was forced to maintain the story for the rest of his life.

Afterword

The Silent Witnesses

Of the aeroplanes that were used by Wilkins and Byrd in the air race to the Poles, a number have been preserved in museums and may be viewed by the public today.

The Fokker Trimotor, the *Josephine Ford*, used by Byrd and Bennett on their North Pole flight in 1926 is displayed at the Henry Ford Museum at Dearborn, Michigan.

At the end of his first expedition to Antarctica Byrd left the Ford Trimotor *Floyd Bennett* and the single-engine Fairchild *Stars and Stripes* at Little America. When he returned in 1933 he dug the planes out of the ice and, at the end of the expedition, took them back to America. The Ford Trimotor is also at the Henry Ford Museum. The Fairchild is at the Virginia Aviation Museum.

After his 1929–1930 expedition to Antarctica, Wilkins gave his two Lockheed Vegas to the government of Argentina on the understanding that they would fly an exhibition tour around the country before being placed in a museum. Wilkins' first Vega, the *Los Angeles*, which he and Eielson flew across the Arctic Ocean in 1928, was damaged in a crash in 1930. It was taken to a military airbase in Buenos Aires and stored outdoors. It was discovered in 1948, but by that time the wooden fuselage and wings were rotten and the plane beyond salvage.

The second Lockheed Vega, the *San Francisco* was also crashed in 1930 and was a total wreck.

The remains of the single-engined Fokker that Wilkins called the *Alaskan* and flew to Barrow, Alaska, in 1926 is in Hatton, North Dakota. Wilkins gave the fuselage (the wing had been irreparably damaged) to Ben Eielson's father after the death of his son. Today it is held at the family home, which has become a permanent museum to the pilot who was the first to fly a plane in the Antarctic and across the Arctic Ocean.

The Fokker Trimotor that Wilkins named the *Detroiter* and flew to Barrow in 1926 is on display in Brisbane, Australia. In 1928, wanting to reduce his debt to the Detroit Aviation Society and pay for his Lockheed Vega, Wilkins sold the plane to three Australians intending to fly from America to Australia. The trio thought the name *Detroiter* inappropriate to attract Australian sponsors and renamed the plane the *Southern Cross*. Two of them, Charles Kingsford Smith and Charles Ulm, flew the plane across the Pacific Ocean in May 1928. Kingsford Smith then went on to fly the plane into the history books. 'Smithy' and the *Southern Cross* have since become Australian icons, appearing at various times on bank notes, coins and other symbols of national identity. Today, the *Detroiter/Southern Cross* stands in its own purpose-built museum near Brisbane Airport. Nowhere in the museum is there any mention of Sir Hubert Wilkins or the plane's pioneering flights in the Arctic.

Acknowledgements

The Byrd Polar Research Center Archival Program is a collaborative effort of the Ohio State University and the Byrd Polar Research Center. The archive is the first port of call for anyone wanting to research either Byrd or Wilkins. Here, Laura Kissel, the polar curator, has cheerfully answered my many requests and been an enormous help over the decade during which this book evolved. Dr Raimund Goerler also receives my gratitude. The hard work of these two people ensures researchers such as myself have an excellent resource.

Because information has been collected over such a long period of time, sadly, some people have passed away without the opportunity to see the completed work to which they contributed. For anyone wanting to know more about the life of Lincoln Ellsworth, I recommend the late Beekman Pool's *Polar Extremes*. Bernt Balchen's widow, Audrey, died while the book was in the final stages of production. The majority of his papers are now held at the Library of Congress, Washington, DC.

Not everyone is going to agree with my conclusions, or my readiness to air matters they would have preferred remained private. I feel I have done so with integrity. Many of the things I learnt did not make it into the book because I felt to include them would be only chasing cheap sensationalism, and not relevant to the story. Above all, Byrd and Wilkins were heroes. Flawed in some respects, but heroes nevertheless.

For information, guidance in my research, or permission to quote from unpublished sources I would also like to thank

Ian Affleck, Sheldon Bart, Paul Dalrymple, John Davies, Ray Drakea, Patrick Dunne, Al Greco, Bob Headland, John Levinson, William Michael, Eileen Mork, Darren Reale, Paul Rodzianko, Michael Ross, Dick Smith, Lowell Thomas Jr., Bess Urbahn, Chris Venema and James Waldron.

The original manuscript benefited from the editorial pen of Genna Gifford, who shaped and refined its structure. At Random House, Meredith Curnow and Julian Welch provided further valuable insights and suggestions. My agent, Andrew Lownie, has been supportive throughout the whole process.

I suspect that Sir Hubert continues to send his 'thoughts through space' and I trust he gets some satisfaction from my efforts.

The debt I owe my family can never be measured. Above all, this book would be no more than an idea if it were not for Zoe.

Notes

In the references that follow, BPRC refers to the Byrd Polar Research Center, Ohio State University. The numbers following BPRC refer to the box and folder.

Chapter One: An Unspeakable Secret

p. 6   'A book with Lowell's name . . .'
Letter from Suzanne Wilkins to E. P. F. Eagon, 7 October 1959, BPRC 2/8

p. 7   'I am sorry to say . . .'
Letter from Harold Sherman to Winston Ross, 9 May 1981, BPRC 21/18

p. 11   'Explain the degree of evasion . . .'
Rodgers, Eugene, *Beyond the Barrier*, Naval Institute Press, Annapolis, Maryland, 1990, p. xi

p. 11   'The late twenties and early . . .'
Montague, Richard, *Oceans Poles and Airmen*, Random House, New York, 1971, p. vii

p. 11   'Was an effort to keep . . .'
Ibid., p. vii

p. 11   'That Byrd's claim . . .'
Ibid., p. 283

p. 12   'When the committee of experts . . .'
Ibid., p. 282

Chapter Two: The Seeds of Disaster

p. 18   'We have at great length . . .'

A. Markham quoted in Holland, Clive, *Farthest North*, Carroll & Graf, New York, 1999, p. 80

p. 25 'I am frankly a hero worshipper . . .'
Ellsworth, Lincoln, *Beyond Horizons*, William Heinemann, London, 1938, p. 115

p. 26 'Thus I came to Amundsen . . .'
Ibid., p. 116

p. 26 'Failing to do that . . .'
Ibid., p. 117

p. 28 'At 3,000 feet of altitude . . .'
Ibid., p. 148

Chapter Three: Aviation Will Conquer the Arctic

p. 33 'And in the following week . . .'
Byrd, Richard E., *Skyward*, G. P. Putnam's Sons, New York, 1928, p. 62

p. 34 'Meanwhile . . . with fading hopes . . .'
Ibid., p. 75

p. 35 'Red tape was cut . . .'
Ibid., p. 81

p. 36 'Byrd spent the afternoon . . .'
Ibid., p. 86

p. 36 'The situation was pretty critical . . .'
Ibid., p. 92

p. 36 'I grasped at this straw.'
Ibid., p. 91

p. 38 '. . . the American Navy – bless her . . .'
Ibid., p. 99

p. 43 'Good weather has come at last.'
R. E. Byrd quoted in Goerler, Raimund E., (ed.), *To the Pole*, Ohio State University Press, Columbus, 1998, p. 36

Chapter Four: The Ice Queen

p. 45   'Adjusters reach their human subjects . . .'
Urantia Book, Urantia Foundation, Chicago, Revised Edition, 1975, 108:2:1

p. 46   'My youth was spent on a large ranch . . .'
Speech by Sir Hubert Wilkins, 'Polar Exploration for Adventure', *Economics, Sport and Science*, (Undated), BPRC B22/32

p. 47   'George was always very aggressive.'
Letter from C. E. 'Buzz' Simmons to Thomas Wilkins, 15 February 1959, BPRC uncatalogued

p. 48   'Three years is a long time . . .'
Letter from G. H. Wilkins to Thomas Wilkins, 5 April 1914, Venema Family Collection

p. 51   'All the time the Explorer Man . . .'
Wilkins, Sir Hubert, *An Antarctic Fairy Story*, unpublished, BPRC 22/5

p. 52   'During the five battles . . .'
Australian War Memorial, War Records Section, 11 October 1917, Collection 2, Box 22, Folder 4

p. 53   'Even amid all this destruction . . .'
Wilkins, Sir Hubert quoted in Thomas, Lowell, *Sir Hubert Wilkins: His World of Adventure*, Readers Book Club, London, 1961, p. 89

p. 54   'The greatest advantage we can gain . . .'
Speech by Sir Hubert Wilkins 'Next Steps Toward Civilisation', April 1941, BPRC 20/12

p. 56   'I finally decided to go with . . .'
Letter from G. H. Wilkins to Louisa Wilkins, 7 August 1921, BPRC 13/14

Chapter Five: The Men Who Took the Airship

p. 67   'This gave control to Amundsen . . .'
Ellsworth, *Beyond Horizons*, p. 186

p. 69   'All morning long we have . . .'
Balchen, Bernt, *Come North With Me*, E. P. Dutton &
Co., New York, 1958, p. 14

p. 70   'All work at our base . . .'
Ibid., p. 16

Chapter Six: Let George Do It

p. 73   'I don't suppose the English papers . . .'
Letter from G. H. Wilkins to Miss Strenberg, 26
January 1926, State Library of New South Wales, MSS
Set 472

p. 73   'Most Australians are well off . . .'
Wilkins, Captain Sir G. H., *Adventures in Undiscovered
Australia*, Ernest Benn Ltd., London, 1928, p. 15

p. 74   'I proposed to take only one . . .'
Wilkins, Captain George H., *Flying the Arctic*, G. P.
Putnam's Sons, New York, 1928, p. 9

p. 75   'I want to say to you very sincerely . . .'
Letter from R. E. Byrd to G. H. Wilkins, 22 January
1926, BPRC 17/12

p. 75   '[Amundsen's] aerial experience . . .'
Letter from G. H. Wilkins to A. Page Cooper, 6
October 1927, BPRC 14/27

p. 76   'Not having ridden in . . .'
Wilkins, *Flying the Arctic*, p. 14

p. 77   '. . . the Detroit Aviation Society is planning . . .'
Letter reproduced in pamphlet, undated. State Library
of New South Wales, MSS Set 472

p. 77   'A few years ago the Federal . . .'
         New York Times, 7 March 1926

p. 81   'A brave man has gone out to fight . . .'
         Radio transcript, undated, BPRC 14/11

p. 82   'We climbed steadily and steadily . . .'
         Wilkins, *Flying the Arctic*, p. 50

p. 83   'I leaned over to Eielson . . .'
         Ibid., p. 56

p. 84   'Hello folks. Here I am again.'
         Radio transcript, undated, BPRC 14/11

p. 88   'We soon came to clouds . . .'
         Wilkins, *Flying the Arctic*, p. 98

p. 88   'We filled our tanks with gasoline . . .'
         Ibid., p. 100

p. 89   'The greatest polar drive in history . . .'
         New York Times, 7 March 1926

Chapter Seven: Everything Was Staked on One Card

p. 91   'Lieut. Commander Richard E. Byrd . . .'
         New York Times, 7 March 1926

p. 91   'Captain Amundsen, after his attempt . . .'
         Ibid.

p. 93   'The least Byrd would receive . . .'
         Goerler, *To the Pole*, p. 46

p. 94   'Spent last night weighing . . .'
         Byrd quoted in *To the Pole*, p. 68

p. 94   'Please arrange for our ship . . .'
         Byrd to Amundsen quoted in *To the Pole*, p. 72

p. 95   'The *Heimdal* . . . was busy taking on . . .'
         Amundsen, Roald and Ellsworth, Lincoln, *First Crossing of the Polar Sea*, George H. Doran, New York, 1927, p. 48

p. 95   'I watch the party work its way . . .'
          Balchen, *Come North With Me*, p. 22

p. 97   'Commander Byrd pushes back . . .'
          Ibid., p. 26

p. 98   'I then requested that he let us . . .'
          Goerler, *To the Pole*, p. 73

p. 98   'The only thing for us to do . . .'
          Byrd, *Skyward*, p. 175

p. 99   'Involuntarily we all held our breath . . .'
          Amundsen and Ellsworth, *First Crossing of the Polar Sea*,
          p. 50

p. 99   'When the plane was pulled over . . .'
          Byrd, *Skyward*, p. 178

p. 100   'Earlier this morning, as I crossed . . .'
          Balchen, *Come North With Me*, p. 35

p. 100   'The Plane's first attempt . . .'
          Byrd, *Skyward*, p. 179

p. 101   'In the back of my mind . . .'
          Balchen, *Come North With Me*, p. 36

p. 102   'Of all the men in the room . . .'
          Ibid., p. 25

p. 102   'At noon, in the machine shop . . .'
          Ibid., p. 36

p. 103   'Took lunch with Amundsen . . .'
          Goerler, *To the Pole*, p. 26

p. 103   'Amundsen was not worried . . .'
          Nobile, General Umberto, *The Red Tent*, New English
          Library, London, 1972 (Originally published as *My
          Polar Flights*, Frederich Muller Ltd., 1961), p. 45

p. 105   'All the rest of the night . . .'
          Balchen, *Come North With Me*, p. 43

p. 105   'We are in the middle . . .'
          Ibid., p. 44

p. 106   'The men of the Byrd expedition . . .'
          Ibid., p. 45

Chapter Eight: The Big Trip

p. 108   'How light I felt . . .'
          Nobile, *The Red Tent*, p. 51

p. 111   'Soon they came to tell me . . .'
          Ibid., p. 60

p. 112   'In this brief respite . . .'
          Ibid., p. 61

p. 113   'I cannot attempt to give . . .'
          Ibid., p. 69

p. 114   'The *Norge* was lying lifeless . . .'
          Ibid., p. 76

Chapter Nine: Beyond a Reasonable Doubt

p. 115   'We were in constant touch . . .'
          Wilkins, *Flying the Arctic*, p. 100

p. 119   'The distances depend on . . .'
          National Geographic Magazine, September 1926, p. 387

p. 121   '. . . wholly due to errors . . .'
          Ibid., p. 387

p. 122   'At 8 hours 58 minutes . . .'
          Ibid.

p. 122   'These four observations confirmed . . .'
          Ibid., p. 388

p. 123   'At the moment when the sun . . .'
          Ibid.

p. 123   '. . . had an even more satisfactory verification . . .'
          Ibid.

p. 124   'The wind began to freshen . . .'
          Byrd, *Skyward*, p. 199

p. 127   'We circle the Detroit air strip . . .'
          Balchen, *Come North With Me*, p. 66

Chapter Ten: Tempting Fate a Second Time

p. 129   'Together we had crossed . . .'
          Nobile, *The Red Tent*, p. 81

p. 131   'At the end of Wilkins' 1926 expedition . . .'
          All costs quoted are from Minutes of Meeting, Detroit
          Aviation Society, 22 November 1926, BPRC 14/11

p. 133   'I went carefully over the possibilities . . .'
          Wilkins, *Flying the Arctic*, p. 123

p. 134   'They were soon lost to sight . . .'
          Mason, Howard H., 'Arctic Adventure', (article),
          publication details unknown, BPRC 14/3

p. 135   'I was much astonished to find . . .'
          Letter from G. H. Wilkins to W. L. G. Joerg, 26
          October 1927, BPRC 12/16

p. 137   'Along the afternoon . . .'
          Mason, *Arctic Adventure*

p. 137   'We were in no desperate hurry.'
          Letter from G. H. Wilkins to A. Smith (undated),
          BPRC 14/8

p. 138   'We battled over rough broken packs . . .'
          Ibid.

p. 138   'Any hope of locating Wilkins . . .'
          Telegram (transcribed, undated), BPRC 14/22

p. 139   'Wilkins told me one chance . . .'
          Ibid.

p. 139   'So we at Barrow sat around helpless . . .'
          Mason, *Arctic Adventure*

p. 139   'I am sending this by Eskimo . . .'
Wilkins to A. Smith (undated), BPRC 14/8

p. 141   'You must go on this flight . . .'
Glines, Carrol V., *Bernt Balchen: Polar Aviator*, Smithsonian Institution Press, Washington, 1999, p. 41

p. 142   'Slowly the great ship gained altitude . . .'
Byrd, *Skyward*, p. 252

p. 144   'The crew of the America visits . . .'
Ibid., p. 283

Chapter Eleven: Spitsbergen Bound

p. 145   'There was at one time a possibility . . .'
Letter from Wilkins to A. M. Smith, 5 October 1927,
BPRC 14/8

p. 146   '[After taking off, I propose] making . . .'
Letter from Wilkins to I. Bowman, (undated), BPRC
14/22

p. 146   '[*The Detroit News*] were so disappointed . . .'
Letter from Wilkins to E. S. Evans, 19 December
1927, BPRC 14/8

p. 147   'With one or two exceptions . . .'
Wilkins, *Flying the Arctic*, p. 202

p. 147   'Then came a time when my girl friend . . .'
Wilkins, *Flying the Arctic*, (unpublished draft), BPRC
14/22

p. 147   'I gave the question much thought . . .'
Letter from Wilkins to E. S. Evans, 19 December
1927, BPRC 14/8

p. 149   'I put out my charts, tested both . . .'
Wilkins, *Flying the Arctic*, p. 272

p. 150   'We had been in the air . . .'
Ibid., p. 282

p. 150   'We were above a small local storm . . .'
Ibid., p. 287

p. 152   'Then we learned how fortunate we were . . .'
Ibid., p. 322

p. 152   'I began sending the message from Spitsbergen . . .'
Wilkins, *Flying the Arctic*, (unpublished draft), BPRC
14/22

p. 155   '. . . leave . . . without any prearranged route . . .'
Nobile, *The Red Tent*, p. 128

p. 157   'It will be remembered that the British . . .'
Letter from Wilkins to A. Page Cooper, 6 October
1927, BPRC 14/27

p. 157   'In all his polar travels Amundsen . . .'
Ibid.

p. 158   'While the Amundsen–Ellsworth expedition . . .'
Ibid.

p. 159   'It seemed that death was very near . . .'
Nobile, *The Red Tent*, p. 146

p. 159   '. . . left me indifferent.'
Ibid., p. 150

Chapter Twelve: The Hares and the Tortoise

p. 168   'Wilkins willing accept total . . .'
Cablegram from T.V. Ranck to W. R. Hearst, 5 July
1928, BPRC 14/8

p. 169   'Now I discovered that success . . .'
Byrd, *Skyward*, p. 208

p. 169   'The greatest hardship I have ever . . .'
Wilkins, *Flying the Arctic*, p. 24

p. 171   'The Soviet Union has informed . . .'
McKee, Alexander, *Ice Crash*, Granada Publishing,
London, 1979, p. 254

Chapter Thirteen: Opposite to the Bear

p. 184   'Byrd's main base latitude . . .'
          Radio message transcript from Hearst Organisation to
          Wilkins, 5 January 1929, BPRC 14/8

p. 186   'Do you intend to drop British or Australian . . .'
          Letter from R.G. Casey to Wilkins, 21 August 1928,
          BPRC 14/8

p. 187   'Deception is a tiny dot . . .'
          Wilkins quoted in Thomas, *Sir Hubert Wilkins: His
          World of Adventure*, p. 184

p. 190   'Ahead of us this land . . .'
          Ibid., p. 191

p. 194   'We pulled off our furs . . .'
          Smith, Dean C., *By the Seat of My Pants*, Little, Brown
          & Co., Boston, 1961, p. 198

Chapter Fourteen: Winter in America

p. 200   'I solemnly swear on my word . . .'
          Rodgers, *Beyond the Barrier*, p. 145

p. 200   '. . . that in the case of disloyalty . . .'
          Ibid., p. 145

p. 201   'The Byrd expedition was not a scientific . . .'
          Smith, *By the Seat of My Pants*, p. 190

p. 203   'This little submarine with the . . .'
          Magazine article, (undated), BPRC OV-16

p. 208   'Smith remained in the cockpit . . .'
          Byrd, Richard E., *Little America*, G.P. Putnam's Sons,
          New York, 1930, p. 317

p. 211   'Next morning I am the one . . .'
          Extract edited from *Come North With Me*, published in
          Oceans, Poles and Airmen, p. 295

Chapter Fifteen: Where Amundsen Stood

p. 214   'Eielson and I together had seen . . .'
          Wilkins quoted in Thomas, *Sir Hubert Wilkins: His World of Adventure*, p. 211

p. 214   'When I left Montevideo . . .'
          Ibid., p. 210

p. 215   'Thinking back on it later . . .'
          Ibid., p. 211

p. 216   'In its 10 o'clock report the . . .'
          Byrd, *Little America*, p. 325

p. 217   'At 9:15 o'clock we had the eastern . . .'
          Ibid., p. 332

p. 219   'The Liv Glacier is like a great frozen . . .'
          Balchen, *Come North With Me*, p. 189

p. 219   'Whenever I noted any change . . .'
          Byrd, *Little America*, p. 338

p. 220   'The right engine backfires . . .'
          Balchen, *Come North With Me*, p. 190

p. 221   'For a few seconds we stood . . .'
          Byrd, *Little America*, p. 341

p. 222   'The skis touched the surface . . .'
          Ibid., p. 345

Chapter Sixteen: The Last Place Left to Explore

p. 236   'I returned from a flight one day . . .'
          Email from J. E. Waldron to the author, 24 August 1996

p. 236   'Sir Hubert said he was going . . .'
          Phone conversation between Paul Dalrymple and the author, 20 October 1999.

p. 238   'The majority of your aims . . .'
          Calvert, James, *Surface at the Pole*, Hutchinson, London, 1961, p.133

p. 238 'Sir Hubert remained on board . . .'
        Ibid., p. 143

p. 239 'The *Skate* would be honoured . . .'
        Ibid., p. 150

p. 240 'On this day we pay humble . . .'
        Ibid., p. 185

p. 241 'Hello Sherman. It is not easy . . .'
        Sherman, Harold M., *The Dead Are Alive*, Fawcett
        Gold Medal, New York, 1981, p. 145

p. 242 'It was clear from the outset . . .'
        Email from Paul Rodzianko to the author, 11 February
        2008

Chapter Seventeen: We Should Be at the Pole

p. 245 'This much should be understood . . .'
        Byrd, Richard E., *Alone*, G. P. Putnam's Sons, New
        York, 1938, p. 3

p. 247 'The Antarctic has ceased . . .'
        New York Times, 13 March 1957

p. 248 'Take the strange contradictions . . .'
        Extract edited from *Come North With Me*, published in
        Oceans, Poles and Airmen, p. 297

p. 250 'In contrast to his lustrous public career . . .'
        Goerler, *To the Pole*, p. 3

p. 251 'The diary's organisation is confusing . . .'
        Ibid., p. 4

p. 251 'I made notes in my log . . .'
        Byrd, *Skyward*, p. 252

p. 252 'Dennis Rawlins, an astronomer . . .'
        Goerler, *To the Pole*, p. 56

p. 254 'We are making good speed . . .'
        This and subsequent quotations are from the Byrd

diary which is reproduced as a fascimile edition in
Goerler's *To the Pole*.

p. 256 'Soon after leaving the Pole . . .'
National Geographic Magazine, September 1926, p. 388

p. 257 'Byrd spent the afternoon . . .'
Byrd, *Skyward*, p. 86

p. 264 'The landing was made . . .'
Amundsen and Ellsworth, *First Crossing of the Polar Sea*,
p. 121

p. 265 'In Bennett and me mothers . . .'
Byrd, *Skyward*, p. 214

Bibliography and Further Reading

Richard Byrd

Byrd, Richard E., *Alone,* G. P. Putnam's Sons, New York, 1938.

Byrd, Richard E., 'Flying over the Arctic', *National Geographic Magazine,* November 1925.

Byrd, Richard E., *Little America,* G. P. Putnam's Sons, New York, 1930.

Byrd, Richard E., *Skyward,* G. P. Putnam's Sons, New York, 1928.

Byrd, Richard E., 'The First Flight Over the North Pole', *National Geographic Magazine,* September 1926.

Goerler, Raimund E. (ed.), *To the Pole: The Diary and Notebook of Richard E. Byrd 1925–1927,* Ohio State University Press, Columbus, 1998.

Rodgers, Eugene, *Beyond the Barrier: The Story of Byrd's First Expedition to Antarctica,* Naval Institute Press, Annapolis, Maryland, 1990.

Staff writer, 'Commander Byrd Receives the Hubbard Gold Medal', *National Geographic Magazine,* September 1926.

Sir Hubert Wilkins

Grierson, John, *Sir Hubert Wilkins: Enigma of Exploration,* Robert Hale Limited, London, 1960.

Nasht, Simon, *The Last Explorer,* Hodder Australia, Sydney, 2005.

Sherman, Harold M., *The Dead Are Alive*, Fawcett Gold Medal, New York, 1981.

Thomas, Lowell, *Sir Hubert Wilkins: His World of Adventure*, Arthur Barker, London, 1961.

Wilkins, Captain George H., *Adventures in Undiscovered Australia*, Ernest Benn Limited, London, 1928.

Wilkins, Captain George H., *Flying the Arctic*, G. P. Putnam's Sons, New York, 1928.

Wilkins, Sir Hubert and Sherman, Harold M., *Thoughts Through Space*, House-Warven, Hollywood, 1951.

Wilkins, Sir Hubert, *Under the North Pole*, Brewer, Warren & Putnam, New York, 1931.

Amundsen, Ellsworth and Nobile

Amundsen, Roald, *My Life as an Explorer*, Doubleday, Doran & Co., New York, 1928.

Amundsen, Roald, *The North-West Passage*, Dutton, New York, 1908.

Amundsen, Roald, *The South Pole*, L. Keedick, New York, 1913.

Amundsen, Roald and Ellsworth, Lincoln, *First Crossing of the Polar Sea*, George H. Doran, New York, 1927.

Amundsen, Roald and Ellsworth, Lincoln, *Our Polar Flight*, Dodd, Mead & Co., New York, 1925.

Arnesen, Odd, *The Polar Adventure: The Italia Tragedy Seen at Close Quarters*, Victor Gollancz Ltd, London, 1929.

Cross, Wilbur, *Ghost Ship of the Pole*, William Heinemann, London, 1959.

Ellsworth, Lincoln, *Beyond Horizons*, William Heinemann, London, 1938.

Huntford, Roland, *The Last Place on Earth*, Modern Library, New York, 1999.

McKee, Alexander, *Ice Crash*, Granada, London, 1979.

Nobile, Umberto, *My Polar Flights*, Frederick Muller Ltd, London, 1961.

Pool, Beekman H., *Polar Extremes: The World of Lincoln Ellsworth*, University of Alaska Press, Fairbanks, 2002.

Balchen and Eielson

Balchen, Bernt, *Come North With Me*, E. P. Dutton & Co., New York, 1958.

Glines, Carroll V., *Bernt Balchen: Polar Aviator*, Smithsonian Institution Press, Washington, 1999.

Page, Dorothy G., *Polar Pilot: The Carl Ben Eielson Story*. Danville, Interstate Publishers, Inc., Illinois, 1992.

Wambheim, H. G. (ed.), *Ben: The Life Story of Carl Ben Eielson*, self-published, Hatton, North Dakota, 1930.

General

Ayres, Philip, *Mawson: A Life,* Melbourne University Press, Melbourne, 1999.

Botting, Douglas, *Dr Eckener's Dream Machine*, HarperCollins, London, 2001.

Calvert, James, *Surface at the Pole*, Hutchinson, London, 1961.

Holland, Clive (ed.), *Farthest North*, Carroll & Graf Publishers, New York, 1999.

McKinlay, William Laird, *The Last Voyage of the Karluk*, St Martin's Griffin, New York, 1999.

Montague, Richard, *Oceans, Poles and Airmen*, Random House, New York, 1971.

Smith, Dean C., *By the Seat of My Pants*, Little, Brown & Co., Boston, 1961.

Uversa Corps of Superuniverse Personalities acting by authority of the Orvonton Ancients of Days (and others), *The Urantia Book*, Urantia Foundation, Chicago, 1955.

Index

Index